Lecture Notes of the Institute for Computer Sciences, Social Informatics and Telecommunications Engineering 188

More information about this series at http://www.springer.com/series/8197

Leandros A. Maglaras · Helge Janicke
Kevin Jones (Eds.)

Industrial Networks and Intelligent Systems

Second International Conference, INISCOM 2016
Leicester, UK, October 31 – November 1, 2016
Revised Selected Papers

 Springer

Editors
Leandros A. Maglaras
School of Computer Science Informatics
De Montfort University
Leicester
UK

Kevin Jones
Airbus Group
Cardiff
UK

Helge Janicke
Faculty of Technology
De Montfort University
Leicester
UK

ISSN 1867-8211   ISSN 1867-822X (electronic)
Lecture Notes of the Institute for Computer Sciences, Social Informatics
and Telecommunications Engineering
ISBN 978-3-319-52568-6   ISBN 978-3-319-52569-3 (eBook)
DOI 10.1007/978-3-319-52569-3

Library of Congress Control Number: 2016963647

Printed on acid-free paper

This Springer imprint is published by Springer Nature
The registered company is Springer International Publishing AG
The registered company address is: Gewerbestrasse 11, 6330 Cham, Switzerland

Preface

The Second International Conference on Industrial Networks and Intelligent Systems (INISCom 2016) provided a successful forum for practitioners and researchers from diverse backgrounds to interact and exchange experiences about the latest technology, advancement, and future directions and trends in industrial networks and intelligent systems. We received over 22 technical papers from around the world. All submissions received high-quality reviews from the Technical Program Committee (TPC) members or selected external reviewers. According to the review results, we accepted 15 regular papers for inclusion in the technical program of the main conference.

The main technical program included five technical sessions and two inspiring keynote speeches: "Energy Optimization for Nano-, Micro- and Large-Scale Computer Systems and Networks" by Prof. Erol Gelenbe, Imperial College, UK, and "The Internet of (Somewhat Secure) Things: To Boldly Go ...?" by Prof. Awais Rashid, University of Lancaster, UK. The conference successfully inspired many innovative directions in the fields of (a) industrial networks and applications, (b) intelligent systems and applications, (c) information processing and data analysis, (d) hardware and software design and development, and (e) security and privacy.

It is our distinct honor to mention here the best paper of INISCom 2016: "Latency in Cascaded Wired/Wireless Communication Networks for Factory Automation." The paper was voted based on the reviewers' recommendations and on the papers' significance, originality, and potential impact. The technical program was the result of the hard work of many individuals. We would like to thank all the authors for submitting their outstanding work to INISCom 2016.

We offer our sincere gratitude to the TPC members and external reviewers, who worked hard to provide thorough, insightful, and constructive reviews in a timely manner. We are grateful to the Steering Committee and Organizing Committee of INISCom 2016, and especially to the TPC chairs, Dr. Dimitrios Katsaros from the University of Thessaly, Greece, Dr. Tiago J. Cruz from the University of Coimbra, Portugal, Prof. Jianmin Jiang from Shenzhen University, China, and Prof. Athanasios Maglaras from T.E.I. of Thessaly, Greece. Recognition should go to the local chair, who worked extremely hard on the details of important aspects of the conference program and social activities. Finally, we are grateful to all the participants at INISCom 2016.

November 2016

Leandros A. Maglaras
Helge Janicke
Kevin Jones

Organization

Steering Committee

Imrich Chlamtac	CREATE-NET, Italy (Chair)
Lei Shu	Guangdong University of Petrochemical Technology, China
Carlo Cecati	University of L'Aquila, Italy
Song Guo	University of Aizu, Japan

Organizing Committee

General Chairs

Leandros A. Maglaras	De Montfort University, UK
Helge Janicke	De Montfort University, UK
Kevin Jones	Airbus Group

Technical Program Committee Co-chairs

Dimitrios Katsaros	University of Thessaly, Greece
Tiago J. Cruz	University of Coimbra, Portugal
Jianmin Jiang	Shenzhen University, China
Athanasios Maglaras	Technological Educational Institute of Thessaly, Greece

Web Chair

Yu Lu	Cranfield University, UK

Publicity and Social Media Chair

Vasilis Sourlas	University College London, UK

Workshops Chair

Richard Smith	De Montfort University, UK

Sponsorship and Exhibits Chair

Leandros Maglaras	De Montfort University, UK

Publications Chair

Ying He	De Montfort University, UK

Local Chair

Francois Siewe   De Montfort University, UK

Conference Manager

Barbara Fertalova   European Alliance for Innovation (EAI)

Contents

Spatial Keyword Query Processing in the Internet of Vehicles

Yanhong Li[1], Lei Shu[2], Jianjun Li[3], Rongbo Zhu[1(✉)], and Yuanfang Chen[2]

[1] College of Computer Science, South-Central University for Nationalities,
Wuhan, China
liyanhong@mail.scuec.edu.cn, rbzhu@mail.scuec.edu.cn
[2] Guangdong University of Petrochemical Technology, Maoming, China
{lei.shu,yuanfang_chen}@ieee.org
[3] School of Computer Science and Technology,
Huazhong University of Science and Technology, Wuhan, China
jianjunli@hust.edu.cn

Abstract. This paper takes the first step to address the issue of processing Spatial Keyword Queries (SKQ) in the Internet of Vehicles (IoV) environment. As a key technique to obtain location-aware information, the Spatial Keyword Query (SKQ) is proposed. It can search qualified objects based on both keywords and location information. In the IoV, with the popularity of the GPS-enabled vehicle-mounted devices, location-based information is extensively available, and this also enables location-aware queries with special keywords to improve user experience. In this study, we focus on Boolean kNN Queries. And a Spatial Keyword query index for IoV environment (SKIV) is proposed as an important part of the algorithm design to be used to improve the performance of this type of SKQ. Extensive simulation is conducted to demonstrate the efficiency of the SKIV based query processing algorithm.

Keywords: Spatial keyword queries · Internet of vehicles · Wireless data broadcast

1 Introduction

The Internet of Vehicles (IoV) as a new emerging technology has caught widely attention, and has become a research hotspot [1–3]. In a IoV environment, vehicles communicate with each other for data sharing and processing [4–6]. With the prevalence of the geographical applications and devices deployed on vehicles, e.g., vehicle-mounted GPS and Web GIS, the data used in the IoV is associated with location information [7–9]. For example, a driver can locate a restaurant based on its position and some keywords *Japanese seafood takeaway*. Compared with traditional restaurant searching, such restaurant locating provides better user experience. In this scenario, Spatial Keyword Queries (SKQ) are proposed, which can search qualified objects based on keywords and location information [10–12].

© ICST Institute for Computer Sciences, Social Informatics and Telecommunications Engineering 2017
L.A. Maglaras et al. (Eds.): INISCOM 2016, LNICST 188, pp. 1–13, 2017.
DOI: 10.1007/978-3-319-52569-3_1

A spatial textual index is an important part in the SKQ processing [13, 14]. Zhou *et al.* [9] did relevant work by combining inverted indexes with R-trees. Three different combining schemes are studied: (i) inverted file and R*-tree double index, (ii) first inverted file then R*-tree, and (iii) first R*-tree then inverted file. The second scheme is better than the other two. As an improvement, Felipe *et al.* [15] proposed an index structure (IR2-tree) that integrates an R-tree and signature files. For each node of the tree, it employs a signature file, in the form of bitmap, to indicate the present of a given term (keyword) in the sub-tree of the node. IR-tree structure proposed by Cong *et al.* [10] augments an R-tree node with inverted lists. It has more powerful pruning ability since it combines R-tree and inverted lists to jointly prune the search space.

In this paper, we propose an algorithm for the spatial keyword query processing in the IoV environment, and we focus on Boolean kNN Queries.

The scientific contributions of this paper are summarized as follows:

- The paper takes the first step to deal with SKQ in IoV. Specifically, we propose an index, SKIV, to deal with SKQ in IoV under wireless broadcast environments.
- By using SKIV, an efficient algorithms is designed for Boolean kNN queries in the IoV environment.
- Extensive simulations are conducted to evaluate the performance of the SKIV based query processing algorithm on a real road network in the IoV environment. The experimental results show that the proposed SKIV based method outperforms the Fixed Partition Based method (FPB) on tuning time and access latency.

The remainder of this paper is organized as follows. Section 2 reviews related work. Section 3 gives some descriptions and preliminaries. Section 4 presents and describes the SKIV index. Section 5 introduces the algorithm for processing BkQ. Section 6 is the evaluation of the proposed algorithm, and we analyze the results in detail. In Sect. 7, we conclude this paper.

2   Related Work

Zhou *et al.* [9] proposed a hybrid index structure, which integrates inverted files and R*-trees, to handle spatial keyword queries. Cong *et al.* [10] proposed an index structure called IR-tree which augments each node of the R-tree with an inverted file. Moreover, a variant of the IR-tree, the DIR-tree, was proposed to incorporate document similarity when computing Minimum Bounding Rectangles.

In [12], Huang *et al.* discussed the problem of processing the moving top-k spatial keyword query. Given a moving spatial query and a set of keywords, it continuously finds the k best objects ranked according to both spatial proximity and text relevance. Li *et al.* [13] discussed the issue of direction-aware spatial keyword query. Given a query with a location, a direction, and a set of keywords, it finds the k nearest neighbors of the query which are in the query direction and contain all the input keywords.

João et al. [16] explored top-k spatial keyword query processing on road networks and described how to rank objects with respect to both network distance and text relevance. Gao et al. [11] discussed reverse top-k Boolean spatial keyword query processing in road networks, and proposed filter-and-refinement frame work based algorithms for giving query result sets. To improve the query performance, several pruning heuristics and a data structure called count tree were proposed.

Wang et al. [17] discussed spatial query processing in road network for wireless data broadcast and proposed a novel index called ISW. Li et al. [14] discussed the problem of processing continuous nearest neighbor queries in road networks on the air. They proposed an NVD-based distributed air index (NVD-DI) to support query processing. Sun et al. [18] presented an air index called Network Partition Index (NPI) to support efficient spatial query processing in road networks on the air.

3   Definitions and Preliminaries

3.1   Definitions

In this study, we assume that each geo-textual object has a spatial location and a set of keywords, and we consider Boolean kNN queries in the IoV, under wireless broadcast environments. The frequently used symbols and their definitions are summarized in Table 1.

Table 1. Symbols and definitions

Notation	Definition
D	a set of points with keywords on a road network
q	a spatial query point with a set of keywords
$d_N(p,p')$	the network distance between two points p and p'
$d_E(p,p')$	the Euclidean distance between two points p and p'
$d_N^{min}(R_i, R_j)$	the minimum network distance between regions R_i and R_j
$d_N^{max}(R_i, R_j)$	the maximum network distance between regions R_i and R_j
$d_E^{min}(R_i, R_j)$	the minimum Euclidean distance between regions R_i and R_j

Dataset Setting. Let D be a set of geo-textual objects locating on the edges of a road network. Each geo-textual object $o \in D$ is defined as a tuple $(o.l, o.\varphi)$, where $o.l$ is a spatial location and $o.\varphi$ is a set of keywords.

Boolean kNN query (BkQ). Given a BkQ $q = < l, \varphi, k >$, where $q.l$ is q's location, $q.\varphi$ is a set of keywords, and $q.k$ is the number of result objects, the result of q, $BkQ(q)$ contains k objects such that $\forall o \in BkQ(q)$, there does not exist $o' \in D \backslash BkQ(q)$ such that $d_N(o'.l, q.l) \leq d_N(o.l, q.l) \wedge q.\varphi \subseteq o'.\varphi$.

3.2   Preliminaries

Adaptive Partition and Kd-Tree. There are many space partition methods, such as fixed partition and adaptive partition. The fixed partition method divides the search space into fixed-size grid cells. This method is simple and efficient when the data objects are evenly distributed in the search space. However, in the real world, the objects are usually unevenly distributed in the space. To adapt to skewed object distributions, the adaptive partition scheme adaptively partitions the space by using a kd-tree like partition method [19]. Specifically, it divides the search space into grid cells such that each grid cell contains nearly the same number of data objects.

The adaptive partition method works as follows. The space is partitioned alternatively between horizontal division and vertical division. Suppose the vertical partition is employed, we first use a straight line parallel to x-axis, denoted by $y = y_1$, to partition the whole space into two regions, and make sure that the upper and the lower regions have equal number of objects. Next, these two regions are partitioned by two lines $x = x_1$ and $x = x_2$, respectively. This process is repeated until every grid cell contains the required data objects. As an illustration, Fig. 1 shows an example of adaptive partition and its corresponding kd-tree index structure.

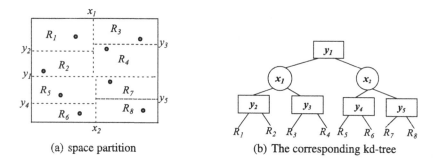

(a) space partition   (b) The corresponding kd-tree

Fig. 1. Space partition and the corresponding kd-tree

4   Index for Spatial Keyword Queries in the IoV

In this section, we present a index, SKIV, to deal with SKQ in the IoV under wireless broadcast environments. By SKIV, the mobile client can reduce the data needed to be retrieved for query processing, while keeping the access latency within a reasonable range, and thus can reduce the energy consumption.

4.1   A Road Network with a Set of Geo-Textual Objects

The graph model is often used to simulate road networks. In this work, we model a road network in the IoV environment as an undirected weighted graph which includes an edge set and a node set. The graph nodes and edges represent road nodes and road segments respectively. Specifically, each node is a road intersection or an end-point in the road network. Each edge has a non-negative weight which represents the length (network distance) of the road segment.

Figure 2 gives a road network and a set of geo-textual objects $D = \{o_1, \cdots, o_{16}\}$ (depicted as solid points) which lie on the edges of the road network. Table 2 shows the word frequencies for each objects. For example, the text information of object o_1 includes three terms "fish", "pizza" and "bread", whose frequencies are 3, 5 and 2, respectively.

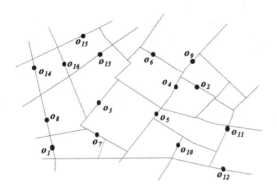

Fig. 2. A road network and a set of geo-textual objects

Table 2. Text information of the objects

Obj	Terms and term frequencies	Obj	Terms and term frequencies
o_1	(fish, 3) (pizza, 5) (bread, 2)	o_9	(pizza, 4) (Italian, 5) (coffee, 2)
o_2	(pizza, 5) (Italian, 5) (bread, 1)	o_{10}	(Italian, 4) (coffee, 3) (bread, 1)
o_3	(coffee, 4) (Italian, 2) (fish, 3)	o_{11}	(Italian, 4) (fish, 3) (bread, 2)
o_4	(coffee, 4) (Italian, 4) (bread, 3)	o_{12}	(pizza, 4) (bread, 4)
o_5	(Italian, 1) (coffee, 2) (fish, 4) (pizza, 3)	o_{13}	(coffee, 3) (pizza, 2) (bread, 4) (Italian, 2)
o_6	(coffee, 3) (fish, 3) (bread, 4)	o_{14}	(pizza, 3) (bread, 3) (coffee, 2)
o_7	(coffee, 2) (fish, 3) (Italian, 4)	o_{15}	(Italian, 3) (pizza, 2) (bread, 4) (fish, 2)
o_8	(Italian, 4) (pizza, 3) (coffee, 2)	o_{16}	(pizza, 4) (Italian, 5)

4.2 SKIV Index

The proposed SKIV index is required to support network space pruning and textual pruning simultaneously The structure of SKIV index includes two components. The first component defines partitions, and maps coordinate points into regions, while the second one specifies minimum/maximum ST scores of the objects between regions.

Firstly, we partition the road network into several disjoint regions. Note that the geo-textual objects may unevenly distributed on the edges of the road network, and we adapt the adaptive partition to divide the search space into grid cells such that each grid cell contains equal number of data objects, and use a kd-tree to keep the partition result [19]. In this way, we can get the partition result and the kd-tree of the road network in Fig. 2, as shown in Fig. 3.

In the client-side, the client needs some information to identify the regions based on coordinate values. Specifically, the first component of the SKIV index includes the splitting values of the kd-tree, which are transmitted in the breadth-first order, and then the client retrieves this index information to reconstruct the tree in Fig. 3(b). Let us go back to the example in Fig. 2, it can be observed that the splitting values is a sequence $< y_1, x_1, x_2, y_2, y_3, y_4, y_5, x_3, x_4, x_5, x_6, x_7, x_8, x_9, x_{10} >$. For ease of query processing at the client side, each node (region) in the kd-tree is assigned an identifier. In particular, the identifier of each region is determined from the leftmost leaf to the rightmost. That is, the identifier of the leftmost leaf is R_1, and increment the region number for the region just at its right side. The derived region numbers are shown in Fig. 3(a).

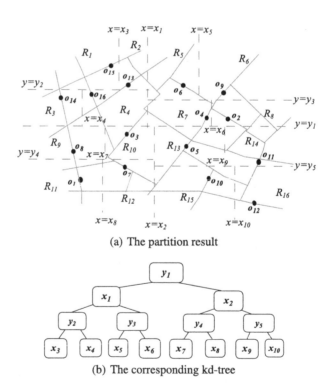

(a) The partition result

(b) The corresponding kd-tree

Fig. 3. The partition result and kd-tree of the road network in Fig. 2

To efficiently prune the search space during spatial query processing, we need to keep two kinds of information: (i) the road network distance, and (ii) the textual relevance between objects and the query. Firstly, the SKIV index provides the minimum and maximum distances between every pair of regions. This distance part is essentially an $n \times n$ array A, where n is the total number of regions. Every element A_{R_i,R_j} of array A contains two values: the minimum and the maximum network distances from any point in R_i to any point in R_j, i.e., $d_N^{min}(R_i, R_j)$ and $d_N^{max}(R_i, R_j)$[1]. To create array A, we need to pre-calculate the shortest path distances between all possible pairs of nodes from different regions, and the largest weight of the edges in each region. The time complexity of this pre-calculation operation is $O(|N|^3 + |E|)$, where $|N|$ and $|E|$ are the total number of nodes and edges in the road network, respectively.

Secondly, for each region R_i, we keep the following items: (i) the total number of objects in R_i, and (ii) the set of inverted lists containing the objects within R_i. Specifically, one list per different keyword in the description of the objects. The content of each inverted list (for term t_i) includes the id of each object o in R_i that have a term t_i in its description. To efficiently search objects which meet the textual requirement of query q, for each region, its inverted lists are arranged in non-increasing order of the number of objects in each list.

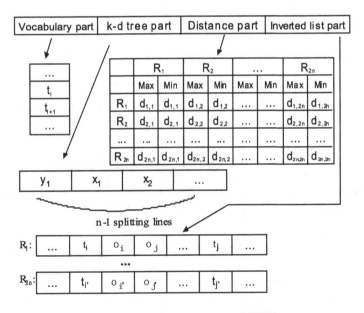

Fig. 4. The index structure of SKIV.

---

[1] In particular, $d_N^{min}(R_i, R_j)$ equals the minimum network distances from any node in R_i to any node in R_j, and $d_N^{max}(R_i, R_j)$ equals the sum of the maximum network distances from any node in R_i to any node in R_j, the largest weight of the edges in R_i, and the largest weight of the edges in R_j.

In this way, we can get the index segment which includes four parts: the vocabulary file, the k-d tree, the distance array, and the inverted lists. In particular, the k-d tree part includes $n-1$ splitting lines from which the clients can easily reconstruct the space consisting of n regions. For each region R_i, in addition to the network distance bounds from R_i to any other region R_j ($i \neq j, i, j \in [1, n]$) and the textual relevant information, it also contains a pointer to the data of R_i, which is denoted by the offset – the number of packets before the data of R_i is broadcast. The final index structure is shown in Fig. 4. For the sake of clarity, we omit to depict the pointers to the data of the regions.

5   Processing Spatial Keyword Queries on the Client Site

Before discussing the BkQ query processing algorithm in detail, we first introduce three lemmas, which will be used to prune the search space.

Lemma 1. *Given a BkQ query* $q =< l, \varphi, k >$ *and a region* R_i*, if* $q.\varphi \nsubseteq R_i.\varphi$*, then* R_i *can be safely pruned.*

Proof. For any object o in region R_i, we have $o.\varphi \subseteq R_i.\varphi$. Then by $q.\varphi \nsubseteq R_i.\varphi$, we can get $q.\varphi \nsubseteq o.\varphi$, which means o cannot be a result object of query q. Hence, R_i can be safely pruned.

Lemma 2. *Given a BkQ query* $q =< l, \varphi, k >$ *and a region* R_i*, if* R_i *does not include any object* o *which belongs to all the invert lists, each of which corresponds to each item in* $q.\varphi$*, then* R_i *can be safely pruned.*

Proof. If R_i does not include any object which belongs to all the invert lists corresponding to each item in $q.\varphi$, then for any object o in R_i, the condition $q.\varphi \subseteq o.\varphi$ does not hold, thus R_i can be safely pruned.

Lemma 3. *Given a BkQ query* $q =< l, \varphi, k >$ *and a region* R_i*, if* $d_N^{\min}(R_q, R_i) > d_k$*, then* R_i *can be safely pruned. In particular,* d_k *is the minimum* $d_N^{\max}(R_q, R_j)$ ($j \in [1, n]$)*, where* R_j *satisfies the condition that region* R_j *together with regions* R_l ($l \in [1, n], j \neq l$) *(which meet the condition that* $d_N^{\max}(R_q, R_l) \leq d_N^{\max}(R_q, R_j)$*) contain at least* k *objects* o*,* $q.\varphi \subseteq o.\varphi$*.*

Proof. Based on the definition of d_k, we know for query q, there exists a set of regions $\mathbb{R}$, and for each region $R \in \mathbb{R}$, there is $d_N^{\max}(R_q, R) \leq d_k$. Moreover, these regions contain at least k objects o which satisfies $q.\varphi \subseteq o.\varphi$. Hence, we can derive that the maximum distance between q and an object that can be the BkQ result of q is d_k. Since $d_N^{\min}(R_q, R_i) > d_k$, we know for any object o' in R_i, there is $d_N(q, o') > d_k$. Therefore, o' cannot be a BkQ object of q, which means R_i does not contain any BkQ object of q and thus can be safely pruned.

Algorithm 1 gives the pseudo-code of BkQ query processing. S is used to keep the regions, which may contain result objects, O_{cand} is used to to keep candidate objects, and float d_k, which is initialized to be infinity, is used to keep the maximum distance value of the k-th nearest neighbor of a query q.

Algorithm 1. BkQ processing

---

1 **begin**

2   //**Step 1:** Get the qualified regions;

3   $S = \emptyset$, $O_{cand} = \emptyset$, $d_k = \infty$;

4   Tune into the broadcast channel and receive the index;

5   List all regions R_i ($1 \le i \le n$) in ascending order of $d_N^{\min}(R_q, R_i)$;

6   **for** *each region R_i which are listed orderly* **do**

7   **if** $d_N^{\min}(R_q, R_i) > d_k$ **then**

8           $\lfloor$ break; //Lemma 3

9   **if** $q.\varphi \nsubseteq R_i.\varphi$ **then**

10          $\lfloor$ prune R_i; //Lemma 1

11   **if** *R_i includes any object o belonging to all the invert lists, each of which corresponds to each item in $q.\varphi$* **then**

12   insert each qualified object o into O_{cand} in the form of $(o, d_N^{\max}(R_q, R_i))$;

13              $d_k = d_N^{\max}(R_q, \mathcal{R})$, where $\mathcal{R}$ is the region where the k-th object in O_{cand} resides in;

14              $\lfloor$ insert R_i (R_i, $d_N^{\min}(R_q, R_i)$) into S;

15   **else**

16              $\lfloor$ prune R_i; //Lemma 2;

17   //Step 2: Selectively receive the data and process the query;

18   **for** *each region R_i in S* **do**

19   **for** *each object o in O_{cand} (o belong to R_i)* **do**

20   calculate $d_N(q, o)$ and arrange the object in ascending order of $d_N(q, o)$;

21   Put the first k objects in O_{cand} into $BkQ(q)$;

22   Return $BkQ(q)$;

---

6 Performance Evaluation

6.1 Experimental Setup

This section evaluates the performance of SKIV that is used to support BkQ in the IoV under wireless broadcast environments. All the experiments were executed on a PC with the following configuration: Intel Core 2 Quad, Q8200 2.33 GHz processor and 2 GB main memory, running Linux Ubuntu 9.10. The implementation was written by CPP and compiled by GNU C++ 4.3.3. Each set of experiments was executed on a real road network. Specifically, to model the real-world road network, we used the real data of the traffic network of Oldenburg in Germany (http://www.cs.fsu.edu/lifeifei/spatialdataset.htm), which consists of 6105 nodes and 7035 edges.

To our best knowledge, there is no other work on dealing with spatial keyword queries in the IoV. Hence, we will compare our SKIV with a fixed partition based method (FPB). In FPB, we divide the search space into several equal-sized grid cells. For each grid cell, we employ inverted files to index the description of the geo-textual objects lying within the cell. Moreover, we calculate and keep the minimum and maximum distances between the cell and any other cells in the road network. In order to reduce the waiting time for receiving the head of the forthcoming index, we also employ the well-known(1, m) interleaving scheme. Suppose the bandwidth of the broadcast channel is fixed, we use the number of bytes transferred over the broadcast channel as the time unit, instead of the real clock time. Moreover, the packet size is set to 256 bytes. We used the generator proposed in [20] to obtain a set of data objects. The description of the objects is obtained from Twitter (http://twitter.com), one tweet per object. We created two data sets namely T_1 and T_2 whose cardinalities (number of objects) are $1k$ and $4k$, respectively. Distinct tweets are used to construct the data set. Table 3 shows the parameters under investigation and the values in bold font are the default values in the experiments. Table 4 gives the characteristics of the data sets.

Table 3. Parameters evaluated in the experiments

Data set	T_1, T_2
Number of NNs (k)	1, 5, **10**, 15, 20
Number of keywords	1, 2, **3**, 4
Number of regions	16, 32, **64**, 128, 256

Table 4. Characteristics of the data sets

Attribute	T_1	T_2
Total size (MB)	2.58	9.98
Total no. of objects	1 k	4 k
Total no. of words	5579	23304
Total no. of distinct words	429	1275
Size of FPB (MB) (64 regions)	0.14	0.60
Size of SKIV (MB) (64 regions)	0.16	0.65

6.2   Experimental Results

We evaluate the performance of SKIV and FPB method for processing BkQ, in terms of tuning time and access latency.

Firstly, the tuning time of the SKIV and FPB method is evaluated. Figure 5(a) depicts the tuning time for BkQ as a function of region number. When we increase the region number, the tuning time of our SKIV first decreases and then increases clearly, and the performance is best at the point of 64 regions. This is because that larger region number means larger index size, thus the time needed to retrieve the index part increases. On the other hand, if the granularity of region is smaller, more objects are pruned by the pruning power of our method. Similarly, the tuning time of FPB first decreases and then increases as the number of regions increases, and it reaches optimal performance when region number is 128. Our SKIV outperforms FPB. Figure 5(b) plots the tuning time as a function of the keyword number. The cost of these two methods increases as the number of keywords increases, since more query keywords means the result objects may locate in a larger range of the road network. Since SKIV has a strong power to prune unqualified objects both on distance and keyword similarity, its increase tendency is much gentle compared to that of FPB method. Figure 5(c) illustrates the tuning time for BkQ as the value k increases from 1 to 20. The cost of these two method increases for larger k, since larger k means larger search region, larger number of candidate objects, and larger result size.

Then, we also evaluate the access time for BkQ processing. Figure 6(a) depicts the access time for BkQ as a function of region number for data sets T1 and T2. The figure shows that the access time of SKIV and FPB first decreases, and then increases slowly as the number of regions increases, and the access time of FPB is higher than that of our SKIV. On the average, SKIV incurs only 66.4% and 66.8% of access time compared to FPB method for the T1 and T2 data sets, respectively. Figure 6(b) plots the access time as the number of keywords increases. The access time of these two methods increases, when we increase keyword number. The reason lies in that more query keywords means the result

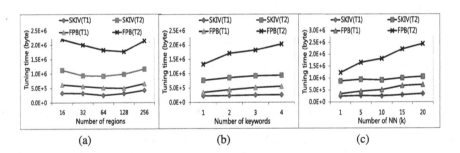

Fig. 5. Tuning time for BkQ

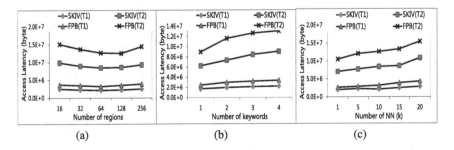

Fig. 6. Access time for BkQ

objects may locate in a larger range of the road network, thus more time is needed to wait for the required data to arrive. Figure 6(c) illustrates the access time for BkQ processing as the value k increases from 1 to 20, and the result shows that the access latency of these two methods grows for larger k value.

7   Conclusion

This paper addresses the issue of processing SKQ in IoV environments. Particularly, we focus on Boolean kNN Queries. A novel SKIV index which includes two parts is proposed. The first part defines space partitions and provides a mapping of coordinate points into regions, while the second part specifies minimum/maximum ST scores of the objects between regions. With the SKIV index, the search space can be efficiently pruned. Based on the SKIV index, a query processing algorithm is developed. Finally, experimental study on a real road network in IoV and two geo-textual data sets demonstrates the efficiency of the proposed index and query processing algorithm. The results show that the proposed method is more efficient than its competitor in both tuning time and access latency.

Acknowledgments. This work is supported by National Science Foundation of China (No. 61309002, No. 61272497).

References

1. Balazs, J.A., Velsquez, J.D.: Opinion mining and information fusion: a survey. Inf. Fusion **27**(C), 95–110 (2016)
2. Yang, F., Wang, S., Li, J., Liu, Z., Sun, Q.: An overview of internet of vehicles. Chin. Commun. **11**(10), 1–15 (2014)
3. Kumar, N., Rodrigues, J.J.P.C., Chilamkurti, N.: Bayesian coalition game as-a-service for content distribution in internet of vehicles. IEEE Internet Things J. **1**(6), 544–555 (2014)
4. Kumar, N., Misra, S., Rodrigues, J., Obaidat, M.S.: Coalition games for spatio-temporal big data in internet of vehicles environment: a comparative analysis. IEEE Internet Things J. **2**(4), 1–1 (2015)
5. Alam, K.M., Saini, M., Saddik, A.E.: Toward social internet of vehicles: concept, architecture, and applications. Access IEEE **3**, 343–357 (2015)
6. Yu, R., Kang, J., Huang, X., Xie, S.: Mixgroup: accumulative pseudonym exchanging for location privacy enhancement in vehicular social networks. IEEE Trans. Dependable Secure Comput. **13**(1), 93–105 (2016)
7. Chen, Y.Y., Suel, T., Markowetz, A.: Efficient query processing in geographic web search engines. In: ACM SIGMOD International Conference on Management of Data, Chicago, Illinois, USA, pp. 277–288, June 2006
8. Christoforaki, M., He, J., Dimopoulos, C., Markowetz, A., Suel, T.: Text vs. space: efficient geo-search query processing. In: ACM Conference on Information and Knowledge Management, CIKM 2011, Glasgow, United Kingdom, pp. 423–432, October 2011

9. Zhou, Y., Xie, X., Wang, C., Gong, Y., Ma, W.-Y.: Hybrid index structures for location-based web search. In: Proceedings of the 14th ACM International Conference on Information and Knowledge Management, pp. 155–162 (2005)
10. Cong, G., Jensen, C.S., Wu, D.: Efficient retrieval of the top-k most relevant spatial web objects. Proc. VLDB Endow. **2**(1), 337–348 (2009)
11. Gao, Y., Zheng, B., Chen, G.: Efficient reverse top-k boolean spatial keyword queries on road networks. IEEE Trans. Knowl. Data Eng. **PP**(99), 1–14 (2014)
12. Huang, W., Li, G., Tan, K.-L., Feng, J.: Efficient safe-region construction for moving top-k spatial keyword queries. In: Proceedings of the 21st ACM International Conference on Information and Knowledge Management, pp. 932–941 (2012)
13. Li, G., Feng, J., Xu, J.: Desks: direction-aware spatial keyword search. In: Proceedings of the 28th International Conference on Data Engineering, pp. 474–485 (2012)
14. Li, Y., Li, J., Shu, L., Li, Q., Li, G., Yang, F.: Searching continuous nearest neighbors in road networks on the air. Inf. Syst. **42**(2014), 177–194 (2014)
15. De Felipe, I., Hristidis, V., Rishe, N.: Keyword search on spatial databases. In: Proceedings of ICDE, pp. 656–665. IEEE (2008)
16. Rocha-Junior, J.B., Nørvåg, K.: Top-k spatial keyword queries on road networks. In: Proceedings of the 15th International Conference on Extending Database Technology, pp. 168–179 (2012)
17. Wang, Y., Xu, C., Gu, Y., Chen, M., Yu, G.: Spatial query processing in road networks for wireless data broadcast. Wirel. Netw. **19**(4), 477–494 (2013)
18. Sun, W., Chen, C., Zheng, B., Chen, C., Liu, P.: An air index for spatial query processing in road networks. IEEE Trans. Knowl. Data Eng. **27**(2), 382–395 (2015)
19. Möhring, R.H., Schilling, H., Schütz, B., Wagner, D., Willhalm, T.: Partitioning graphs to speedup Dijkstra's algorithm. J. Exp. Algorithmics (JEA) **11**, 2–8 (2007)
20. Brinkhoff, T.: A framework for generating network-based moving objects. GeoInformatica **6**(2), 153–180 (2002)

Recovering Request Patterns to a CPU Processor from Observed CPU Consumption Data

Hugo Lewi Hammer[(✉)], Anis Yazidi, Alfred Bratterud, Hårek Haugerud, and Boning Feng

Department of Computer Science,
Oslo and Akershus University College of Applied Sciences, Oslo, Norway
{hugo.hammer,anis.yazidi,alfred.bratterud,
harek.haugerud,boning.feng}@hioa.no

Abstract. Statistical queuing models are popular to analyze a computer systems ability to process different types requests. A common strategy is to run stress tests by sending artificial requests to the system. The rate and sizes of the requests are varied to investigate the impact on the computer system. A challenge with such an approach is that we do not know if the artificial requests processes are realistic when the system are applied in a real setting. Motivated by this challenge, we develop a method to estimate the properties of the underlying request processes to the computer system when the system is used in a real setting. In particular we look at the problem of recovering the request patterns to a CPU processor. It turns out that this is a challenging statistical estimation problem since we do not observe the request process (rate and size of the requests) to the CPU directly, but only the *average* CPU usage in disjoint time intervals.

In this paper we demonstrate that, quite astonishingly, we are able to recover the properties of the underlying request process (rate and sizes of the requests) by using specially constructed statistics of the observed CPU data and apply a recently developed statistical framework called Approximate Bayesian Computing.

Keywords: Classification · Co-occurrence information · Text mining · Tweets

1 Introduction

Scaling of computer systems is one of the most fundamental tasks in computer science. A popular approach is to assume that requests to a computer system follow some statistical queuing model, see e.g. [5, 11, 14, 16, 21–23] for a few representative examples. The typical approach in such papers is to run artificial stress tests on the systems by sending requests to the system and vary the rate and sizes of the requests. A challenge with such an approach is that we do not

© ICST Institute for Computer Sciences, Social Informatics and Telecommunications Engineering 2017
L.A. Maglaras et al. (Eds.): INISCOM 2016, LNICST 188, pp. 14–28, 2017.
DOI: 10.1007/978-3-319-52569-3_2

know if the rates and sizes used in the stress tests are realistic compared that what the computer system are faced with in a real setting. A natural strategy, of course, is to observe how well the system performs in real live settings. Unfortunately, such observations do not reveal the properties of the underlying real live request process to the system which contains important information on how the computer system should be constructed, see more below.

In this paper we address this challenge and focus on requests to a CPU processor. We use real observed CPU consumption data to recover the properties of the underlying request processes (queuing process) to the CPU processor. More specifically we want to recover the size and rate of the requests to the CPU processor. If we know the time point for every request to the CPU processor (arrival times) and when the system finished processing the requests (departure times), the estimation of the properties of the queuing process can usually be easily done by standard statistical estimation techniques like maximum likelihood estimation. Unfortunately, such information is far from available for observed CPU consumption data. In fact, it is not even possible to observe the current CPU load (number of active CPU cores), but only the *average* load in disjoint time intervals (e.g. five minute intervals). Consequently, a process consisting of many small requests to the CPU and a process consisting of only a few large requests may look similar since the two processes *on average* consume the same amount of CPU resources. Even though we only observe the average CPU consumption we show that by using the statistical framework called Approximate Bayesian Computing (ABC) we are, quite astonishingly, able to estimate the properties of the underlying queuing process, i.e. rates and sizes of requests to the CPU processor.

From a practical point of view, being able to recover the properties of the underlying queuing process can be quite useful. E.g. if the request pattern turns out to consist of many small tasks (in stead of a few large) it can easily be parallelized and the computer system can be constructed to take advantage of this.

2   Related Work

Applying queuing models for analyzing resource usage for different computer systems have received a lot of attention. We shall review some representative studies on this topic.

In [16], a double renting scheme that combines short term renting and long term renting is proposed. The service system is modeled as $M/M/m + D$ queuing model. An optimal configuration for profit optimization is derived subject to guaranteeing the service quality of all requests. Many optimization factors are considered for the profit optimization problem which includes the market demand, the workload of requests, the server-level agreement, the rental cost of servers, the cost of energy consumption etc. The authors treat the case of homogeneous cloud environment and the case of heterogeneous is left for future work as it is more involved.

In [15], Liu and his colleagues study the effect of cloud scheduling on service performance. Unlike most legacy models, the service rate is not considered fixed but rather depends on the schedule strategy. Each server is modeled as an $M/G/1$ queuing system, while a semi-Markov model is used to model the cloud computing center.

In [20], an open Jackson network is used to model a cloud platform and used to provide SLA guarantee in terms of response time. A sequential model composed of $M/M/1$ and $M/M/m$ in sequence was proposed to model the cloud platform. The work is particularly useful for dimensioning the cloud as it is able to determine the system bottleneck parameters that needs to be adjusted so that to guarantee the desired response time. The work can be applied to enable dimensioning cloud platform to host different types of services (education, production, e-health, etc.).

In [18], a queue model for multimedia cloud is proposed. The model is composed of three concatenated queues: are the schedule queue, the computation queue, and the transmission. The aim is to efficiently host multi-media services in the cloud by optimizing the quality of service QoS and resource cost. queue.

Bouterse and Perros [4] developed a model inspired from the realm of circuit switched telephony models, namely the model of blocking of Erlang, in order to develop reserve capacity model.

Parameter estimation in queuing models have a long tradition going back to the David Cox paper from [6]. Most papers rely on the likelihood principle in one way or another, see e.g. [1,8,13], but there are some situations where standard estimation techniques can not be used. E.g. Heggland and Frigessi [12] estimate the parameters of a $G/G/1$ queue model when only the departure times are known applying a method called indirect inference.

A disadvantage of the indirect inference approach is that it is difficult to get reliable uncertainty estimates of the parameter estimates. Over the recent years the indirect inference framework has been generalized and casted in to a Bayesian framework. The approaches are typically referred to as Approximate Bayesian Computing (ABC). See e.g. [3,7] for very nice reviews of the different approaches available within the ABC framework. Due to the complexity of the estimation problem considered in this paper, we resort to the ABC framework.

3   CPU Consumption Data

In this paper we apply the methodology described in the introduction on real CPU consumption data collected from a laptop with a Windows 7 operating system used by an office worker. We observed the office worker for 19 whole working days (i.e. weekends removed) with the average CPU usage in five minutes intervals, i.e. 288 observations every day. The CPU data for four arbitrary days are shown in Fig. 1. A value of one is equivalent to one CPU core constantly running. We observe that the CPU consumption typically is largest during the day and with some occasional computations during the evening. We observe little CPU consumption during the night. Large tasks are visible in the real data with a constant CPU usage around 1, e.g. in the evening of the upper left panel. In the same panel we observe that the CPU consumption is around 2 right after 8 PM (value 20 on the x axis) meaning that two CPU cores run some larger tasks. We also observe large time spans in which the CPU usage is far below one meaning that in this periods a number of smaller requests are sent to the CPU processor. Even though we do not observe the CPU requests directly we see that we still are able to say something about the amount of request and the sizes of them just by inspecting the CPU consumption data.

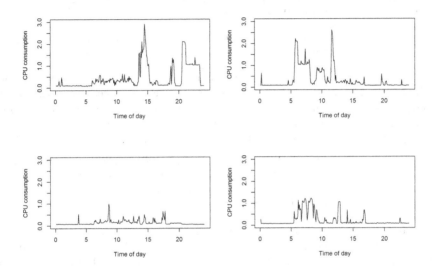

Fig. 1. The CPU consumption data for four arbitrary days.

In the next section we will present a statistical model for how such CPU consumption data are generated. The model will then be used to recover unobserved properties of the underlying request process to the CPU processor.

4   Data Generating Model

The laptop, in which the data was collected from, was equipped with a four core CPU processor. We assume that the number of available cores are more than the number of current requests that need to processed such that requests are never queued. More specifically we assume that the request process can be modeled by a $M/G/\infty$ queue process.

4.1   Notation

We assume that we have CPU consumption data for D days. We divide each day in T equidistant intervals by the time points $\tau_0, \ldots, \tau_T$ and define the length of each time interval by $\Delta\tau = \tau_t - \tau_{t-1}$. We let the measurement unit be in days so that $\tau_0 = 0$ and $\tau_T = 1$. Let $\overline{y}_{dt}$, $d = 1, \ldots D$, $t = 1, \ldots T$ denote the average CPU consumption on the time interval $[\tau_{t-1}, \tau_t]$ at day d. Recall from the sections above that this is in fact our observations. Further let $y_d(\tau)$ denote the current CPU usage at time τ on day d and recall that is unobservable since we only observe the average CPU consumptions $\overline{y}_{dt}$. Let N_d be the number of requests to the CPU processor on day d and let $a_{d1}, \ldots, a_{dN_d}$ denote the arrival times for each of these request. Finally let $s_{d1}, \ldots, s_{dN_d}$ denote the size (processing time) for the requests $a_{d1}, \ldots, a_{dN_d}$. Since we assume a $M/G/\infty$ model, the departure time for request, h_{dn}, will simply be $h_{dn} = a_{dn} + s_{dn}$.

4.2 Statistical Queuing Model

We assume that N_d, $d = 1, \ldots, D$ are independent Poisson distributed stochastic variables with expectation λ. For a homogeneous Poisson process we assume that the requests are uniformly distributed throughout the day. From a practical point of view this is rarely the case and not for the data analyzed in this paper were we observed most of the requests during the day (Sect. 3). In stead we assume an inhomogeneous (time varying) Poisson process and assume that the arrival times of the requests are independent Beta distributed stochastic variables

$$a_{d1}, \ldots, a_{dN_d} \sim \text{Beta}(\alpha, \beta), \ d = 1, \ldots, D$$

By varying the shape parameters α and β most of the arrivals (CPU requests) will happen at different times during the day. E.g. if high values are chosen for both shape parameters, e.g. $\alpha = \beta = 20$, almost all arrivals (CPU requests) will happen within a short time period in the middle of the day. Setting $\alpha = \beta = 1$ the arrivals will be uniformly distributed throughout the day (homogeneous Poisson process). For more details on the Beta distribution, see e.g. [10]. Finally we assume that the processing time of each request is an independent stochastic variable from a Log-normal distribution

$$s_{d1}, \ldots, s_{dN_d} \sim \text{LogN}(\mu, \sigma), \ d = 1, \ldots, D$$

If X is a normally distributed stochastic variable with expectation μ and standard deviation σ, then $Y = \exp(X)$ will be Log-normal distributed with parameters μ and σ. Of course other distributions could be used in the model, but for the data analyzed in this paper, the Log-normal distribution performed well. Since the requests to the CPU can be both very small (short processing time) and very large tasks, we need a distribution that captures this. Taking the exp of outcomes from the normal distribution we potentially get both very small values and very large values and thus the Log-normal distribution is suitable. We also experimented with both an exponential and gamma distribution, but the results were less promising.

Given the arrivals and processing times as described above, and recalling that we assume a $M/G/\infty$ model, the current CPU consumption at time τ on day d is given by

$$y_d(\tau) = \sum_{n=1}^{N_d} I(a_{dn} < \tau < h_{dn})$$

where $I(A)$ is the indicator function returning one if A is true and zero else. We see that $y_d(\tau)$ is simply the sum of the requests being processed at time τ. Finally the CPU observations, $\bar{y}_{dt}$, can be computed from $y_d(\tau)$. Recall that $\bar{y}_{dt}$ is the average CPU consumption on the time interval $[\tau_{t-1}, \tau_t]$ which gives

$$
\begin{aligned}
\bar{y}_{dt} &= \frac{1}{\Delta\tau} \int_{\tau_{t-1}}^{\tau_t} y_d(\tau)\,d\tau \\
&= \frac{1}{\Delta\tau} \int_{\tau_{t-1}}^{\tau_t} \sum_{n=1}^{N_d} I(a_{dn} < \tau < h_{dn})\,d\tau \\
&= \frac{1}{\Delta\tau} \sum_{n=1}^{N_d} \int_{\tau_{t-1}}^{\tau_t} I(a_{dn} < \tau < h_{dn})\,d\tau \\
&= \sum_{n=1}^{N_d} [F(\tau_t; a_{dn}, h_{dn}) - F(\tau_{t-1}; a_{dn}, h_{dn})]
\end{aligned}
\tag{1}
$$

where

$$
F(\tau; a_{dn}, h_{dn}) = \begin{cases}
0 & \text{if } \tau \leq a_{dn} \\
\dfrac{\tau - a_{dn}}{\Delta\tau} & \text{if } a_{dn} < \tau \leq h_{dn} \\
\dfrac{h_{dn} - a_{dn}}{\Delta\tau} & \text{if } \tau > h_{dn}
\end{cases}
$$

4.3 Likelihood Function

Given both the observations (Sect. 3) and the statistical model presented in the previous section, the natural next step is the use the observations to estimate the unknown parameters in the statical model $\lambda, \alpha, \beta, \mu$ and σ. The parameters characterize the properties of the underlying request process to the CPU processor and estimating these parameters is thus the goal of this paper. The most common way to estimate parameters in statistical models is to optimize the likelihood functions which in this case can be written as

$$
L(\lambda, \alpha, \beta, \mu, \sigma \,|\, \bar{\mathbf{y}}_1, \ldots, \bar{\mathbf{y}}_D) = \prod_{d=1}^{D} \left(\int\int \sum_{N_d=0}^{\infty} \text{Poisson}(N_d; \lambda) \times \right.
$$

$$
\left. \left[\prod_{n=1}^{N_d} \text{Beta}(a_{dn}; \alpha, \beta)\,\text{LogN}(s_{dn}; \mu, \sigma) \right] G(\bar{\mathbf{y}}_d \,|\, \mathbf{a}_d, \mathbf{s}_d) d\mathbf{a}_d\,d\mathbf{s}_d \right)
$$

where $\overline{\mathbf{y}}_d = \overline{y}_{d1}, \ldots, \overline{y}_{dt}$, $\mathbf{a}_d = a_{d1}, \ldots, a_{dN_d}$, $\mathbf{s}_d = s_{d1}, \ldots, s_{dN_d}$ and $G(\overline{\mathbf{y}}_d \mid \mathbf{a}_d, \mathbf{s}_d)$ refers to the relation in (1). Here $G(\overline{\mathbf{y}}_d \mid \mathbf{a}_d, \mathbf{s}_d)$ is a delta function since the relation (1) is deterministic. Hence all possible combinations of $N_d, \mathbf{a}_d, \mathbf{s}_d$ that can give rise the the observed data need to be identified. If we knew N_d and also in which time interval $[\tau_{t-1}, \tau_t]$ each a_{dn} and s_{dn} occurred, (1) can be be solved. Unfortunately the number of ways to position the N_d arrivals and N_d departures on T time intervals is given by

$$\binom{2N_d + T - 1}{2N_d}$$

[9] which explodes as either N_d or T increases and the likelihood function thus is infeasible except for in the most simple cases.

5   Approximate Bayesian Computing

Since the likelihood function is infeasible, we resort to a more indirect way to estimate the parameters. Intuitively, if we generate outcomes from the statistical model in Sect. 4.2 using the true parameter values (that generated the real data), we expect that outcomes from the statistical model should be similar to the real data. Fortunately, it is simple to generate outcomes from the statistical model in Sect. 4.2 which means that such an indirect approach is possible. We rely of the framework called Approximate Bayesian Computing (ABC). See [3,7] for nice reviews on the different ABC approaches.

The methodology can be described as follows. Suppose that we have a statistical model with parameter θ. Let $p(\theta)$ denote the prior distribution of the parameter and let Υ_o denote the observations, which were generated from the statistical model with the unknown parameter θ_o. The goal is thus to estimate θ_o. The estimation procedure can then be described as follows.

1. Generate a large set of samples $\theta_1, \ldots, \theta_M$ from the prior distribution $p(\theta)$.
2. For each sample θ_i, generate an outcome from the statistical model Υ_i.
3. Compute a set of K different statistics (sample mean, variance etc.) for each outcome Υ_i, $S_1(\Upsilon_i), \ldots, S_K(\Upsilon_i)$. These statistics summarize the main properties of the data.
4. Compute the same statistics for the observations $S_1(\Upsilon_o), \ldots, S_K(\Upsilon_o)$. Intuitively, if $S_1(\Upsilon_i), \ldots, S_K(\Upsilon_i)$ is close to $S_1(\Upsilon_o), \ldots, S_K(\Upsilon_o)$ using some suitable metric, we expect that θ_i is close to the unknown true parameter θ_o.
5. Fit a statistical model to the relation between the parameters and the statistics using the samples θ_i and $S_1(\Upsilon_i), \ldots, S_K(\Upsilon_i)$, $i = 1, \ldots, M$. We let θ be the response of the model (although the opposite is also possible).
6. Use the statistical model to get inference on the the unknown parameter θ_o. A simple approach is to just plug the observed statistics $S_1(\Upsilon_o), \ldots, S_K(\Upsilon_o)$ into the statistical model and use the output from the model as the estimate of θ_o.

The interested reader is referred to [3,7] for more details. In our case θ refers to the parameters $\lambda, \alpha, \beta, \mu, \sigma$ and Υ to the outcomes from the model in Sect. 4.2, i.e. $\overline{\mathbf{y}}_d$, $d = 1, \ldots, D$.

6 CPU Data Statistics

A crucial part of the ABC methodology, described in the previous section, is to choose statistics that are able to distinguish properties of samples from the model in Sect. 4.2 for different values of the parameters $\lambda, \alpha, \beta, \mu, \sigma$. Thus we started by generating samples from the model for different values of the parameters. We fixed the expected CPU consumption for outputs from the model to be equal to the value in the observations, i.e.

$$E(N_d)E(s_{dn}) = \frac{1}{D} \sum_{d=1}^{D} \overline{y}_d$$

$$\lambda \exp\left(\mu + \sigma^2/2\right) = \frac{1}{D} \sum_{d=1}^{D} \overline{y}_d \tag{2}$$

where the expectations on the left hand side follows from the properties of the Poisson and Log-normal distributions. We thus choose combinations of λ, μ and σ satisfying this relation. We start by setting $\lambda = 50$, μ equal to the four values $-6, -7.5, -9$ and -10.5 and σ were chosen to satisfy (2). Finally we sat $\alpha = \beta = 3$ which resulted in a little more requests happening during day which is in accordance with the real data. To study the effects of adjusting the parametric values, we ran several samples from the model for the different parametric choices. One sample from each of the values of μ are shown i Fig. 2. We see that setting $\mu = -6$ (upper left panel) each CPU request is small and about the same size. For $\mu = -9$ (lower left panel) we see that the output from the model contains both very small tasks and large tasks (the CPU consumption is high for long time periods). For $\mu = -10.5$ (lower right panel) this happens in an even larger degree. Comparing to the real data in Fig. 1, it seem like the lower left panel in Fig. 2 is the most similar to the real data. However it seem to be more spikes in the real data, indicating that $\lambda = 50$ is a too low value to replicate the properties of the real data.

Figure 3 shows the same as Fig. 2 except that we increased λ to 1000. Since we now get far more requests to the CPU, the expected size of each request must be smaller and we set $\mu = -9, -11, -13$ and -15. Comparing Figs. 2 and 3 we see that by increasing λ we get more spiky data which is in accordance with the real data. The lower right panel of Fig. 3 seem to replicate properties of the real data quite well.

Figures 2 and 3 show that by adjusting the parameters of the model we end up with CPU data with different properties. We saw that the ABC method relies on finding suitable statistics of the real data. In the experiments we use the following the statistics.

– Average CPU consumption.

$$\overline{y} = \frac{1}{D} \sum_{d=1}^{D} \overline{y}_d$$

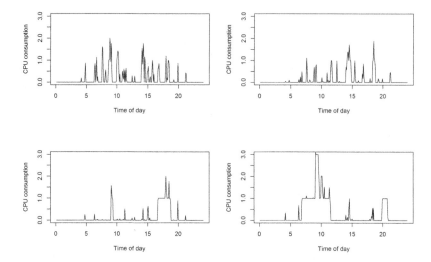

Fig. 2. Samples from the model in Sect. 4.2 for $\lambda = 50$. For the panels from upper left to lower right, $\mu = -6, -7.5, -9$ and -10.5, respectively.

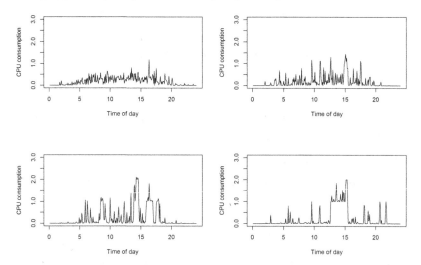

Fig. 3. Samples from the model in Sect. 4.2 for $\lambda = 1000$. For the panels from upper left to lower right, $\mu = -9, -11, -13$ and -15, respectively.

– Cumulative probabilities. Define

$$P_q = \frac{1}{DT} \sum_{d=1}^{D} \sum_{t=1}^{T} I(\overline{y}_{dt} < q)$$

being the portion of observations with a value less than q (quantile). We see that with $\lambda = 50$ compared to $\lambda = 1000$ it is far more common with a CPU consumptions equal to zero, one and two since we have less disturbances from zero, one or two cores running. The same is observed if we use a lower value of μ (lower right panel in Figs. 2 and 3). Thus choosing values of q close to these values seem reasonable. In the estimation procedure we therefore use the following values of q: 0.01, 0.1, 0.5, 0.9, 0.99, 1.01, 1.1, 1.5, 1.9 and 1.99. 2.01. 2.1 and 2.5.

– To measure the degree of spikiness we compute the change in CPU consumption from one time step to the next

$$\frac{1}{D(T-1)} \sum_{d=1}^{D} \sum_{t=2}^{T} |\bar{y}_{dt} - \bar{y}_{dt-1}|$$

– We expect that the spikiness measure above will be higher if the average CPU consumption is high. Therefore we also compute the relative change from one time step to the next.

$$\frac{1}{D(T-1)} \sum_{d=1}^{D} \sum_{t=2}^{T} \frac{|\bar{y}_{dt} - \bar{y}_{dt-1}|}{MA(t)}$$

where $MA(t)$ is a moving average estimate of the expected CPU consumption at different times during the day

$$MA(t) = \frac{1}{D(2L-1)} \sum_{d=1}^{D} \sum_{l=-L}^{L} \bar{y}_{d(t-l)}$$

In the experiments we used $L = 5$. We use the moving average in stead of the CPU consumption observations directly since the observations is very spiky resulting in unstable estimates.

– Changes in average load from one day to another. From Fig. 1 we see that in the real data the average load varies quite much from one day to another and we should have the same property in the model. We there include the standard deviation in the daily averages

$$SD_{\bar{y}} = \sqrt{\frac{1}{D-1} \sum_{d=1}^{D} (\bar{y}_d - \bar{y})^2}$$

Typically choosing μ and σ such that the Log-normal distribution gets more heavy tailed, like the lower right panels in Figs. 2 and 3, the standard deviation of the daily average increases.

– Finally we need some statistics to capture the inhomogeneity in requests during the day, i.e. to estimate the parameters α and β. Let V be a stochastic variable with probabilities

$$P(V = \tau_t) = \frac{MA(t)}{\sum_{t=1}^{T} MA(t)}, \quad t = 1, 2, \ldots, T$$

which can be interpreted as the probability of requests to the CPU at different times during the day. We now compute the expectation and standard deviations of V and use these values as statistics

$$E(V) = \sum_{t=1}^{T} \tau_t \, P(V = \tau_t)$$

$$SD(V) = \sqrt{\sum_{t=1}^{T} (\tau_t - E(V))^2 \, P(V = \tau_t)}$$

If most of the requests happens early (late) during the day, $E(V)$ will have low (high) value. The parameters α and β are directly related to the statistics $E(V)$ and $SD(V)$.

7   Experiments

In the previous sections we have built a reliable model for the CPU consumption data and an estimation strategy based on the ABC framework. In this Section we will evaluate to what extent we are able to recover the request patterns to the CPU processor. To use the ABC procedure, we establish the following.

– Prior distributions. The ABC procedure requires that we have prior distributions for the unknown parameters. We assume that we have little prior information and chose wide uniformly distributed priors as follows

$$p(\lambda) = \text{Unif}(50, 10000)$$
$$p(\alpha) = \text{Unif}(0.5, 10)$$
$$p(\beta) = \text{Unif}(0.5, 10)$$
$$p(\mu) = \text{Unif}(-25, -5)$$
$$p(\sigma) = \text{Unif}(0.5, 7)$$

where $\text{Unif}(a, b)$ denotes the uniform distribution on the interval between a and b.
– Generate samples. We know follow the first three steps of the ABC procedure described in Sect. 5 by generating $M = 4 \cdot 10^6$ samples and computing the statistics presented in Sect. 6.
– In the fifth step of the procedure different statistical models can be used like partial least square [19], neural net [2] or ridge regression [17]. We evaluated both the neural net and the ridge regression approach and both approaches resulted in very similar results. The results below are based on the neural net approach.

In the rest of the paper we set $D = 19$ and $T = 288$ meaning that we have 288 observations per day (every five minutes) for 19 days. This is in accordance with the real data presented in Sect. 3.

7.1   Synthetic Data Example

We start by generating a synthetic dataset from the model with parameter values $\lambda = 500, \alpha = 8, \beta = 8, \mu = -10, \sigma = 2.2$ and compute the statistics from Sect. 6. If the estimation procedure performs well we should get reliable estimates of the parameters used to generate the synthetic data. Figure 4 shows histogram of outcomes from the ABC posterior distribution for the different parameters. We see that the procedure, quite astonishingly, estimates the parameters of the underlying queue process very well.

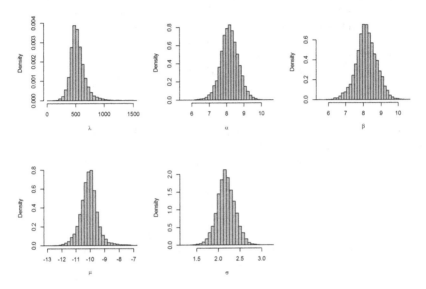

Fig. 4. Synthetic example: Samples from the posterior distribution for the different parameters of the model.

7.2   Real CPU Consumption Data Example

We now run the estimation procedure for the real data. Figure 5 show samples from the posterior distribution for the different parameters. We see that we are able to get fairly precise and reliable estimates of the underlying request process to the CPU processor. In particular the results reveal that the expected number of requests to the CPU processor during a day is somewhere between 1000 (a request about every 1.5 min) and 5000 (a request about every 15 s). We see $\alpha \approx \beta \approx 3.5$ meaning that most of the requests to the CPU processor happens in the middle of the day (office hours), but 3.5 is not a very high value so a fair amount of the requests also happens at other times during the day.

Figure 6 shows four arbitrary samples from the stochastic model using the estimated parameters with the highest posterior probability (the MAP parameters). We see that outcomes from the statistical model replicates the properties of the real CPU consumption data very well.

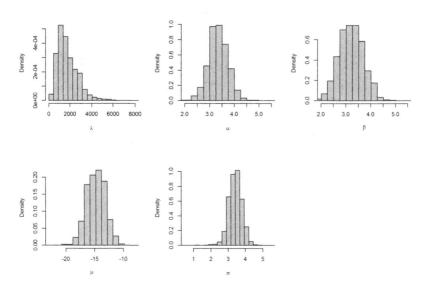

Fig. 5. Real data example: Samples from the posterior distribution for the different parameters of the model.

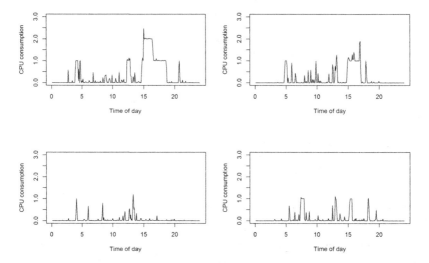

Fig. 6. Real data example: Samples from the statistical model in Sect. 4.2 using the MAP estimate of the unknown parameters.

8   Closing Remarks

In this paper we build a statistical model to replicate how observed CPU consumption data are generated. We demonstrate that by adjusting the parameters of the statistical model, the outcomes from the model have different properties. Next we build statistics that quantify these differences which are used to estimate the parameters of the statistical model to replicate the properties of real CPU consumption data. Our results show that we are able to recover the properties of the underlying request patterns to the CPU processor.

There are several interesting directions for future research. We want to apply the framework to other types of data like single core CPU processors. This adds another complexity since processes may be queued until the CPU is finished with other tasks. If the load is so high that the CPU processor runs continuously, of course recovering of the request pattern is impossible. We may also apply the methodology to other types of data like network data.

References

1. Acharya, S.K.: On normal approximation for maximum likelihood estimation from single server queues. Queueing Syst. **31**(3–4), 207–216 (1999)
2. Blum, M.G.B., François, O.: Non-linear regression models for approximate Bayesian computation. Stat. Comput. **20**(1), 63–73 (2010)
3. Blum, M.G.B., Nunes, M.A., Prangle, D., Sisson, S.A., et al.: A comparative review of dimension reduction methods in approximate Bayesian computation. Stat. Sci. **28**(2), 189–208 (2013)
4. Bouterse, B., Perros, H.: Scheduling cloud capacity for time-varying customer demand. In: 2012 IEEE 1st International Conference on Cloud Networking (CLOUDNET), pp. 137–142. IEEE (2012)
5. Christodoulopoulos, K., Gkamas, V., Varvarigos, E.A.: Statistical analysis and modeling of jobs in a grid environment. J. Grid Comput. **6**(1), 77–101 (2008)
6. Cox, D.R.: The statistical analysis of congestion. J. R. Stat. Soc. Ser. A (Gen.) **118**(3), 324–335 (1955)
7. Drovandi, C.C., Pettitt, A.N., Lee, A., et al.: Bayesian indirect inference using a parametric auxiliary model. Stat. Sci. **30**(1), 72–95 (2015)
8. Fearnhead, P.: Filtering recursions for calculating likelihoods for queues based on inter-departure time data. Stat. Comput. **14**(3), 261–266 (2004)
9. Feller, W.: An introduction to probability theory and its applications. vol. i (1950)
10. Forbes, C., Evans, M., Hastings, N., Peacock, B.: Statistical Distributions. John Wiley & Sons, Hoboken (2011)
11. Guo, L., Yan, T., Zhao, S., Jiang, C.: Dynamic performanceoptimization for cloud computing using M/M/m queueing system. J. Appl. Math. **2014**, 8 (2014)
12. Heggland, K., Frigessi, A.: Estimating functions in indirect inference. J. R. Stat. Soc. Ser. B (Stat. Methodol.) **66**(2), 447–462 (2004)
13. Jain, S.: Relative efficiency of a parameter for a M/G/1 queueing system based on reduced and full likelihood functions. Commun. Stat. Simul. Comput. **21**(2), 597–606 (1992)
14. Kim, J., Shin, K.G.: Execution time analysis of communicating tasks in distributed systems. IEEE Trans. Comput. **45**(5), 572–579 (1996)
15. Liu, X., Li, S., Tong, W.: A queuing model considering resources sharing for cloud service performance. J. Supercomput. **71**(11), 4042–4055 (2015)
16. Mei, J., Li, K., Ouyang, A., Li, K.: A profit maximization scheme with guaranteed quality of service in cloud computing. IEEE Trans. Comput. **64**(11), 3064–3078 (2015)
17. Muniz, G., Kibria, B.M.G.: On some ridge regression estimators: an empirical comparisons. Commun. Stat. Simul. Comput. **38**(3), 621–630 (2009)

18. Nan, X., He, Y., Guan, L.: Queueing model based resource optimization for multimedia cloud. J. Vis. Commun. Image Representation **25**(5), 928–942 (2014)
19. Sjöström, M., Wold, S., Lindberg, W., Persson, J.Å., Martens, H.: A multivariate calibration problem in analytical chemistry solved by partial least-squares models in latent variables. Anal. Chim. Acta **150**, 61–70 (1983)
20. Vilaplana, J., Solsona, F., Teixidó, I., Mateo, J., Abella, F., Rius, J.: A queuing theory model for cloud computing. J. Supercomput. **69**(1), 492–507 (2014)
21. Xiong, W., Altiok, T.: Queueing analysis of a server node in transaction processing middleware systems. Comput. Oper. Res. **35**(8), 2561–2578 (2008)
22. Yuzukirmizi, M., Smith, J.M.: Optimal buffer allocation in finite closed networks with multiple servers. Comput. Oper. Res. **35**(8), 2579–2598 (2008)
23. Zhang, Z., Fan, W.: Web server load balancing: a queueing analysis. Eur. J. Oper. Res. **186**(2), 681–693 (2008)

Impacts of Radio Irregularity on Duty-Cycled Industrial Wireless Sensor Networks

Mithun Mukherjee[1], Lei Shu[1(✉)], Likun Hu[1,2], and Der-Jiunn Deng[3]

[1] Guangdong Provincial Key Lab of Petrochemical Equipment Fault Diagnosis,
Guangdong University of Petrochemical Technology, Maoming 525000, China
{m.mukherjee,lei.shu}@ieee.org
[2] College of Information and Computer Engineering,
Northeast Forestry University, Harbin, China
likun.hu@outlook.com
[3] Department of Computer Science and Information Engineering,
National Changhua University of Education, Changhua, Taiwan
djdeng@cc.ncue.edu.tw

Abstract. With rapid adoption of advanced wireless sensors in last decades, industrial wireless sensor networks (IWSNs) are increasingly deployed in the industries for various applications. Sleep scheduling is a common approach in IWSNs to overcome network lifetime problem due to energy-constrained sensor nodes. However, in real-environment, node's transmit power varies in different directions due to non-isotropic nature of electromagnetic transmission, path-loss, noise, and temperature. Thus, radio irregularity results in link asymmetry, thereafter, affects the performance of sleep scheduling in IWSNs. In this paper, we evaluate the impacts of radio irregularity on sleeping probability and lifetime performances of well-known connected k-neighborhood (CKN)-based sleep scheduling algorithms in duty-cycled IWSNs. We derive the upper-limit of sleep probability with radio irregularity variables. From the extensive simulations, we show that radio irregularity increases the number of awake nodes in duty-cycled sensor networks, therefore, network lifetime decreases with increasing values of link asymmetry parameters. Finally, an adverse impact of radio irregularity is observed in higher k-value in CKN-based algorithm due to more awake nodes to satisfy the k-connectivity in presence of link asymmetry.

Keywords: Industrial wireless sensor networks · Radio irregularity · Duty-cycled IWSNs · CKN-based sleep scheduling

1 Introduction

Recently, with the fast development of various emerging technologies in sensing devices and towards Industry 4.0 of traditional factories, industrial wireless sensor networks (IWSN) has become a global interconnection between management and factory products in large-scale industries [3,5]. Wireless sensor nodes

© ICST Institute for Computer Sciences, Social Informatics and Telecommunications Engineering 2017
L.A. Maglaras et al. (Eds.): INISCOM 2016, LNICST 188, pp. 29–38, 2017.
DOI: 10.1007/978-3-319-52569-3_3

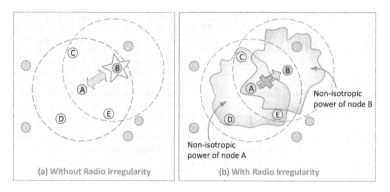

Fig. 1. Link asymmetry due to radio irregularity. (a) B, C, D, and E nodes are 1-hop neighbor of node. Node B decides to wake up at a given instance. (b) However, $link_{A \to B}$ is significantly different from $link_{B \to A}$ due to the link asymmetry.

are widely deployed to many applications, e.g., robotics, large-scale pipeline and equipment monitoring, fault diagnosis, and toxic gas leakage detection. Due to their advantage of low cost, ease of deployment, energy efficiency, and mobility compared to the traditional wired field-bus, an IWSN is a promising approach for manufacturers as well as plant designers.

Constrained by limited physical sensor size, difficult access (e.g., heat exchange tube and rotating machines), and limited energy harvesting possibilities, IWSNs inherit limited lifetime problem of traditional WSNs. Sleep scheduling is one of the effective approaches to prolong network lifetime. Sleep scheduling allows a sub-set of deployed nodes to be awaken, while other nodes go to sleep for a certain amount of time to conserve their energy.

Among the extensive studies in duty-cycled WSNs [1,6], connected k-neighborhood (CKN) [4]-based approach has drawn a significant interest due to the following reasons: (1) each node have at least $min(N_u, k)$ awake neighbors in each epoch, where N_u is the set of 1-hop neighbors of node u and k is any positive integer, (2) all awake nodes will be connected, (3) every node (awake or sleep) has an awake neighbor, and (4) the set of awake nodes changes from epoch to epoch. The CKN algorithm efficiently reduces the number of active nodes while keeping the network k-connected. Recently, we proposed several CKN-based sleep scheduling schemes such as energy-consumption-based CKN (EC-CKN) [8], geographic routing-oriented sleep scheduling (GSS) [13], geographic-distance-based connected k-neighborhood for first path (GCKNF) [13] and geographic-distance-based CKN for all paths (GCKNA) [13], collaborative location-based sleep scheduling (CLSS) [11], and priority-based sleep scheduling (PSS) [12] in duty-cycled WSNs.

Since the low-power link quality in IWSNs strongly depends on the radio characteristics of the sensor nodes, radio irregularity [10] has a heavy impact on the performance of IWSNs. In the literature, several experimental studies have been presented in [2,7,9] to characterize the low-powered link through real-world

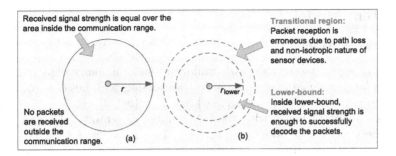

Fig. 2. (a) Example of binary perfect-reception within the transmission range. (b) However, the links are highly unreliable due to *transitional* region in real-deployment.

measurement with different assumptions and scenarios. However, apart from the cross-technology interference due to coexisting wireless devices with IEEE 802.11 b/g (WiFi), IEEE 802.15.1 (bluetooth), and IEEE 802.15.4 (ZigBee) standards, path loss, non-isotropic nature such as diffraction, scattering, and reflection of electromagnetic (EM) transmission, temperature, equipment noise are responsible for radio irregularity in low-powered IWSNs. This radio irregularity often results in link asymmetry as shown in Fig. 1. Link asymmetry is not always correlated with distance, rather is mainly located at the transitional region [14] where the received power is not good enough to correctly decode the packet. As shown in Fig. 2, a large number of links are unreliable in the transitional region in the dense deployments due to high-variance in reception rates and asymmetric connectivity. In addition, the transitional region of any nodes creates interference to its neighbor nodes, and leads to packet-error-reception (PER). Although the sleep scheduling algorithms [1,4,6,8,11–13] provide the efficient way to increase the network lifetime, however, none of them consider effects of the radio irregularity [2,9,10] in their schemes.

The focus of this paper is to investigate the effect of radio irregularity on the duty-cycled IWSNs. We evaluate the performance of sleeping probability with the link asymmetry and number nodes that have this asymmetric problem in the CKN-based sleep scheduling. We further derive the upper-limit of sleeping probability for the CKN-based sleep scheduling algorithms in presence of the radio irregularity.

The rest of the paper is organized as follows. Section 2 presents the system model. The analysis of CKN-based schemes with radio irregularity is conducted in Sect. 3. The simulation results are presented in Sect. 4. Finally, conclusions are drawn in Sect. 5.

2   System Model

2.1   Network Model

We consider a multihop WSN with uniformly and randomly deployed sensor nodes in a large-scale 2-dimensional industrial sensing field. Let $G = (S, E)$ be a network graph, where $S = \{s_1, s_2, \ldots s_N\}$ and $E = \{e(1,2), e(1,3), \ldots, e(N,N)\}$ are the set of sensor nodes with total N number of sensor nodes and the set of edges between sensor nodes, respectively. Two sensor nodes $\{u, v\} \in S$ are called 1-hop neighbor if they are within the transmission region of each other and $e(u, v) \in E$. We assume bi-directional communication between 1-hop neighbors. It is assumed that MAC layer will mask the unidirectional links and pass the bidirectional links. Any two nodes $\{u, v\} \in S$ belong to 2-hop neighbor if $e(u, v) \notin E$, however, there exists a node $k \in S$ with $\{e(u, k), e(k, v)\} \in E$. The location of any sensor node along with its 1-hop neighbors can be obtained by possibly using the global positioning system (GPS) or other techniques such as triangulation or localization. The sink node knows the location and IDs of all nodes. We also do not consider the energy consumption aspect in this research work as we assume that the industrial sensor nodes can harvest energy from environment by using additional device, e.g., solar power panel. It is also assumed that each node has the same functionality and sensing capability. With a very large number of sensor nodes, we ensure a well-connected WSN in deployed area.

2.2   Radio Irregularity Model

We consider radio irregularity model (RIM) in [10]. Assume that each node u loses its unidirectional link $\texttt{link}_{u \rightarrow v}$ to any node v $\forall v \in N_u$ with a probability $\alpha(u)$ at each instant due to time-varying nature of radio irregularity. Since we assume RTS/CTS-based link scheduling, quality of the bi-directional link $l(u, v)$ strongly depends on $\alpha(u)$ and $\alpha(v)$ $\forall v \in N_u$. Let β be the ratio of the number of nodes with link asymmetry and the total number of deployed nodes in a given area $\mathcal{A}$. We observe that quality of bi-directional link depends on individual loosing connection, i.e., $\alpha(u)$ as well as number of nodes that suffer from link asymmetry, which is related to β. Without loss of generality, we denote $\alpha(u)$ and β as link asymmetry and node asymmetry, respectively. For the sake of simplicity, we drop u from $\alpha(u)$ in the rest of the paper.

3   Performance Analysis of CKN-Based Sleep Scheduling with Radio Irregularity Model

3.1   Sleep Probability Without Radio Irregularity

The probability that any node u has n neighbors in uniformly and randomly distributed WSNs with N nodes within an area $\mathcal{A}$ is given as

$$P(|N_u| = n) = \frac{\left(\rho \pi r^2\right)^n}{n!} \exp\left(-\rho \pi r^2\right), \tag{1}$$

where $\rho = N/\mathcal{A}$ is the node density. Thus, the expectation of the 1-hop neighbors of u is given as $\mathbb{E}\left[\|N_u\|\right] = \rho\pi r^2$. We denote N_u and N'_u are the set of the uth 1- and 2-hop neighbors, respectively. The probability that the graph G is k-connected is

$$P(G)_{\text{k-connected}} = \left(1 - \sum_{n=0}^{k-1} \frac{\left(\rho\pi r^2\right)^n}{n!} \exp\left(-\rho\pi r^2\right)\right)^N \tag{2}$$

Similarly, we deduce the probability that the graph $G_{C_u+C'_u}$ is connected as follows

$$\text{Prob}_1 = P\left(G_{C_u+C'_u}\right)_{\text{1-connected}} = \left(1 - \exp\left(-\rho'\pi r^2\right)\right)^{\left(|C_u|+|C'_u|\right)}, \tag{3}$$

where $\rho' = |S'|/\mathcal{A}$, C_u, C'_u, and S' are the subset of N_u, N'_u, and S whose rank $\leq \text{rank}_u$, where rank_u is the random rank that the senor node u picks randomly. Therefore, the probability that the graph G_{N_u} is k-connected in C_u is expressed as

$$\text{Prob}_2 = P\left(G_{N_u\sim C_u}\right)_{\text{k-connected}} = \left(1 - \sum_{n=0}^{k-1} \frac{\left(\rho'\pi r^2\right)^n}{n!} \exp\left(-\rho'\pi r^2\right)\right)^{|C_u|} \tag{4}$$

Therefore, the sleep probability of the node u in CKN-based sleep scheduling is expressed as $P_{\text{sleep}}(u) = \text{Prob}_1 \times \text{Prob}_2$, where Prob_1 and Prob_1 consider the two conditions of the CKN algorithm as (1) the graph $G_{C_u+C'_u}$ is connected and (2) the graph G_{N_u} is connected by C_u nodes, respectively.

3.2   Sleep Probability with Radio Irregularity

The probability that any node u with loosing neighbor connection probability $\alpha(u)$ has n neighbors with a uniformly and randomly distributed WSN in an area $\mathcal{A}$ is given as

$$\begin{aligned} P(|N_u| = n)^{\text{Irregular}} &= \frac{\left(\beta(1-\alpha)\rho\pi r^2 + (1-\beta)\rho\pi r^2\right)^n}{n!} \\ &\quad \times \exp\left(-\beta(1-\alpha)\rho\pi r^2 - (1-\beta)\rho\pi r^2\right) \\ &= \frac{\left((1-\beta\alpha)\rho\pi r^2\right)^n}{n!} \times \exp\left(-(1-\beta\alpha)\rho\pi r^2\right) \end{aligned} \tag{5}$$

Thus, the probability that the graph G is connected in presence of radio irregularity is given as

$$P(G)_{\text{k-connected}}^{\text{Irregular}} = \left(1 - \sum_{n=0}^{k-1} \frac{\left((1-\beta\alpha)\rho\pi r^2\right)^n}{n!} \exp\left(-(1-\beta\alpha)\rho\pi r^2\right)\right)^N. \tag{6}$$

Table 1. Simulation parameters

Parameters	Values
Network size	$600 \times 600 \, \text{m}^2$
Number of sensor nodes	200 to 1000
k-value in CKN	1 to 10
Transmission radius	$60 \, \text{m}$
E_{elec}	$50 \, \text{nJ/bit}$
E_{amp}	$50 \, \text{nJ/bit/m}^2$
Initial energy	$100000 \, \text{mJ}$
Time epoch	$1 \, \text{min}$
Packet size	12 byte
Packet number	$1000 \times 32768^{32768}$

Using (3), (4), (5), and (6), the sleep probability of the node u with the link asymmetry becomes

$$P_{\text{sleep}}(u)^{\text{Irregular}} = \left(1 - \exp\left(-(1 - \beta\alpha)\rho'\pi r^2\right)\right)^{\left(|C_u| + |C'_u|\right)}$$

$$\times \left(1 - \sum_{n=0}^{k-1} \frac{\left((1 - \beta\alpha)\rho\pi r^2\right)^n}{n!} \exp\left(-(1 - \beta\alpha)\rho\pi r^2\right)\right)^{|C_u|}. \quad (7)$$

Note that the sleep probability in presence of radio irregularity is less than that without radio irregularity. Therefore, more number of nodes are awakened to satisfy the k-connectivity in duty-cycled WSNs with radio irregularity.

4   Simulation Results

In this section, we evaluate the impact of radio irregularity on sleeping rate and network lifetime of the CKN-based sleep scheduling in WSNs.

4.1   Simulation Setup

We conducted extensive simulation using the WSN simulator NetTopo[1]. For each number of deployed sensor nodes, we average the results over 100 network topologies with different seeds. The number of sensor nodes ranges from 200 to 1000 (each time increased by 100). The simulation parameters are summarized in Table 1. The network lifetime is defined as the instant from the network deployment to the instant when the first sensor node runs out of energy.

---

[1] NetTopo (online at http://sourceforge.net/projects/nettopo/) is an open source software for simulating and visualizing WSNs.

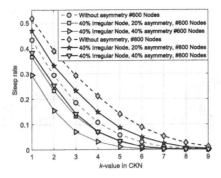

Fig. 3. Sleep rate with probability of link and node asymmetry in 600 and 800 numbers of deployed nodes with different k-value in CKN-based sleep scheduling.

4.2 Sleep Rate vs. k-Value with Different Node Density

To illustrate the impact of radio irregularity, Fig. 3 shows sleeping probability of CKN-based sleep scheduling with $\alpha = 0.4$, and $\beta = 0.2$ and 0.4. As observed in Fig. 3, the sleep-rate degrades with higher k-value due to more number of awaken node to satisfy the k-connectivity. Since less number of nodes are awaken to maintain k-value in CKN algorithm, the sleeping rate is higher in 800 node deployment compared to 600 nodes. The sleeping probability degrades with the irregularity parameter $\alpha = 0.4$ and $\beta = 0.2$ for both 600 and 800 node deployment. The reason is that more nodes have to be awaken to maintain k-connectivity due to link asymmetry nature. Furthermore, as β, which is the probability that how many nodes with asymmetric link, increases from 0.4 to 0.2, the impact is more compared to the previous value. To obtain a sleeping rate about 0.07, the maximum k-value can be satisfied upto 4 and 3 for $\{\alpha = 0.4, \beta = 0.2\}$ and $\{\alpha = 0.4, \beta = 0.4\}$, respectively with 600 nodes.

4.3 Sleeping Rate vs. Radio Irregularity Variable

Figure 4 illustrates sleep rate for CKN-based sleep scheduling with different probabilities of link and node asymmetry in duty-cycled IWSNs. From Fig. 4, we observe that sleep rate reduces with higher values of irregularity variables α and β. As observed in Fig. 4(a) and (b), sleep probability is 0.07 with $\alpha = 0.4$ and $\beta = 0.4$ with a number of node deployment of 200 with $k = 1$. We observe that almost all the nodes are awaken beyond $\alpha = 0.5$ and $\beta = 0.6$ for $k = 3$. Thus, the sleeping probability tends to zero as shown in Fig. 4(b). Accordingly, from the Fig. 4(c) and (d), we see that the sleeping rate is higher in 600 node deployment compared to 200 node deployment with $k = 1$ and $k = 3$, respectively, due to more number of sensor deployment. However, at higher k-value, the sleep rate degrades due to the increasing probabilities of link asymmetry and nodes with asymmetric nature. The performances of 1000 node deployment are shown in Fig. 4(e) and (f) with $k = 1$ and $k = 8$, respectively. The sleeping probability is

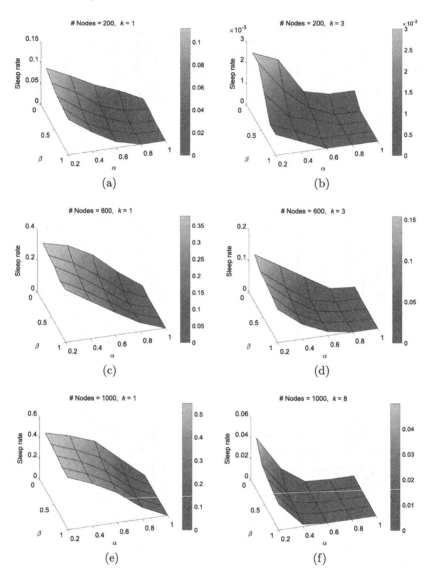

Fig. 4. Sleep rate with probability of asymmetric node and different link asymmetry at various numbers of deployed nodes with k value in CKN-based sleep scheduling.

higher compared to the previous node density, however, at a high deployment cost. We also observe that the k-value can be maintained upto 8 with $\alpha = 0.4$ and $\beta = 0.8$ with 1000 nodes. From the results we confirm that impact of radio irregularity is more in higher k-value in CKN algorithm since more number of deployed nodes are awaken to maintain k-connectivity in asymmetric nature of the radio link.

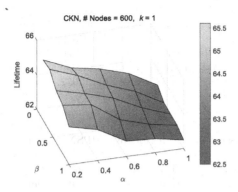

Fig. 5. Network lifetime with the probability of asymmetric node and different link asymmetry in the CKN-based sleep scheduling.

4.4   Life Time vs. Irregularity Variables

In order to see the relationship between the network lifetime and radio irregu-larity variables, we present the simulation results in Fig. 5. The network lifetime decreases with the increasing values of radio irregularity parameters α and β. As the link asymmetry becomes more serious with higher α value with more number of asymmetric nodes, i.e. β, the round of duty cycle decreases due to more number of awake nodes.

5   Conclusion

In this paper, we investigated the impact of radio irregularity on sleep prob-ability for CKN-based duty-cycled IWSNs. We observed that more number of deployed nodes are awakened to satisfy higher k-constraint in presence of radio irregularity. The extensive simulation results further support the adverse impact of link asymmetry of the nodes as well as the number of nodes that have link asymmetry. In addition, our analysis shows that sleeping probability decreases when the radio links become more asymmetric in duty-cycled IWSNs.

Acknowledgments. This work is supported by Guangdong University of Petrochem-ical Technology through Internal Project 2012RC106, 2013 Special Fund of Guang-dong Higher School Talent Recruitment, Educational Commission of Guangdong Province, China Project 2013KJCX0131, Guangdong High-Tech Development Fund 2013B010401035, and National Natural Science Foundation of China Grant 61401107. Lei Shu is the corresponding author.

References

1. Berman, P., Calinescu, G., Shah, C., Zelikovsky, A.: Power efficient monitoring management in sensor networks. In: Proceedings of the IEEE WCNC, pp. 2329–2334. Atlanta, Georgia USA, April 2004

2. Cerpa, A., Wong, J.L., Kuang, L., Potkonjak, M., Estrin, D.: Statistical model of lossy links in wireless sensor networks. In: Proceedings of the IEEE IPSN, pp. 81–88. Los Angeles, California, April 2005

3. Evans, P.C., Annunziata, M.: Industrial internet: pushing the boundaries of minds and machines. Technical report, November 2012. www.ge.com/docs/chapters/Industrial_Internet.pdf

4. Nath, S., Gibbons, B.: P.: Communicating via fireflies: geographic routing on duty-cycled sensors. In: Proceedings of the IEEE/ACM 6th International Symposium on Information Processing in Sensor Networks (IPSN), Cambridge, MA, pp. 440–449, April 2007

5. Sasajima, H., Ishikuma, T., Hayashi, H.: Future IIoT in process automation – Latest trends of standardization in industrial automation. In: Proceedings of the IEEE 54th Annual Conference on Social Instrumentation Control Engineers of Japan (SICE), Hangzhou, China, pp. 963–967, July 2015

6. Tian, D., Georganas, N.: A coverage-preserving node scheduling scheme for large wireless sensor networks. In: Proceedings of the ACM International Workshop on Wireless Sensor Networks and Application, Atlanta, Georgia, USA, pp. 32–41 (2002)

7. Wang, L., Washington, W., Gilmore, K., Liu, C.: Impact of radio irregularities on connectivity of wireless networks with log-normal shadowing. In: Proceedings of the 11th IEEE International Conference on Mobile Ad-hoc and Sensor Networks (MSN), Shenzhen, pp. 250–257, December 2015

8. Wang, L., Yuan, Z., Shu, L., Shi, L., Qin, Z.: An energy-efficient CKN algorithm for duty-cycled wireless sensor networks. Int. J. Distrib. Sensor Netw. **2012**, 1–15 (2012)

9. Zhao, J., Govindan, R.: Understanding packet delivery performance in dense wireless sensor networks. In: Proceedings of the ACM Sensor System, Los Angeles, California, pp. 1–13, November 2003

10. Zhou, G., He, T., Krishnamurthy, S., Stankovic, J.A.: Models and solutions for radio irregularity in wireless sensor networks. ACM Trans. Sensor Netw. **2**(2), 221–262 (2006)

11. Zhu, C., Leung, V.C.M., Yang, L.T., Shu, L.: Collaborative location-based sleep scheduling for wireless sensor networks integratedwith mobile cloud computing. IEEE Trans. Comput. **64**(7), 1844–1856 (2015)

12. Zhu, C., Sheng, Z., Leung, V.C.M., Shu, L., Yang, L.T.: Toward offering more useful data reliably to mobile cloud from wireless sensor network. IEEE Trans. Emerg. Topics Comput. **3**(1), 84–94 (2015)

13. Zhu, C., Yang, L.T., Shu, L., Leung, V.C.M., Rodrigues, J.P.C., Wang, L.: Sleep scheduling for geographic routing in duty-cycled mobile sensor networks. IEEE Trans. Ind. Electron. **61**(11), 6346–6355 (2014)

14. Zuniga, M., Krishnamachari, B.: Analyzing the transitional region in low power wireless links. In: Proceedings of the IEEE SECON, Santa Clara, California, pp. 517–526, October 2004

Security Visualization: Detecting Denial of Service

Glen Hawthorne, Ying He$^{(\boxtimes)}$, Leandros Maglaras, and Helge Janicke

De Montfort University, Leicester LE1 9BH, UK
grhawthorne@googlemail.com,
{ying.he,leandros.maglaras,heljanic}@dmu.ac.uk

Abstract. Denial Of Service attacks are notorious attack methods used to target servers of IT systems and Industrial Control Systems to prevent them from working or to reduce efficiency, hence decreasing user experience. Visualization is the method of taking data, processing and displaying data in an easy to view format. Visualization could be used to identify Denial Of Service attacks by monitoring the data sent to clients and being displayed to the users. Manipulating the type of data shown and the format it is shown in can help users spot potential attacks by seeing outliers in the data sets. This research develops novel software that can run on an web server. It processes the web access logs, displays the data to users and identify potential attacks in access logs. The software has been tested, with the majority of tests passing. Further development of the project is discussed and the main areas for development are also explored.

Keywords: Denial of service attack · Security visualization · Web logs · Intrusion detection

1 Introduction

Denial Of Service and Distributed Denial Of Service attacks have been proven to be constant threats as over two thousand attacks are launched daily and can be purchased via the black market, allowing those who lack technical skills to launch attacks [17]. According to previous research, speed is an important feature and the software will need to match reading 70000 records a second from a web log [18]. The data need to be presented in a clear way that allows quick reading by the user and operate independently of web server applications. Tools are available for monitoring web servers but can only operate with specific web servers. This paper reviews the most popular web servers (Apache, nginx, Microsoft IIS and Google Server), and identifies the format they utilize to save the web logs that allow software to process them.

In the three main control systems of a Critical Infrastructure, the SCADA is the central nerve system that constantly gathers the latest status from remote units. Many researchers have applied Internet technologies in order to improve

© ICST Institute for Computer Sciences, Social Informatics and Telecommunications Engineering 2017
L.A. Maglaras et al. (Eds.): INISCOM 2016, LNICST 188, pp. 39–49, 2017.
DOI: 10.1007/978-3-319-52569-3_4

certain functions in a SCADA system. Authors in [19] present a web-based SCADA display system which is implemented based on the client/server architecture that can control the operation of a substation on the server side. Authors in [20] present a Web-based power quality monitoring system that is allowing users to operate the system through the browser. SCADA systems are vulnerable to many attacks [21, 24] and new Intrusion Detection Systems that can monitor both the network traffic [23] or the web server activity [22] are of great need.

In order to help users identify when their server is targeted by a Denial Of Service attack, this article presents a novel software to analyze web server access logs. Using the data extracted from the access logs, graphs are created and visually displays users different loads on the web server. The developed application is also capable of detecting possible HTTP Flood denial (and distributed) of service attacks.

This paper is structured as follows. Section 2 reviews related work of Denial Of Service attacks; Sect. 3 presents existing products, web server applications and logs; Sect. 4 introduces the software developed that can extract information from the logs to detect attacks and visualize information to the users and Sect. 5 summarizes the paper and discusses future work.

2 Related Work

Denial Of Service attacks can render online resources inaccessible/unavailable to users [2]. They are not designed to breach security but can be used as a distraction technique for other malicious practices. Being a high profile form of attack, Denial Of Service attack is a popular method used by hacktivists, cyber vandals and other similar groups. The attacks are capable of lasting for extended periods of time and can be damaging to the victim organisation in terms of monetary loss, loss of customer trust and damage to reputation.

Denial Of Service attacks are attacks sent from a single host, however, when an attack is sent from multiple hosts it is classed as a Distributed Denial Of Service attack [1]. Distributed Denial Of Service attacks are usually launched via the use of a botnet.

UDP Flood Denial Of Service attacks use IP packets that contain UDP datagrams [3]. When the targeted machine receives the packets it checks for programs associated with the received datagrams. When no associated program can be found the victim machine sends a destination unreachable response. As more and more UDP packets are sent to the target machine and are responded too, the victim will eventually become overwhelmed and unable to respond to user requests.

SYN Flood is a form of Denial Of Service attack that exploits vulnerabilities in the TCP three way handshake protocol and is designed to abuse resources on the targeted machine [4]. The attacking machine(s) will send TCP connection requests faster than the victim is capable of processing them. The attack works via the attacker sending repeated SYN packets to all ports on the targeted server, the server in turn replying to each sent packet with a SYN ACK packet while the attacking machine is not responding to the SYN ACK packets as would normally happen. The server then waits for acknowledgment (for the SYN ACK) and while waiting for this response the connection cannot be closed. Before the connection times out more SYN packets are received resulting in an increasing amount of open connections. This leads to the server maxing out on the amount of connections it can handle and legitimate users being denied access to resources. SYN packets can be sent with fake IP addresses by the attacker, making the victim server respond to fake addresses.

HTTP Flood attack is another form of Denial Of Service attack that often utilize botnets [5]. For a HTTP Flood attack to be successfully executed, knowledge of the target is required, meaning that each attack must be specifically designed, making it hard to detect. This form of attack utilizes GET and POST methods. The POST method is the most effective for this attack as the parameters passed require dynamic processing on the server side absorbing greater resources from the victim. The GET method can be used to get static content from the target server. POST is a more effective form of HTTP Flood due to the extra processing that is required on server side, however, GET is a more scalable in distributed denial of service attacks.

The Ping of Death is a Denial Of Service attack that allows malicious users to send IP packets greater than the 65532 byte limit [6]. Fragmentation is a feature offered with TCP packets that allows the packets to be broken down into smaller segments. It is possible to send packets that exceed the 65536 byte limit with the use of fragmentation. When operating systems receive a packet that exceed the limit, they would freeze, crash or reboot. It also allows for attackers to remain anonymous as the identify of the attacker can be easily falsified. The only detail an attacker would need to know about the victim machine is the IP address.

3   Existing Products

Logstalgia is marketed as a website traffic visualization tool that is capable of watching live as well as replaying requests made to a web server, it is designed to be in the style of the classic computer game Pong [7]. The log formats supported by Logstalgia are NCSA Common Log Format, NCSA Common Log Format with Virtual Host, NCSA Extended/Combined Log Format and NCSA Extended/Combined Log Format with Virtual Host. However, the software is dependent upon OpenGL and is recommended to run on a workstation rather than the web server. The traffic is represented via coloured blocks traveling across the screen, from the clients on the left to the web server on the right of the screen.

Nginx is a popular web server. The nginx Plus version provides the user with a real time monitoring interface that provides information on key load and performance issues [8]. The monitoring interface can provide a range of information on the server and running details. It provides administrative information on the server including the version number running and its IP address. It also shows the amount of connections to the server, number of requests, detailed information on server zones and up-streams as well as the amount of traffic going through the TCP zones.

The Webalizer is a web server log analyzer that produces reports in HTML format [9]. It is fast and claims to be able to process roughly 70000 records per second on a 1.6 GHZ laptop [9]. It supports a wide range of web server log file layouts which includes Common Log File Format, several variations of NCSA Combined Logfile format, wu-ftp/proftpd xferf format logs, Squid proxy server native format and W3C Extended log formats. The Webalizer is capable of analyzing compressed web logs without the need of uncompressing them. When analyzing log files there is no limit to the size of the file being analyzed and is also capable of analyzing partial logs. The Webalizer is capable of generating reports via command line, supports IPv4 and IPv6 addressing and has built in geolocation services.

Imperva Incapsula is a piece of software that provides Distributed Denial Of Service attack mitigation and aims to protect against layer 3, 4 and 7 Denial Of Service attacks [10]. It can be installed in less than five minutes, offering automatic detection and activation with an extremely low rate of false positives. Running in real time it is capable of blocking multi-gigabit attacks and can also prevent SQL injection and cross site scripting attack. The claim is that it will not slow down the site running it, but make the site run faster and more efficiently, using less resources by offering various acceleration techniques. No server down time is required during installation of the software.

3.1   Web Server Applications

There are numerous web server applications and they can run on a variety of operating systems. Table 1 shows that Apache is currently the most widely used web server application as of January 2015. Table 2 shows the most popular (for the top one million domains as of 2012) operating system to run when a hosting web server is Linux.

Table 1. Most popular web servers

Web server application	Percentage of market share [12]
Apache	39.74 %
Microsoft	27.52 %
nginx	14.47 %
Google	2.30 %
Other	15.83 %

3.2   Web Server Logs

There are numerous standardized ways in which web servers can store their logs, each variety having different information and different way of storing it. The

Table 2. Operating systems running web server applications

Operating systems	Percentage of operating systems running web servers [13]
Linux	46.30 %
CentOS	16.60 %
RedHat	10.90 %
Ubuntu	9.00 %
Debian	7.67 %
ebian	7.67 %
Fedora	3.51 %
FreeBSD	2.06 %
Windows	1.27 %
SUSE	1.05 %

Table 3. Explanation of fields in NCSA common log file format

Format	Meaning [14]
remotehost	The remote host name of IP address of the client
rfc931	Remote log name of the client
authuser	The name the client is authorised with
date	Date and time the request was made
request	Request line as it came from the client
status	The HTTP status code returned to the user
bytes	The content length of the document transferred

NCSA Common Log File Format is a standardized way to layout web logs. It is outlined below and explained in Table 3. In some web servers, such as Apache, a hyphen is used in the log-in indicating a field is not available for the log [11].

The W3C Extended Log Format is another standardized way in which a web server can store its logs, it was designed to be an improved format of the Common Log File Format for storing web logs [15]. It allows for additional information to be included (compared to the Common Log Format) in the logs or selected information to be omitted from the logs. Table 4 below outlines and explains what each of the possible fields in the W3C Extended Log Format is used for.

The W3C Extended Log Format also provides additional information at the start of the log [15], It holds the version of the W3C Extended Log Format being used, the fields recorded in the log, the software that generated the logs, the date and time the log was started, the date and time the log ended, the date and time in which the entry was added and a comment section [15].

The Combined Log Format offers the same information as the common log format, plus additional fields [16]. The extra data offered includes: the name of the site that the user was on if they followed a link, information about the user

Table 4. Explanation of fields in WC extended log format

Field	Explanation
Date	Date at which transaction was completed
Time	Time at which transaction was completed
Time-taken	Time taken for transaction to compete, measured in seconds
Bytes	Amount of bytes transferred
Cached	Whether a cache hit occurred
IP	The IP address and port
DNS	The DNS name
Status	The status code returned
Comment	The comment returned with the status code
Method	The method
URI	The URI
URI-stem	Stem part of the URI
Count	The number of entries for the listed data
Time-from	Time that the sampling began
Time-to	Time that the sampling ended
Interval	Length of time that sampling occurred for, recorded in seconds

i.e. browser and browser version and operating system used as well as information on cookies that we sent by the HTTP server [16].

3.3   Web Servers and Web Logs

Having discovered the most popular web server applications used and some common standardized web log layouts, the web log layout that web severs offer, needs to be researched also.

Google allows members of the public to host their websites on Google servers. It is thought that these servers run a custom web server built and maintained by Google. Due to the proprietary nature of this web server it will not be possible to discover how Google layout their web logs.

The Apache web server supports Common Log Format, Combined Log Format and Conditional Logs. The nginx web server supports Combined Log Format and Modified/custom variation of the Combined Log Format. Microsoft IIS supports W3C Extended Log File Format, W3C Centralised Logging, NCSA Common Log File Format, IIS Log File Format, ODBC Logging, Centralised Binary Logging and HTTP.sys Error Log Files.

4   Proposed Software Application

The main functionality of this software product is to extract information from the logs to detect an attack and manipulate the data from the access logs to present information to the user that is useful and can visually identify attacks on the server.

4.1   Software Introduction

The software allows users to enter the path to web access logs, view the data contained in the logs, filter the data to view and receive and alert to address that could contain denial of service attacks. It was decided to investigate the data available in the logs after an attack on a web server as the access logs are usually overlooked by some products on the market and could contain useful information. The software processes NCSA Common Log File Format and Combined Log Format web logs.

Figure 1 displays an example of the graph that is used to show the total load on the web server. Figure 2 shows the class diagram for the main classes used by the produced software. The diagram shows how classes interact. By examining the diagram it is obvious that the program abides with Model View Controller (MVC) [26] principles. More classes were used in the construction of the software, however, these are items such as file readers and data structures that would crowd the diagram and are not necessary to show the flow of the program. Figure 3 displays the point chart of addresses. Each address has a different color, allowing for easy identification of addresses.

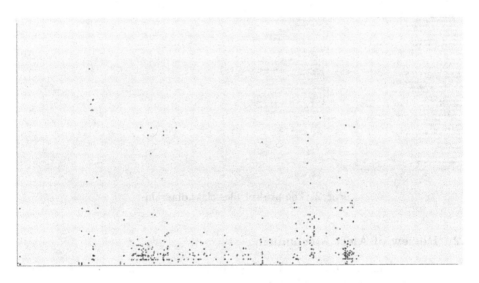

Fig. 1. The total load on the web server

The software has been designed to help build learned actions during repeated use, allowing experienced users to quickly navigate the menus effectively. As explained by [25], once actions have been completed repetitively they start to become learned behaviour and can be performed without the need to think about how to achieve the task.

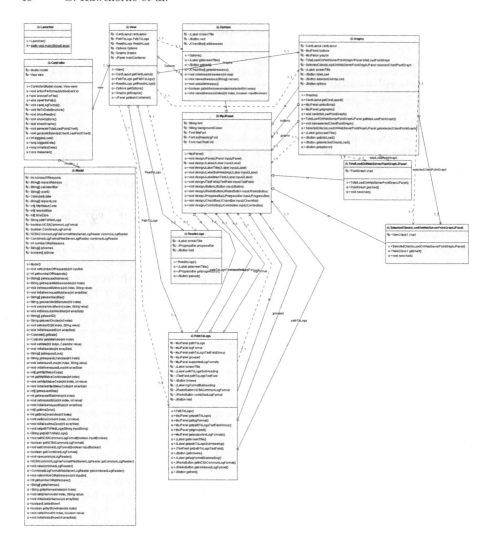

Fig. 2. The project files class diagram

4.2 Review of Alert Mechanism

The alert mechanism runs after the web server access logs have been processed and saved into the memory. The total load of the server is calculated by taking the sum of all pages sent by the web server. This value is divided by the number of unique addresses found in the provided web access log in order to calculate the average load per address. Although this may seem to be a primitive way of detecting an attack, HTTP Flood attacks swamp the server with too many requests, which means that any address that initiates an HTTP Flood attack produces a load on the web server that is way above average.

Fig. 3. The point chart of addresses

The addresses that are identified as potential Denial Of Service attack sources, are displayed in an application modal pop up. The pop up is effective for delivering the information for the application in its present format, however, for a log file with a small number of addresses it may prove to be inaccurate. The more addresses there exist in the network, the more effective the attack detection is. In the future when application will be adapted to run in real time, a log file for the application could be used to store the detected attacks. This will allow the user to store the information for future reference and offer other software the choice to access the information found.

4.3 Review of Testing

There were three branches of the testing: Specification Testing, Manual Testing Of Software and Automated Testing. The testing of the software has been positive, meeting the important areas in the specification, behaving as expected during use and passing all automated testing meaning the software produced is robust with a minimum chance of bugs.

The Specification Testing had mixed results during the test. The majority of tests in the Required Specification Test Report were passed. The project was written in Java and is compliant with MVC specification while being platform independent. Files used in the project are documented with JavaDoc. The developed software can process the NCSA Common Log File Format and is capable of reading more than 70000 line from web logs per second. The software is capable of comparing multiple selected clients load on the web server, and all clients load on the web server. HTTP Flood attacks can be automatically detected and visualized via the graphs made. SYN Flood attacks and UDP Flood attacks cannot be detected via the software as they are not saved into the web logs.

5   Summary and Future Work

This paper has explored the problems that Denial Of Service attacks can cause, the products that are currently on the market and the features that they offer. The most popular web logs are examined along with the percentage of operating systems that host web server applications. The format of the most commonly used web logs are examined and the format of web logs that web servers can save in are listed. The article also presents a novel software application that can be used in order to detect UDP Flood, SYN Flood and HTTP Flood attacks on a web server that runs the proposed software. The application can extract information from the logs and use them in order to detect an attack and can use the data from the access logs in order to visualize attack information to the users. The software has been tested, and the results are positive.

The main focus of further development would be to modify the software to enable it to run in real time. This would provide a greater usability feature as it could be used to identify attacks as they are taking place. Different log formats could be supported by the software, allowing compatibility with more set ups and providing the opportunity of greater market share. More graph types could be added to the application, such as the three dimensional graph, providing more ways to visualize the data. Different filtering methods could also be used, such as filtering on the HTTP status code of a request, providing sophisticated mechanisms for filtering out misleading or irrelevant data before creating the graphs.

References

1. Bartholemy, A., Chen, W.: An examination of distributed denial of service attacks. In: 2015 IEEE International Conference on Electro/Information Technology (EIT), pp. 274–279. IEEE (2015)
2. Garber, L.: Denial-of-service attacks rip the Internet. Computer **33**(4), 12–17 (2000)
3. Wan Mohd Ghazali, K., Hassan, R.: Flooding distributed denial of service attacks-a review. J. Comput. Sci. **7**(8), 1218–1223 (2011)
4. Lemon, J.: Resisting SYN flood DoS attacks with a SYN cache. In: BSDCon, vol. 2002, pp. 89–97 (2002)
5. Yatagai, T., Isohara, T., Sasase, I.: Detection of HTTP-GET flood attack based on analysis of page access behavior. In: IEEE Pacific Rim Conference on Communications, Computers and Signal Processing, PacRim 2007, pp. 232–235. IEEE (2007)
6. Kenney, M.: Ping of death. Insecure.org (1996)
7. Logstalgia (2015). http://logstalgia.io/. Accessed 31 Oct 2015
8. Nginx: Logging AND monitoring (2015). https://www.nginx.com/resources/admin-guide/logging-and-monitoring/. Accessed 31 Oct 2015

9. Webalizer: The Webalizer (2014). http://www.webalizer.org/. Accessed 30 Oct 2015
10. Imperva: Why Incapsula? (2015). https://www.incapsula.com/ddos/why-incapsula/. Accessed 13 Nov 2015
11. The Apache Software Foundation: Log files (2015). https://httpd.apache.org/docs/trunk/logs.html#page-header. Accessed 30 Oct 2015
12. Netcraft: January 2015 web server survey (2015). http://news.netcraft.com/archives/2015/01/15/january-2015-web-server-survey.html. Accessed 20 Oct 2015
13. SolveDNS statistics (2015). http://www.solvedns.com/statistics/. Accessed 27 Oct 2015
14. World Wide Web Consortium: Logging control In W3C httpd (1995). http://www.w3.org/Daemon/User/Config/Logging.html#common-logfile-format. Accessed 30 Oct 2015
15. World Wide Web Consortium: Extended log file format (2015). http://www.w3.org/TR/WD-logfile.html. Accessed 31 Oct 2015
16. Ogbuji, U.: Working with web server logs (2009). IBM. http://www.ibm.com/developerworks/library/wa-apachelogs/. Accessed 01 Nov 2015
17. Sauter, M.: LOIC will tear us apart the impact of tool design and media portrayals in the success of activist DDOS attacks. Am. Behav. Sci. **57**(7), 983–1007 (2013)
18. Kenkre, P.S., Pai, A., Colaco, L.: Real time intrusion detection and prevention system. In: Satapathy, S.C., Biswal, B.N., Udgata, S.K., Mandal, J.K. (eds.) Proceedings of the 3rd International Conference on Frontiers of Intelligent Computing: Theory and Applications (FICTA) 2014. AISC, vol. 327, pp. 405–411. Springer, Heidelberg (2015). doi:10.1007/978-3-319-11933-5_44
19. Qiu, B., Gooi, H.B.: Web-based SCADA display systems (WSDS) for access via Internet. IEEE Trans. Power Syst. **15**(2), 681–686 (2000)
20. Leou, R.-C., Chang, Y.-C., Teng, J.-H.: A web-based power quality monitoring system. In: Power Engineering Society Summer Meeting, vol. 3. IEEE (2001)
21. Maglaras, L.A., Jiang, J.: Intrusion detection in SCADA systems using machine learning techniques. In: Science and Information Conference (SAI). IEEE (2014)
22. Zuech, R., Khoshgoftaar, T.M., Wald, R.: Intrusion detection and big heterogeneous data: a survey. J. Big Data **2**(1), 1–41 (2015)
23. Maglaras, L.A., Jiang, J., Cruz, T.J.: Combining ensemble methods and social network metrics for improving accuracy of OCSVM on intrusion detection in SCADA systems. J. Inf. Secur. Appl., 4 May 2016. ISSN 2214-2126
24. Nicholson, A., Webber, S., Dyer, S., Patel, T., Janicke, H.: SCADA security in the light of cyber-warfare. Comput. Secur. **31**(4), 418–436 (2012)
25. Johnson, J.: Designing with the Mind in Mind: Simple Guide to Understanding User Interface Design Guidelines. Elsevier, Amsterdam (2013)
26. Syromiatnikov, A., Weyns, D.: A journey through the land of model-view-design patterns. In: 2014 IEEE/IFIP Conference on Software Architecture (WICSA), pp. 21–30, IEEE, April 2014

Latency in Cascaded Wired/Wireless Communication Networks for Factory Automation

Steven Dietrich[1(✉)], Gunther May[1], Johannes von Hoyningen-Huene[2], Andreas Mueller[2], and Gerhard Fohler[3]

[1] Bosch Rexroth AG, Lohr am Main, Germany
{Steven.Dietrich,Gunther.May}@boschrexroth.de
[2] Robert Bosch GmbH, Renningen, Germany
{Johannes.Hoyningen-Huene,Andreas.Mueller21}@de.bosch.com
[3] Chair of Real-time Systems, Technical University Kaiserslautern,
Kaiserslautern, Germany
fohler@eit.uni-kl.de

Abstract. Unlike in the areas of process automation and condition monitoring, current wireless technologies cannot be used for many closed-loop control applications in factory automation. These applications require shorter cycle times, precise synchronicity in the microseconds range and higher reliability with low packet error rates. Furthermore, established Industrial Ethernet communication systems will not be completely replaced in the near future. Therefore, a wireless communication system for factory automation also requires seamless integration into existing networks.

However, a resulting cascaded network will lead to additional latencies, which have a negative effect on the overall real-time performance. In this paper, we analyze the effect of frame structure conversion for different subnetworks with respect to the additional latencies they introduce. Therefore, we introduce an abstracted network model representing various subnetworks. We exemplify different protocol implementations and discuss them in terms of the resulting latencies and optimizations.

Keywords: Industrial Ethernet · Closed-loop control · Wireless communication · Cascaded network · ParSec · Latency

1 Introduction

In industrial communication, flexibility and mobility gains more and more importance, especially in the context of connected industries (in Germany also referred to as Industrie 4.0 [1]). In the recent past, communication networks known from

---

The work presented in this paper has been partially supported by the German Federal Ministry of Education and Research BMBF (grant agreement no. 16KIS0225 & 16KIS0224).

© ICST Institute for Computer Sciences, Social Informatics and Telecommunications Engineering 2017
L.A. Maglaras et al. (Eds.): INISCOM 2016, LNICST 188, pp. 50–61, 2017.
DOI: 10.1007/978-3-319-52569-3_5

the office domain have been established in areas like condition monitoring or process automation. They represent an approach to use components off the shelf (COTS).

Nevertheless, for the area of factory automation wireless communication is hardly considered so far, since there is no wireless communication system that covers all the requirements of industrial closed-loop control applications. Here Industrial Ethernet (IE) systems are most widely used. They provide cycle times below 1 ms, high synchronicity with a timing deviation of less than 1 μs, and high reliability with packet error ratios (PER) of $\leq 10^{-9}$ [2].

Since the benefits of wireless communications are desired in the field of factory automation too [3], the German research project ParSec [4] currently develops a wireless real-time system especially for closed loop control applications.

In the near future, wireless communication will not completely replace the established IE systems [5]. Therefore, hybrid communication networks build on cascaded wired and wireless subnetworks will arise. A seamless integration of the wireless subnetwork into existing wired technologies is mandatory.

Due to the cascading the behavior of the communication network is changed. Especially the timing constraints are affected. Therefore, this paper analyses different approaches of data positioning into a secondary network frame to reduce the resulting latency and jitter. The remainder of this paper is structured as follows: Sect. 2 provides work related to hybrid networks and timing constraints. In Sect. 3 we introduce an abstract network model intended to represent many network protocols used in factory automation. Additionally the wired IE and the wireless ParSec subsystem are shortly introduced. In Sect. 4 we discuss the different approaches of frame conversion from one subnetwork into another one. Finally a summary and a short outlook are given in Sect. 5.

2   Related Work

Cascaded networks for industrial communication were investigated already over the last few years. Ackerberg et al. [6] introduces arising latencies and jitter as mayor research challenges for the use of wireless networks in industry. However, most of the investigated cascaded networks do not face the timing constrains or the combination of several hard real-time protocols. The authors of [7,8] introduce a detailed protocol conversion form Industrial Ethernet to CAN, but without any timing constraints. They use unadapted mechanisms for sending and receiving, which results in high jitter transmission latency. The authors of [9] introduce the hybrid network concept of FlexWare with wired field-level backbone and wireless clusters. Unfortunately, this concept cannot guarantee any hard real-time performance as well.

Investigations of timing and synchronization in cascaded hard real-time networks are mostly based on distributed clocks. For example Ferrari et al. [10] show a method of synchronized communication over an intermediate network. However, the mechanism of distributed clocks might not always be available. While reaching the required synchronization for factory automation, the throughput can not be guaranteed since the PROFINET IP protocol in not designed for these requirement. The authors of [3,11] introduce a low jitter point to point wireless communication. Since both investigations are based on basic WLAN, the scaling to multi point communication would result in increased latencies and jitter.

Addad et al. [12] introduce a delay evaluation of networked control systems which includes also the field devices due delay. Since it is based on Switched Ethernet, it does not consider the additional delay arising when using heterogeneous cascaded networks. Accordingly, a gap could still be found in the investigation of timing constraints when combining several hard real-time protocols. Especially the protocol conversion and data placement will have a big influence on the latency and jitter, that was hardly investigated in detail so far.

3   Cascaded Communication System

By combining different communication networks with each other, their individual performances will influence the overall system. Not only every subsystem has to be optimized but also cross attributes needs to be adapted to still meet the requirements of closed-loop control applications. In this section we introduce a model for a subnetwork that enables the analyses detached from any concrete network protocol and shortly present exemplary subsystems.

3.1   Abstract Cascaded Network

A communication network for closed loop control application is often built on master-slave relation. One control unit, the master, operates one or multiple sensor or actuator devices, the slaves. The communication takes place cyclically, such that real-time (RT) performance can be guaranteed. Mostly also non-real-time (NRT) communication can take place whenever there is no RT communication. In this paper, we focus on RT data, since they require higher performance and NRT data can be scheduled with higher latencies and jitter.

We assume full duplex networks, since high throughput and low cycle times (t_{cycle}) are required. Therefore, we can analyze downlink (DL) from master to slave and uplink (UL) from slave to master separately. Here we will focus on the analysis of the DL, since the knowledge about the latencies there are important to set a global network synchronization time. The resulting latencies for UL can be investigated similarly. We do not consider transmission errors, since industrial communication networks often provide advanced mechanisms to minimize the error rate. Remaining errors can then be compensated by the application.

All networks have a limited resource space, in which the DL data are encapsulated (Fig. 1). This can be subdivided into several resource elements (RE) by multiple channel access mechanism and further coding. Thus, one RE consist of n_{BpRE} bits.

We assume that a preamble or header with a size of S_{Pre} RE needs to be transmitted periodically for example for synchronization and signalization.

A frame of S_{Frame} RE consists of S_{Pre} RE for the preamble and S_{Data} RE for the data and is transmitted with a RE rate R_{RE}. A possible idle duration of t_{Idle} can separate two successive frames. For simplification, this could also be seen as a number of RE $S_{\text{Idle}} = t_{\text{Idle}} \cdot R_{\text{RE}}$

A cascaded communication network can now be analyzed with two or more of these models with different parametrization. In Fig. 2 we illustrate the network structure of an exemplary cascaded network built on three subnetworks. The primary subnetwork consists of the primary master (PN-M), several primary slaves (PN-S) and the master of the secondary subnetwork (SN-M). A slave of the secondary subnetwork (SN-S) is then the basis of a tertiary subnetwork with several tertiary slaves (TN-S).

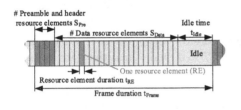

Fig. 1. Frame resource space.

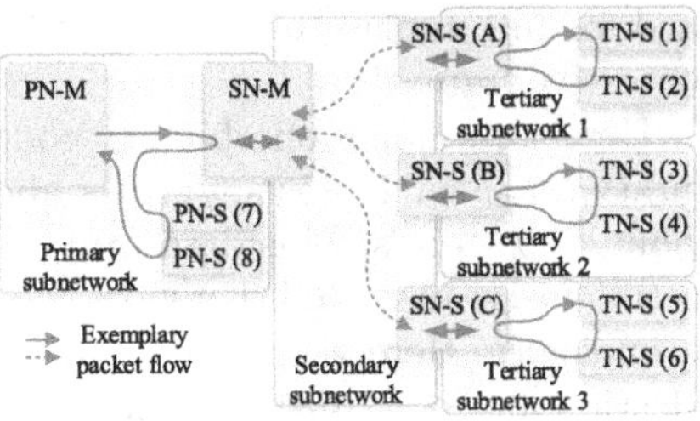

Fig. 2. Schematic network concept with data flow.

3.2   Wired Industrial Ethernet Communication

There are multiple wired IE networks well established in factory automation. The most common IE protocols for closed loop control applications are Sercos III, EtherCAT, and PROFINET IRT [5,13–15]. All of them are based on cyclic master-slave communication.

Sercos III and EtherCAT are mostly organized in a ring or line topology. D_{Down} and D_{Up} are transmitted by summation telegrams carrying data of several slaves. These telegrams are building the DL and the UL. They provide minimal latencies and the required low cycle times within the IE network.

PROFINET on the other hand is not based on summation telegrams. By synchronized clocks, the slave devices are able to generate UL packets on their own. Through special Ethernet switches also star topologies can be build up.

Referring to the abstract model, the frame structure of the introduced IE networks is built on Fast Ethernet [16]. S_{Pre} corresponds to the necessary number of bytes for the Ethernet header and S_{Data} to the payload (max. 1500 RE per frame). The net data rate at the link layer is 100 Mbit/s. A fixed number of one or more frames of individual length each is transmitted per communication cycle. The idle time between successive frames can vary. Once set, these variable parameter are constant in each cycle.

3.3   Wireless ParSec Communication

One exemplary wireless network for industrial closed loop applications we will focus on in this paper will be developed within the ParSec Project [4]. Within this project we focus on the design of a highly deterministic wireless communication network. This includes especially minimum latency and high reliability. This section presents the current working hypothesis regarding integration. The communication is also based on master-slave relations.

Referring to the abstract model, the communication is based on the Parallel Sequence Spread Spectrum (PSSS) technique [17,18]. 255 orthogonal codes can be used in parallel to build up a RE. However, the number of bits per code can be varied to increase the reliability of the communication or the data rate. Either code division duplexing (CDD) or frequency division duplexing (FDD) is used for full duplex transmission of DL and UL. There is no idle time between successive frames.

Here we assume one bit per code and therefore $n_{\mathrm{BpRE}} = 255$. With a RE duration t_{RE} of 14.25 µs, R_{RE} is about 70.175 kHz and, thus, the data rate is about 17.9 Mbit/s. This data rate is further reduced by the necessary error correction mechanism and therefore significantly smaller than 100 Mbit/s used in IE technologies. Here we have to find special approaches for rate conversion, data selection and placements of the IE data into the wireless frame.

Further information about the project will be published soon and can be found on the project homepage [4].

4   Data Positioning into a Secondary Network Frame

According to the cascaded network structure, additional latencies arise due to the placement of the data from the primary subnetwork (PN) into the secondary subnetwork (SN). Latency in this context means the time between the full reception of the PN data and the complete placement into the SN frame. Constant latencies could be partially compensated by the application by adapting the control algorithm. Therefore, they must be completely known and kept as low as possible. In addition, the jitter must be minimal to enable adequate control. Here, jitter means the fluctuation between the best and the worst case latency.

Each PN cycle, only a subset of the PN DL date $D_{\mathrm{Down(PN)}}$ must be transmitted into the SN, since some slaves might be located already in the PN. The resulting amount of SN DL data $D_{\mathrm{Down(SN)}}$ results as $D_{\mathrm{Down(SN)}} \leq D_{\mathrm{Down(PN)}}$. The number of required RE per PN cycle is equal to

$$n_{\mathrm{RE(SN)}} = \left\lceil \frac{D_{\mathrm{Down(SN)}} + M_{\mathrm{(SN)}} \cdot B_{\mathrm{OH(SN)}}}{n_{\mathrm{BpRE(SN)}}} \right\rceil . \tag{1}$$

M denotes the number of slaves to be addressed and B_{OH} the signaling overhead (OH) to address them. With the number of RE for data per frame (S_{Data}), the number of required SN frames per PN cycle is

$$n_{\mathrm{Frames(SN)}} = \left\lceil \frac{D_{\mathrm{Down(SN)}} + M_{\mathrm{(SN)}} \cdot B_{\mathrm{OH(SN)}}}{n_{\mathrm{BpRE(SN)}} \cdot S_{\mathrm{Data(SN)}}} \right\rceil . \tag{2}$$

The required number of RE for data and OH together with the overall number of preamble and idle RE must be smaller or equal to the possible number of RE during one PN cycle, as shown in Eq. (3). Otherwise there will be no balanced relation between data sending and receiving.

$$t_{\text{Cycle(PN)}} \geq \left\lceil \frac{n_{\text{RE(SN)}} + n_{\text{Frames(SN)}}(S_{\text{Pre(SN)}} + S_{\text{Idle(SN)}}) - S_{\text{Idle(SN)}}}{R_{\text{RE(SN)}}} \right\rceil \quad (3)$$

For the following analyses, we assume that this condition is always met.

We propose two different approaches with several variants each to place the received data $D_{\text{Down(SN)}}$ into the SN frame: by static allocation or by a streaming approach. In the following subsections we will analyze them to enable the best choice regarding lowest latency and jitter according to the target application and cascaded network. Figure 3 illustrates the approaches with their different subclasses in their worst case scenario according to the network structure shown in Fig. 2. Here, the PN addresses six slaves (1–6) wireless with one DL and UL frame every cycle. The SN consists of three slaves (A–C). Each of these SN slaves has to receive the data for two of the slaves addressed in the PN (A: 1&2, B: 3&4, C: 5&6). The transmission duration of the packets in the SN is pictured to be longer than in the PN. The number of required frames to transmit the PN data depends on the implementation approach. The data reception time could be seen as constant offset. Therefore, the approaches are independent of the PN structure and the SN indexing could be neglected.

4.1   Static Allocation

Static allocation (Fig. 3.1–4) in this context means, that each SN data packet has a reserved slot within the SN frame and can only be placed there. If this slot is missed, for example when the PN data arrive too late, the next slot has to be awaited. This might be one or multiple frames later. In the meantime, no other RT data can be transmitted, since their order must be satisfied. All SN data placements can be predefined and signaled during startup. The SN-S only need to observe always the same position within the SN frame. Therefore, we

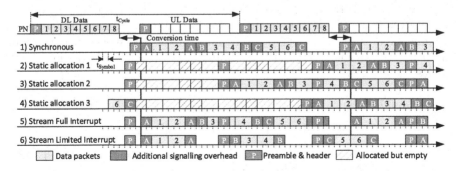

Fig. 3. Exemplary data positioning approaches (worst case).

assume that the signaling overhead for this approach will be lower compared to the other cases.

A further differentiation within the static allocation is possible by the comparison of the SN frame duration with respect to the PN cycle time. If the SN frame duration is smaller or equal to the PN cycle time, one or more SN frames will fit into the time between two successive PN DL frames.

In the simplest case, the duration of one (or several) SN frames is equal to the PN cycle time and we have a *synchronous* cyclic relation (Fig. 3.1). Here, the signaling overhead is minimal since the whole SN frame structure can be predefined and would not change during runtime. If the start of the SN frame is adapted according to the arrival of the DL data, the latency can be minimized. The worst case latency will result as in Eq. (4) and there will be no jitter.

$$t_{\text{Place}}[\text{Synchronous}] = ((n_{\text{Frames}} - 1)(S_{\text{Pre}} + S_{\text{Idle}}) + n_{\text{RE}})R_{\text{RE}}^{-1} \qquad (4)$$

However, either the PN cycle time has to be set according to the SN frame duration or the other way around. Also, despite unsynchronized clocks, there must be no phase drift between the clocks of each subnetwork.

If there is an asynchronous relation between the PN cycle time and the SN frame duration, the reception of the PN data will vary within the SN frame. A possible phase drift provides another additional shift within the SN frame. For the static allocation this means that we cannot use every SN frame for RT data. If the SN frame duration is smaller than the PN cycle time and multiple SN frames are required, we can further distinguish between two different approaches. In the first one, later called *static allocation 1*, all SN frames are statically allocated and have a fixed successive order (Fig. 3.2). If the SN data are only available after the start of the according SN frame is already over, all n_{Frames} frames remain empty for RT transmission. The worst case latency results as in Eq. (5) whereas the jitter is calculated in Eq. (6).

$$t_{\text{Place}}[\text{Static 1}] = (n_{\text{Frames}}(S_{\text{Data}} + 2S_{\text{Pre}} + 2S_{\text{Idle}}) - S_{\text{Pre}} - S_{\text{Idle}} + n_{\text{RE}})R_{\text{RE}}^{-1} \quad (5)$$

$$t_{\text{J}}[\text{Static 1}] = (n_{\text{Frames}}(S_{\text{Data}} + S_{\text{Pre}} + S_{\text{Idle}}) - S_{\text{Idle}})R_{\text{RE}}^{-1} \qquad (6)$$

In the second approach, later called *static allocation 2*, all SN frames still are statically allocated. However, we can mark one frame as empty and repeat its transmission, if the PN data are received too late (Fig. 3.3). Therefore, only one SN frame remains empty for RT transmission, but we need special signalization. This results in an increased OH. The worst case latency results as in Eq. (7) whereas the jitter is calculated in Eq. (8).

$$t_{\text{Place}}[\text{Static 2}] = (S_{\text{Data}} + n_{\text{RE}} + n_{\text{Frames}}(S_{\text{Pre}} + S_{\text{Idle}}) - S_{\text{Idle}})R_{\text{RE}}^{-1} \qquad (7)$$

$$t_{\text{J}}[\text{Static 2}] = (S_{\text{Data}} + S_{\text{Pre}} + S_{\text{Idle}})R_{\text{RE}}^{-1} \qquad (8)$$

If the SN frame duration is larger than the PN cycle time, later called *static allocation 3*, the SN data must fit multiple times completely into the SN frame to avoid congestions (Fig. 3.4). As advantage of this approach, we need to transmit less SN preambles. However, the system must stay highly synchronous even for long intervals without new preambles. We assume that this approach requires a higher signaling overhead than the previous ones. The worst case latency results as in Eq. (9) whereas the jitter is calculated in Eq. (10).

$$t_{\text{Place}}[\text{Static 3}] = (2n_{\text{RE}} + S_{\text{Pre}} + S_{\text{Idle}})R_{\text{RE}}^{-1} \tag{9}$$

$$t_{\text{J}}[\text{Static 3}] = (n_{\text{RE}} + S_{\text{Pre}} + S_{\text{Idle}})R_{\text{RE}}^{-1} \tag{10}$$

4.2   Streaming Approach

In this approach, we consider the SN frames not statically allocated but as continuous stream. Here, we can place the SN data together with according signaling as they arrive. This transmission can be interrupted by the SN preamble. We constitute two different cases how this can be implemented:

– By full interrupt, where the SN preamble can interrupt data arbitrarily, or
– by limited interrupt, where only complete data packets for one PN-S or SN-S can be interrupted.

In both cases, the SN frame duration matters only in the number of SN preambles we have to transmit.

In case of the *full interrupt* (Fig. 3.5), the capacity of the SN frame will be used fully. Since the data from the PN arrive in periodical cycles, we can place the SN data in regular RE distances into the SN frame. This requires that the SN preamble can be identified and subtracted from the number of received RE. However, phase drift might occur in this approach as well. This must be compensated by new resource allocation during runtime and can result in a complete change of the resource plan. Therefore, we assume the signaling OH for a streaming approach higher than with a static allocation. The worst case latency results as in Eq. (11) whereas the jitter is one preamble duration, as shown in Eq. (12).

$$t_{\text{Place}}[\text{Stream}] = (n_{\text{RE}} + n_{\text{Frames}}(S_{\text{Pre}} + S_{\text{Idle}}) - S_{\text{Idle}})R_{\text{RE}}^{-1} \tag{11}$$

$$t_J[\text{Stream}] = (S_{\text{Pre}} + S_{\text{Idle}})R_{\text{RE}}^{-1} \tag{12}$$

In the case of streaming with *limited interruptibility* (Fig. 3.6), it is possible that we have to stall the RT data transmission, since a SN preamble might be privileged. Therefore, we have to delay the transmission of a SN data packet until the SN preamble is sent, if this packet does not fit completely in front of it. Depending on the SN frame duration, this limits the maximum size of SN data packets we are able to transmit. Further, the shift of one SN packet into the next frame will influence subsequent packets, which then might also be shifted. This can lead to an instable communication relation between receiving and sending. Latency calculations cannot be performed in a general manner, since the whole SN DL needs to be analyzed packet by packet at every possible position within the SN frame. Therefore, also the signaling overhead and the additional required computation performance increases. Due to these substantial disadvantages, we will not consider this approach further.

Table 1. Assumed parameters for exemplary application.

Parameter	Value
Number of slaves (M)	20
RE duration (t_{RE})	14.25 µs
Bit per RE (n_{BpRE})	255
Frame size (S_{Frame})	50 RE
Preamble size (S_{Pre})	6 RE
Idle duration (t_{Idle})	0 s

Table 2. Estimated signaling overhead.

Signaling overhead	Bytes per slave
Synchronous	1
Static allocation 1	2
Static allocation 2	2
Static allocation 3	4
Stream 1	10
Stream 2	30

4.3   Comparison of the Approaches

In this section we compare the different approaches with each other with respect to their latency. We assume an exemplary application based on the networks presented in Sect. 3. The parameters used are listed in Table 1 and derived from the current working hypothesis of the ParSec project. Figure 4 illustrates the calculated latency for different amounts of payload per slave. Here, for simplification, we assume that each SN-S has to receive only one payload packet. Thus, for each SN-S the payload and the signaling overhead is transmitted only once. However, the actual size of the SN signaling overhead for the different cases is not yet fully analyzed. Here we assume the conservatively estimated values listed in Table 2.

In Fig. 4 we show that the *synchronous approach* results in the lowest latency. Here we do not have to consider any additional worst case RE for the data placement. Even with higher OH the latency of synchronous data positioning would remain below that of streaming with the same or higher amount of OH. The steps in the calculated curves occur, whenever the amount of SN RE for the according SN data and OH increases that much, that we need one more SN frame. However, as mentioned earlier, this approach will only be hardly implementable.

The approaches for *static allocation 1* and *2* have the same trends as long as we only need one SN frame for the transmission of all PN data. For more SN frames, the latency of the *static allocation 1* takes bigger steps, because we have to transmit in worst case all required SN frames twice. For *static allocation 2* only one frame needs to be retransmitted. As mentioned earlier, the *static allocation 3* requires that the PN data with the SN OH fit at least twice into the SN frame. Therefore, we can only use this approach as long as Eq. (13) holds.

$$\left\lceil \frac{D_{Down} + M \cdot B_{OH}}{n_{BpRE}} \right\rceil \leq \frac{S_{Data}}{2} \qquad (13)$$

Up to this point, the latency is lower than for *static allocation 1* and *2* and the *streaming approach* with high OH. Here we have to consider less SN preambles and the SN frame utilization is higher. However, the latency increases depending

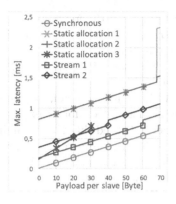
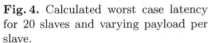
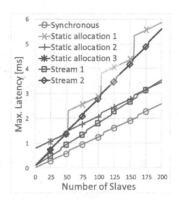

Fig. 4. Calculated worst case latency for 20 slaves and varying payload per slave.

Fig. 5. Calculated worst case latency for a varying number of slaves and 25 byte payload per slave.

on the payload twice as fast than with the other approaches. For implementation reasons the *static allocation* generally has the advantage that the resource allocation for the SN data remains the same even with a phase drift between PN and SN. We only need to consider more frames for worst case estimations.

The *streaming approach with full interrupt* results in the best latency after the *synchronous approach*. Even with the estimated high signaling overhead of 30 bytes per slave and 20 SN-S this approach results in shorter latency times as with the *static allocation*. In comparison to completely empty SN frames, the influence of the OH RE remains insignificant. However, the latency of data positioning with the *streaming approach* increases faster with increasing number of SN-S than with the *static allocation* approach, since we estimate the signalization OH to be higher. This is exemplified in Fig. 5 for a varying number of slaves with 25 byte data per slave (other parameters being equal as before).

As mentioned above, the streaming approach requires the capability of new resource allocation and therefore the implementation will be more challenging than the static allocation.

With help of this comparison, we will now be able to choose the optimal data positioning according to latency and jitter for the investigated application and cascaded network. Considering also the latencies of each subnetwork, we will now be able to calculate the overall latency and the maximum jitter. As a result, we can adapt the control algorithm for the according network structure.

5   Conclusion

In this paper, we focused on the analysis of cascaded real-time communication networks for industrial closed-loop control application with respect to their latencies. We have introduced an abstract model for the subnetworks. This could be used for a wired IE protocols as well as for the currently developed wireless ParSec protocol and simplifies the latency analyses.

Using two combined subnetwork models, we analyzed different approaches to place the data of the primary network into the secondary one with respect to their latencies. We showed that only two approaches are of interest, since a synchronous approach is hard to achieve: Static allocation with only one empty frame, and streaming with full interruptible data.

Within a theoretical evaluation with estimated signaling overhead, we showed that the streaming approach results in shorter latencies, even for conservative assumptions and high numbers of slaves. We further indicated that the streaming approach depends on the ability of the system to reallocate resources during runtime. Therefore, if the latency is less important, we exposed the static allocation approach to be easier to implement. Here, even with phase drift, the resource allocation does not need to be changed during runtime.

Nevertheless, further analyses and real-life implementations have to show how large the signaling overhead for the different data positioning approaches really is, considering also transmission errors. In addition, the ability of resource reallocation needs to be analyzed. Implementations of adjustments in the global synchronization time must prove whether all requirements of the closed-loop control applications still can be met.

References

1. Jazdi, N.: Cyber physical systems in the context of industry 4.0. In: 2014 IEEE International Conference on Automation, Quality and Testing, Robotics, pp. 1–4. IEEE (2014)
2. Frotzscher, A., Wetzker, U., Bauer, M., Rentschler, M., Beyer, M., Elspass, S., Klessig, H.: Requirements and current solutions of wireless communication in industrial automation. In: 2014 IEEE International Conference on Communications Workshops (ICC), pp. 67–72. IEEE (2014)
3. Bauer, M., May, G., Jain, V.: A wireless gateway approach enabling industrial real-time communication on the field level of factory automation. In: Emerging Technology and Factory Automation (ETFA), 2014 IEEE, pp. 1–8. IEEE (2014)
4. BMBF-Project. ParSec. www.parsec-projekt.de
5. Sauter, T.: The three generations of field-level networks - evolution and compatibility issues. IEEE Trans. Ind. Electron. **57**(11), 3585–3595 (2010)
6. Akerberg, J., Gidlund, M., Bjorkman, M.: Future research challenges in wireless sensor and actuator networks targeting industrial automation. In: 2011 9th IEEE International Conference on Industrial Informatics (INDIN), pp. 410–415. IEEE (2011)
7. Zhang, Y., Feng, X., Guo, Y.: Design of ethernet-can protocol conversion module based on STM32. Int. J. Future Gener. Commun. Netw. **7**(1), 89–96 (2014)
8. Eum, S.: Implementation of protocol conversion control board for industrial communication. Int. J. Control Autom. **9**, 201–208 (2016)
9. Sauter, T., Jasperneite, J., Bello, L.L.: Towards new hybrid networks for industrial automation. ETFA **9**, 1141–1148 (2009)
10. Ferrari, P., Flammini, A., Rinaldi, S., Sisinni, E.: On the seamless interconnection of IEEE1588-based devices using a PROFINET IO infrastructure. IEEE Trans. Ind. Inf. **6**(3), 381–392 (2010)

11. Mahmood, A., Ring, F.: Clock synchronization for IEEE 802.11 based wired-wireless hybrid networks using PTP. In: IEEE International Symposium on Precision Clock Synchronization for Measurement, Control and Communication Proceedings, pp. 1–6. IEEE (2012)
12. Addad, B., Amari, S., Lesage, J.-J.: A virtual-queuing-based algorithm for delay evaluation in networked control systems. IEEE Trans. Ind. Electron. **58**(9), 4471–4479 (2011)
13. International Electrotechnical Commission (IEC). IEC 61784–2: 2014 industrial communication networks - profiles - part 2: Additional fieldbus profiles for real-time networks based on ISO/IEC 8802-3-CP 16/3 (Sercos III), 07 2014
14. International Electrotechnical Commission (IEC). IEC 61784–2: 2014 industrial communication networks - profiles - part 2: Additional fieldbus profiles for real-time networks based on ISO/IEC 8802-3-CP 12/1 (EtherCAT Simple IO) and CP 12/2 (EtherCAT Mailbox and Timing Synchronization), 07 2014
15. International Electrotechnical Commission (IEC). IEC 61784–2: 2014 industrial communication networks - profiles - part 2: Additional fieldbus profiles for real-time networks based on ISO/IEC 8802-3-CP 3/4 (PROFINET Conformance Class A), CP 3/5 (PROFINET Conformance Class B) and CP 3/6 (PROFINET Conformance Class C), 07 2014
16. IEEE 802.3 standard for ethernet (2016)
17. Schwetlick, H., Wolf, A.: PSSS-parallel sequence spread spectrum a physical layer for RF communication. In: 2004 IEEE International Symposium on Consumer Electronics, pp. 262–265 (2004)
18. Gowda, K.K., Messinger, T., Wolf, A.C., Kraemer, R., Kallfass, I., Scheytt, J.C.: Towards 100 Gbps wireless communication in THz band with PSSS modulation: a promising hardware in the loop experiment. In: 2015 IEEE International Conference on Ubiquitous Wireless Broadband (ICUWB), pp. 1–5. IEEE (2015)

Network Topology Exploration for Industrial Networks

Andreas Paul$^{(\boxtimes)}$, Franka Schuster, and Hartmut König

Computer Networks Group, Brandenburg University of Technology
Cottbus-Senftenberg, Cottbus, Germany
{andreas.paul,franka.schuster,hartmut.koenig}@b-tu.de

Abstract. Large industrial networks (e.g., plants and grids) are usually characterized by numerous sectors of responsibility and multiple suppliers. Managing these networks is a challenge and requires concrete knowledge of the current network state in terms of device influence and network activities. Here, automated topology exploration is a valuable and very performant measure to provide a wide range of information about devices and their communication relations. Existing exploration methods mostly use active, intrusive methods which have no chance to be applied in sensitive or critical industrial networks. In this paper we present a completely passive approach. It is supplier-independent and provides information that has not been explored before using passive methods.

Keywords: Topology exploration · Industrial networks · Critical infrastructures · Passive network traffic analysis

1 Motivation

In industrial networks a profound knowledge of the current network topology, i.e., the included devices, their roles, and their communication relations with other devices, is essential for the network operator and prerequisite for precise administrative network decisions. Especially, large industrial networks of plants and grids usually involve multiple areas of responsibility and suppliers. Only in rare cases, a well-defined and mandatory documentation process tracks all network configuration changes. Here, topology exploration can provide a direct and reliable picture of the current network configuration and activities as reliable base for various analyses and applications.

Existing methods for network topology exploration either depend on active methods influencing the network by new traffic (which is not acceptable for sensitive or critical industrial networks), are supplier-specific, or lack essential topology information. The proposed approach combines multiple passive methods to provide a high amount of information about devices in the network and their communication independently of the suppliers.

The main contributions of this paper are: (1) we identify multiple (contrary) ways for passively discovering network topologies, (2) we present a fusion of these

© ICST Institute for Computer Sciences, Social Informatics and Telecommunications Engineering 2017
L.A. Maglaras et al. (Eds.): INISCOM 2016, LNICST 188, pp. 62–76, 2017.
DOI: 10.1007/978-3-319-52569-3_6

methods for gaining a maximum of topology information of a network, (3) we present a graph-based approach to the visualization of the gathered topology information, and (4) we demonstrate the outcome of the approach for different industrial networks.

The remainder of the paper is organized as follows: In Sect. 2, we explain our approach on sole passive topology exploration. The involved methods are applied on a series of experiments, whose results are presented in Sect. 3. After putting our work in the context of other research in Sect. 4, we conclude the paper with an outlook on future research in this field.

2   Methodology

The proposed approach for a sole passive topology exploration is outlined in Fig. 1. It consists of three stages: the *network device discovery*, the *communication discovery*, and the *device information discovery*. The first stage searches for the devices currently included in the observed network domain, whereas the second one tries to enrich the exploration by additional information about the devices. The third stage aims to discover communication relations among the devices. For this, two complementary methods are applied which differentiate in the fact which part of the network messages is used as source of information. The *header inspection* (HI) analyses only the message header, while the *deep packet inspection* (DPI) expands the potential of the header inspection by inspecting the message payload.

2.1   Network Traffic Processing

In this section we describe the function and the implementation of the three basic stages of the network traffic processing unit in detail.

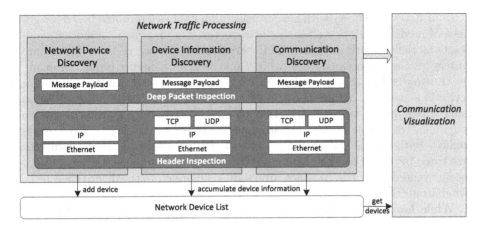

Fig. 1. Topology exploration methodology

Network Device Discovery. As basic method for the network device discovery, we apply header inspection to analyze the source and destination addresses of Ethernet frames and IP packets. However, for indentifying end-to-end communication relations between devices, a strict differentiation between IP packets transported in Ethernet frames and pure Ethernet frames is required. In the case of IP packets, the devices are identified by the IP source and destination addresses. As the Ethernet header stores only the addresses of the point-to-point communication (e.g., routers/gateways or destination device), it is not suitable to use MAC addresses for device identification. Only in case of a pure link-layer communication, it can be assumed that the addresses in the Ethernet header belong to end-to-end communicating devices and can be used for device discovery.

DPI is an advanced method for device discovery because it allows an implicit detection of further network components which are referred to in the message payload. Especially, protocols used for configuration and bootstrap procedures transport information of additional network devices. The principle of implicit device discovery using the ARP protocol is exemplified at the end of this section.

Table 1 summarizes the set of protocols that are currently supported by our device discovery approach. For IP and Ethernet, the header inspection is applied. Implicit device detection is currently performed by decoding ARP, STP, and ICMP. The benefit of the additional application of DPI for device discovery is demonstrated in Sect. 3.2.

Device Information Discovery. Traffic processing also pursues to collect further information about the participating network devices. This can be used to provide operators of industrial networks additional information to recognize unknown devices, e.g., devices identified by (undocumented) MAC addresses. The accumulation of configuration information is also valuable for IT security purposes. It helps to identify existing vulnerabilities and sensitive devices which need a special protection.

Information discovery with header inspection implies a protocol-based assignment of predefined device classes (client, server, router/switch, broadcast/multicast) to the network devices. The Ethernet header is one of the utilized data sources for class assignment (see *(c)* in Table 1). If an Ethernet frame, for example, transports STP (Spanning Tree Protocol) traffic it is assumed that the source device is a switch. This method can be transferred to TCP/IP communication using a port-based protocol detection in combination with a protocol-specific assignment of device classes. Additionally, address-based class assignment is applied. Initially, the vendor of the network device is detected by mapping the first three bytes of the MAC addresses (organizational unique identifier) to the specific vendor (e.g., Cisco) which afterwards is mapped to the device class (e.g., switch/router).

While header-based information derivation is limited to class assignment, the deep packet inspection allows us to derive a more comprehensive set of information. Table 1 indicates that depending on the concrete protocol this also

Table 1. Protocols analyzed in the traffic processing stage

	Protocol	Device discovery		Comm. discovery		Inf. discovery	
		HI	DPI	HI	DPI	HI	DPI
Application layer	NTP						c
	DHCP						c, a
Transport layer	TCP			x		c	
	UDP			x		c	
Internet layer	ICMP		x			c	
	IP	x					
Link layer	Profinet IO						a, o
	CDP						a, o
	STP		x			c	o
	LLDP						c, o
	HP						a, o
	ARP		x		x		a
	Ethernet	x		x		c	

x Inspection is applied.
a Inspection is applied to extract device address information.
c Inspection is applied for device class assignment.
o Inspection is applied to extract other device configuration data.

may include address information *(a)* and other *(o)* device configuration data (e.g., operating system and symbolic names).

Communication Discovery. A useful method for industrial network analysis is the assessment of communication of the network devices. For this, the set of *communication relations* is collected for each discovered device. We define a communication relation through the triple of source address, the destination address, and the protocol type. An explicit header-based communication discovery comprises in case of IP-based communication a straightforward port-based protocol mapping. In case of non-IP traffic, the communication protocol is derived from the type field of the Ethernet header. Implicit communication detection using deep packet inspection represents a protocol interpretation, which is currently implemented for ARP only (cf. Table 1). The following example explains the idea of implicit communication detection in detail.

Exemplary Message Processing. Since ARP supports all features described in the previous sections, an exemplary ARP request outlined in Fig. 2 is used for clarification. Following the presented methodology of the network traffic processing, this frame is handled as follows:

– **Device discovery:** As an ARP frame is recognized by inspecting the *type* field of the Ethernet header, a new network device *(devA)* is detected based on the

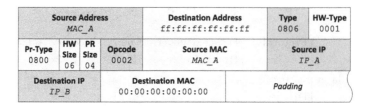

Fig. 2. Exemplary ARP request frame

Ethernet *source address*. The interface function add_device (cf. Listing 1.1) either creates a new device or returns its reference, if it is already part of the current network device list. Moreover, the ARP decoder tries to add a further device *(devB)* based on the *destination IP* address, which belongs to the implicitly requested device.

- **Device information discovery:** ARP requests transport the IP address of the requesting device *(source IP)*. Thus, payload inspection enables an IP address assignment to *devA* by use of the function add_information.
- **Communication discovery:** Whereas the source address of the message header is used to determine the source of the communication, the implicit requested device *(devB)* rather than the Ethernet destination address (Ethernet broadcast) is interpreted as the destination of the communication relation. This is added during ARP payload processing by use of the interface function add_relation. Note that the ARP decoder also determines the specific message type (ARP request) by inspecting the *opcode* field.

```
devA = add_device(device_list, eth.source_address)
process_ARP(devA, device_list, eth.payload)
⟶add_information(devA, arp.source_ip)
⟶devB = add_device(device_list, arp.destination_ip)
⟶add_relation(devA, devB, arp-request)
```

Listing 1.1. Exemplary use of interface functions for network traffic processing

2.2   Visualization of Device Communication

Visualization is considered to be the most effective way to explore the discovered topology. In the following we introduce a graph-based approach to analyze the visualization.

Communication Graphs. We use *communication graphs* for a visual representation of devices and their communication relations. A communication graph is a directed multigraph $G = (V, E)$ with:

- V, a set of vertices, with each vertex $v \in V$ representing a network device discovered in the traffic processing stage.

– E, a set of edges, with each edge $e = ((v_{src}, v_{dst}), M) \in E$ representing a set of communication relations discovered by the network traffic processing between a source device $v_{src} \in V$ and a destination device $v_{dst} \in V$ using the set M of messages consisting of $n \in \mathbb{N}$ different messages.

Visualization Filter. Applying communication graphs results in relative complex visualizations when including the whole set of discovered information. Although this provides a detailed network overview, the analysis should be performed incrementally, e.g., by individual exploration of remarkable devices or specific message types. Hence, *visualization filters* are implemented.

A visualization filter $F = (V_F, M_F)$ consists of a set of vertices V_F, each $v \in V_F$ representing a network device and a set of messages M_F. The application of F to communication graph G results in the subgraph G_{Fw} or G_{Fb} when F works in *whitelist (w)* or *blacklist (b)* mode. While a whitelist filter allows an exclusive visualization of devices and/or messages specified with F, blacklisting operates in the opposite direction for a selective exclusion of specified graph elements. Some characteristics of elements being part of the subgraphs G_{Fw} and G_{Fb} are described in the following.

Characteristics of Network Devices. In case of whitelisting, a discovered device represented by vertex v is specified with V_F, formally described with (1). In contrast, explicit exclusion of a network device from visualization in blacklist mode can be achieved by specifying v with V_F. Thus, v fulfills (2).

$$v \in V \cap V_F \tag{1}$$

$$v \in V \backslash V_F \tag{2}$$

The following characteristics formally describe that v belongs to (is source or destination of) an arbitrary set of communication relations discovered in the network processing stage where at least one communication relation either uses a message specified with M_F (3) or does not use such a message (4) at all.

$$\exists (v_{scr}, v_{dst}, M) \in E : (v_{src} = v \vee v_{dst} = v) \wedge \exists (m \in M : m \in M_F) \tag{3}$$

$$\exists (v_{scr}, v_{dst}, M) \in E : (v_{src} = v \vee v_{dst} = v) \wedge \exists (m \in M : m \notin M_F) \tag{4}$$

With (5), v is characterized to be part of a relation in which the associated communication partner meets (1). To be more restrictive, this assertion can be combined with (3) which results in (6). Whereas these characteristics obviously apply in the context of whitelisting, the adjusted version (7) applies to v in case of communicating to a blacklisted device using a blacklisted message.

$$\exists (v_{scr}, v_{dst}, M) \in E : (v_{dst} = v \wedge v_{src} \in V \cap V_F) \vee \\ (v_{src} = v \wedge v_{dst} \in V \cap V_F) \tag{5}$$

$$\exists (v_{scr}, v_{dst}, M) \in E : ((v_{src} = v \wedge v_{src} \in V \cap V_F) \vee \\ (v_{dst} = v \wedge v_{dst} \in V \cap V_F)) \wedge \\ \exists (m \in M : m \in M_F) \tag{6}$$

$$\exists(v_{scr}, v_{dst}, M) \in E : (\ (v_{src} = v \land v_{src} \in V \backslash V_F) \lor$$
$$(v_{dst} = v \land v_{dst} \in V \backslash V_F)) \land \tag{7}$$
$$\exists(m \in M : m \notin M_F)$$

Characteristics of Communication Relations. Let $e = (v_{src}, v_{dst}, M)$ be a set of communication relations which belongs to the set of visualized edges when applying F to G. Set e is a subset of a set of discovered relations $e' = (v'_{src}, v'_{dst}, M')$ with $v_{src} = v'_{src}, v_{dst} = v'_{dst}$ and $M \subset M'$ with each $m \in M$ matching the characteristics specified with the following assertions.

The first assertions characterize for each e that its communicating devices belong to the set of visualized devices when F operates in whitelist (8) or blacklist (9) mode. As no requirements on the messages are made, all elements of M' are included in M.

$$\exists(v'_{src}, v'_{dst}, M') \in E : (v_{src} = v'_{src} \land v'_{src} \in V_{Fw}) \land$$
$$(v_{dst} = v'_{dst} \land v'_{dst} \in V_{Fw}) \land \tag{8}$$
$$M = \{m | m \in M'\}$$

$$\exists(v'_{src}, v'_{dst}, M') \in E : (v_{src} = v'_{src} \land v'_{src} \in V_{Fb}) \land$$
$$(v_{dst} = v'_{dst} \land v'_{dst} \in V_{Fb}) \land \tag{9}$$
$$M = \{m | m \in M'\}$$

With (10) and (11), e is characterized by the exclusively use of messages specified with M_F or rather by the use of not blacklisted messages. The two most restrictive assertions on a set of communication relations simply combine (8) and (10) to (12), respectively (9) and (11) to (13).

$$\exists(v'_{src}, v'_{dst}, M') \in E : (v_{src} = v'_{src} \land v_{dst} = v'_{dst}) \land$$
$$M = \{m | m \in M' \cap M_F\} \tag{10}$$

$$\exists(v'_{src}, v'_{dst}, M') \in E : (v_{src} = v'_{src} \land v_{dst} = v'_{dst}) \land$$
$$M = \{m | m \in M' \backslash M_F\} \tag{11}$$

$$\exists(v'_{src}, v'_{dst}, M') \in E : (\ (v_{src} = v'_{src} \land v'_{src} \in V_{Fw}) \land$$
$$(v_{dst} = v'_{dst} \land v'_{dst} \in V_{Fw})) \land \tag{12}$$
$$M = \{m | m \in M' \cap M_F\}$$

$$\exists(v'_{src}, v'_{dst}, M') \in E : (\ (v_{src} = v'_{src} \land v'_{src} \in V_{Fb}) \land$$
$$(v_{dst} = v'_{dst} \land v'_{dst} \in V_{Fb})) \land \tag{13}$$
$$M = \{m | m \in M' \backslash M_F\}$$

Characteristics of G_{Fw} and G_{Fb}. For describing the characteristics of the resulting subgraphs when applying a visualization filter F to a graph G, four cases have to be considered with regard to the composition of F:

1. $V_F = \emptyset \land M_F = \emptyset$: In case of an empty filter with no elements specified with V_F and M_F the subgraphs directly correspond to G.

Table 2. Subgraph characteristics

Case	G_{Fw} (Whitelist mode)	G_{Fb} (Blacklist mode)
1	$V_{Fw} = \{v \mid v \in V\}$	$V_{Fb} = \{v \mid v \in V\}$
	$E_{Fw} = \{e = (v_{src}, v_{dst}, M) \mid e \in E\}$	$E_{Fb} = \{e = (v_{src}, v_{dst}, M) \mid e \in E\}$
2	$V_{Fw} = \{v \mid (1) \vee (5)\}$	$V_{Fb} = \{v \mid (2)\}$
	$E_{Fw} = \{e = (v_{src}, v_{dst}, M) \mid (8)\}$	$E_{Fb} = \{e = (v_{src}, v_{dst}, M) \mid (9)\}$
3	$V_{Fw} = \{v \mid v \in V \wedge (3)\}$	$V_{Fb} = \{v \mid v \in V \wedge (4)\}$
	$E_{Fw} = \{e = (v_{src}, v_{dst}, M) \mid (10)\}$	$E_{Fb} = \{e = (v_{src}, v_{dst}, M) \mid (11)\}$
4	$V_{Fw} = \{v \mid (1) \wedge (6)\}$	$V_{Fb} = \{v \mid (2) \wedge (7)\}$
	$E_{Fw} = \{e = (v_{src}, v_{dst}, M) \mid (12)\}$	$E_{Fw} = \{e = (v_{src}, v_{dst}, M) \mid (13)\}$

2. $V_F \neq \emptyset \wedge M_F = \emptyset$: A sole device based filter includes (whitelist) all devices specified with V_F and the belonging communication relations into the visualization, respectively excludes them in case of blacklisting.
3. $V_F = \emptyset \wedge M_F \neq \emptyset$: A message based filter operating in whitelist (or blacklist) mode exclusively considers (or excludes) communication relations that are based on messages specified with M_F and the associated communication partners.
4. $V_F \neq \emptyset \wedge M_F \neq \emptyset$: Device and message based filtering can be combined which results in the most restrictive set of visualized graph elements.

Table 2 summarizes the exact composition of $G_{Fw} = (V_{Fw}, E_{Fw})$ and $G_{Fb} = (V_{Fb}, E_{Fb})$ for each of these cases by implicit specifications of the sets of vertices and edges. For this, the characteristics of their elements are indicated by use of (1)–(13).

Exemplary Communication Visualization. The methodology of device communication visualization is exemplarily explained by the graph presented in Fig. 3. The graph consists of four vertices, three of them represent real network devices labeled with the discovered MAC[1] and/or IP addresses. The virtual device indicated by the dashed frame line results from using a non-interpreted broad or multicast address (e.g., the spanning tree multicast address in case of STP traffic) as destination of a communication relation. Figure 4 shows the graph that results when applying a whitelist filter with the following characteristics:

– $V_F = (switch/router)$: The exclusive visualization of the switch is achieved by using the corresponding device class as a device-based filter. Alternatively, devices can also explicitly be specified with V_F by using MAC or IP addresses. Devices matching a device-based filter are indicated in the graph by green-filled vertices.

---

[1] OUI lookup is used for integration of the manufacturer or the name of well-known broad and multicast addresses into the MAC address label.

– $M_F = (arp)$: A message filter is used for an exclusive visualization of ARP frames. Further possibilities to specify messages of the subgraph are the indication of specific protocol message types (e.g. ARP request) or to filter several protocol classes, e.g., TCP or UDP to indicate the transport protocol.

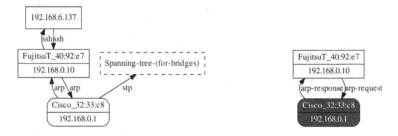

Fig. 3. Complete graph   **Fig. 4.** Subgraph

3   Application and Evaluation

In order to evaluate and test our passive topology exploration approach we applied three datasets (cf. Table 3) from industrial networks. In our evaluation we especially focus on the benefit of applying deep packet inspection and communication visualization.

3.1   Applied Datasets

The applied datasets differ in size and deployment purpose. Dataset 1 is derived from a network used to operate a double-unit lignite power plant. The traffic sensor was placed on one of eight main switches interconnecting several process control and expert systems. Beside standardized IT protocols the communication runs over proprietary vendor specific protocols on top of TCP/IP. Full access to the traffic of the observed domain was realized by port mirroring.

The second dataset was captured from a flexible lignite conveyer system situated in an opencast mine used for bridging the way between the excavator and long-distance vehicles transporting the lignite out of the mine. The sensor was connected to a mirror port of a switch its interconnected devices basically communicate via an Industrial Ethernet based field bus, namely Profinet IO.

Source of dataset 3 is a test system of a power distribution grid. The observed network traffic contains telecontrol communication between a control center, a transformer station, and a local grid using the IEC 60870-5-104 protocol on top of Ethernet as well as IP. Again, the sensor had access to the complete traffic passing the main network switch.

Table 3. Characteristics of the datasets

	Dataset 1		Dataset 2		Dataset 3	
	Total	bc/mc	Total	bc/mc	Total	bc/mc
Size [MB]	1,007	1.2	1,126	1.2	112	84.3
# packets	3,637,652	12,064	5,775,465	7,279	716,655	550,348
Duration [min]	25		19		941	
# devices	133		33		12	

Of course, access to a mirror port cannot be guaranteed in each scenario, especially when applying the exploration to networks which operate in critical infrastructures. For simulating a traffic sensor connected to a default switch port, we extracted broad- and multicast messages from the total captures. The characteristics of the resulting datasets (bc/mc) are also summarized in Table 3.

3.2   Network Device Discovery

For evaluating the device discovery, we first investigate the capabilities of implicit device detection, followed by indicating the potential of a comprehensive topology exploration regarding the proportion of network components discovered by use of passive traffic analysis. The results discussed are presented in Table 4. Here, all disclosed numbers of devices exclusively refer to discovered devices with an assigned IPv4 unicast address.

DPI Benefit. In order to demonstrate the benefit of implicit device detection using deep packet inspection the number of devices detected only by header inspection (n_{HI}) is compared with number of devices detected additionally by means of DPI (n_{DPI}). For this, Table 4 indicates the *DPI benefit* which is defined as follows:

$$DPI\ benefit = \frac{(n_{DPI} - n_{HI}) \cdot 100\%}{n_{HI}} \tag{14}$$

The relatively low DPI benefit in comparison to the total captures with a maximum of about 27% (three more detected network devices in dataset 3) can be explained by the position of the traffic sensors, which were connected to a mirror port of a main network router or switch, respectively. An exclusive consideration of broad- and multicast traffic shows a substantial increase of the DPI benefit which raises up to 1100% in case of dataset 2. Moreover, it should be noted that each device discovered by the full capture could also be identified in the broad- and multicast traffic of datasets 2 and 3.

Device Detection Rate. The underlying infrastructure of the datasets used in the evaluation is characterized by various interconnected networks. To determine meaningful results concerning the device detection rate the sets of *detectable*

Table 4. Discovered network devices

	Dataset 1		Dataset 2		Dataset 3	
	All	bc/mc	All	bc/mc	All	bc/mc
n_{HI}	96	47	21	2	11	3
n_{DPI}	101	62	24	24	14	14
DPI benefit [%]	5.21	31.91	14.29	1100.00	27.27	366.67
n_d	88		22		11	
DDR [%]	81.82	61.36	90.91	90.91	90.91	90.91

devices were determined first. These are subsets of documented devices that belong to the same network as the device on which the traffic sensor was placed. The percentage ratio between detected devices, which are part of the set of detectable devices, and the total number of detectable devices (n_d) is indicated as *device detection rate (DDR)*. As Table 4 indicates, passive device discovery reaches a detection rate up to 90% for the datesets 2 and 3, even if only broad- and multicast messages are considered.

Note that due to differences in quality and completeness of the documentation required to determine the sets of detectable devices, DDR is not seen as a clear criteria for the evaluation. Instead, the occurrence of undocumented devices can be indicated by comparing the sets of detected and detectable devices. As the number of discovered devices n_{DPI} exceeds the number of detectable devices, an out-dated documentation has to be assumed for each of the three datasets.

3.3 Network Analysis Using Communication Visualization

Now we discuss exemplarily the results from applying network topology visualization approach using communication graphs (cf. Sect. 2.2) to the datasets 1 and 2. Due to demands of the network operators, all addresses mentioned in this section had to be anonymized as follows: The pattern $MAC\_ < number >$ $(IP\_ < number >)$ is used to represent a unique MAC (IP) address, whereby equal addresses within a network are represented by equal numbers.

Analysis of Individual Device Communication. The first scenario presents a practical procedure for analyzing devices to which special attention should be paid, e.g., unknown (undocumented) devices discovered by automated topology exploration. It is obvious that in a first step the address of the device to be investigated should be used to whitelist its whole communication. Figure 5 shows the resulting communication graph by use of an exemplary undocumented IP address *IP_04* discovered from dataset 1.

The exclusive discovery of ARP communication indicates, that the assignment of the IP address to the network interface with *MAC_04* was provided by DPI. As presented by the node label, multiple IP addresses are assigned to the

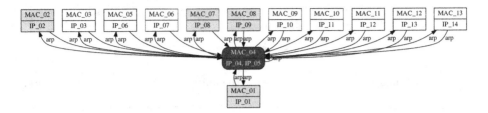

Fig. 5. Communication graph resulting from *device* whitelisting

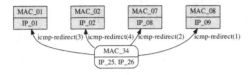

Fig. 6. Communication graph resulting from *protocol* whitelisting

device. The additional IP address *IP_05*, which is also not part of the documentation, was also announced by the device using ARP request frames[2].

The considered device is classified as "switch/router", even though exclusive ARP relations are discovered. In this case, role assignment was applied by the ICMP decoder, more precisely by interpreting the address of a preferable gateway announced from a router using ICMP redirect packets. Applying an edge (protocol) based whitelist filter for an exclusive consideration of ICMP redirect messages results in the graph presented in Fig. 6. The (documented) router with the IP addresses *IP_25* and *IP_26* sends redirect messages to four devices. All of them are also addressed by the undocumented router, which can immediately be recognized by use of the yellow-filled node marking.

Thus, beside identifying an undocumented router the analysis of an individual device also reveals a security lack inside the observed network. As ICMP redirect messages can easily be exploited to launch man-in-the-middle attacks, it is recommended not to use (send and process) them any more.

Analysis of the Complete Network Communication. This scenario evaluates the capability to distinguish between the different roles of the devices by analyzing their communication patterns. For this, the whole unicast communication discovered in the network represented by dataset 2 is represented by the graph shown in Fig. 7. The graph already indicates significant differences in the communication patterns regarding the number of addressed communication partners. Most communication partners by far are addressed by device *MAC_01*. The 17 addressed components include 16 decentralized peripheral devices and one PC

---

[2] Because of space limitations the edges of the graph are not labeled with the full protocol message names. All outgoing arcs of the device *IP_04* represent ARP request frames, while incoming arcs belong to the respective responses.

Fig. 7. Communication graph summarizing the unicast communication of a network.

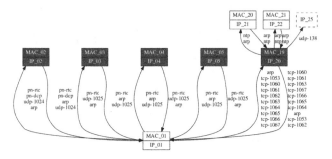

Fig. 8. Communication graph presenting relations of different roles of devices.

used for diagnostics. Decentralized peripheral (devices *MAC_02-17*) are solely identified by the data exchange with its superordinated PLC (device *MAC_01*).

These assumptions regarding the device roles can be confirmed by a more detailed view on the communication patterns by taking the communication protocols into account. For this, Fig. 8 depicts the exclusive communication from devices *MAC_02-05*[3] and the PC *(MAC_19)*. The field layer communication is essentially characterized by a cyclic real-time transfer of process data using the Profinet IO protocol *(pn-rtc)* and a request/response-based query of specific PLC slots via Profinet IO Context Management running over UDP (ports 1024 and 1025). Optionally, devices exchange configuration information by use of the Profinet Discovery and Configuration Protocol *(pn-dcp)*. In contrast, several applications running over TCP are addressed through the communication from the diagnostic PC to the PLC.

4   Related Work

Related work of automated topology exploration comprises a broad research area, but the number of comparable approches is quite limited due to the pure passive character of our approach. Most of the related approaches rely on active techniques, e.g., for device discovery via ICMP [12,13], MAC probe sending [7], and querying intermediate systems with SNMP (e.g., [3,5,8,12]). Partially, the topology exploration even requires specific software installation on the participating network hosts [2,7]. The main advantage of active methods is the possibility to determine wired connections between network devices that enables a

---

[3] Due to space limitations, these devices are chosen to represent the communication patterns of the decentralized periphery. The remaining devices *MAC_05-MAC_17*, however, exhibit similar relations to device *MAC_20*.

reconstruction of the real physical topology. Although this is a valuable skill, the generation of additional network traffic and the installation of further software is not acceptable in the considered area of industrial networks.

Approaches on passive network discovery are very rare. In [4] an algorithm is proposed that uses hop-counts for distance measurements. As the associated information (Time-to-Live value) is modified by network routers, this method can be used exclusively for topology discovery on the internet protocol layer, but it does not work solely on the data link level. Closest to our approach is the network analyzer in [9] that also supports passive device and communication discovery. Header inspection in the internet protocol layer is applied in the two cases. This is not applicable to handle pure Ethernet frames. Since real-time variants of the Industrial Ethernet and other vendor-specific protocols are implemented directly on the data link layer, the processing of the Ethernet protocols is indispensable for a detailed analysis of local industrial networks. Furthermore, we differentiate ourselves from existing solutions by the use of protocol decoders. To the best of our knowledge, our approach exclusively applies deep packet inspection to maximize the potential of passive topology exploration.

5   Final Remarks

Automated network topology exploration is a challenging issue, especially when avoiding interferences resulting from active techniques has top priority. In this paper, we have presented a novel method for passive traffic processing that makes topology discovery suitable for application in the industrial area. Our future research will focus on utilizing the collected topology information to improve industrial network security by means of network-based intrusion detection. In a first step, the set of communication relations can be transformed into a rule set processed by a signature-based intrusion detection system (e.g., Snort [1]). Due to the homogeneity of industrial traffic [6], this provides an initial protection by detecting changes in the topology caused by unknown devices or communication relations. We further plan to combine this rule-based analysis with a more advanced approach on anomaly detection based on machine learning methods presented in [10]. To this end, we will focus on applying rule-based IDS alerts as a replacement of a feature subset with the aim to reduce the feature space and thus increasing the current detection accuracy [11].

Acknowledgements. The authors gratefully acknowledge funding from the German Federal Ministry of Education and Research (BMBF) via the projects INDI (funding code: 16KIS0156) and SICIA (16KIS0158K).

References

1. Snort: Network intrusion detection system (2016). https://www.snort.org
2. Black, R., Donnelly, A., Fournet, C.: Ethernet topology discovery without network assistance. In: Proceedings of the 12th IEEE International Conference on Network Protocols (ICNP 2004), Berlin, Germany, 5–8 October 2004, pp. 328–339 (2004)

3. Breitbart, Y., Garofalakis, M.N., Jai, B., Martin, C., Rastogi, R., Silberschatz, A.: Topology discovery in heterogeneous IP networks: the NetInventory system. IEEE/ACM Trans. Netw. **12**(3), 401–414 (2004)

4. Eriksson, B., Barford, P., Nowak, R.D., Crovella, M.: Learning network structure from passive measurements. In: Proceedings of the 7th ACM SIGCOMM Internet Measurement Conference, IMC 2007, San Diego, California, USA, 24–26 October 2007, pp. 209–214 (2007)

5. Gobjuka, H., Breitbart, Y.: Ethernet topology discovery for networks with incomplete information. IEEE/ACM Trans. Netw. **18**(4), 1220–1233 (2010)

6. Hadžiosmanović, D., Simionato, L., Bolzoni, D., Zambon, E., Etalle, S.: N-Gram against the machine: on the feasibility of the N-Gram network analysis for binary protocols. In: Balzarotti, D., Stolfo, S.J., Cova, M. (eds.) RAID 2012. LNCS, vol. 7462, pp. 354–373. Springer, Heidelberg (2012). doi:10.1007/978-3-642-33338-5_18

7. Kienzle, D.M., Evans, N.S., Elder, M.C.: NICE: endpoint-based topology discovery. In: Cyber and Information Security Research Conference, CISR 2014, Oak Ridge, TN, USA, 8–10 April 2014, pp. 97–100 (2014)

8. Lowekamp, B., O'Hallaron, D.R., Gross, T.R.: Topology discovery for large ethernet networks. In: SIGCOMM, pp. 237–248 (2001)

9. Moussadek-Kabdania, A., Soilli, A.: Grassmarlin, an open-source tool for passive ICS network mapping (2016). http://www.securityinsider-solucom.fr/2016/03/en-grassmarlin-open-source-tool-for.html

10. Schuster, F., Paul, A.: A distributed intrusion detection system for industrial automation networks. In: Proceedings of 2012 IEEE 17th International Conference on Emerging Technologies & Factory Automation, ETFA 2012, Krakow, Poland, 17–21 September 2012, pp. 1–4. IEEE (2012)

11. Schuster, F., Paul, A., Rietz, R., König, H.: Potentials of using one-class SVM for detecting protocol-specific anomalies in industrial networks. In: IEEE Symposium Series on Computational Intelligence, SSCI 2015, Cape Town, South Africa, 7–10 December 2015, pp. 83–90. IEEE (2015)

12. Wang, Y., Li, D., Han, C., Zhu, Z.: Research and application on automatic network topology discovery in ITSM system. In: Proceedings of the 9th International Conference on Hybrid Intelligent Systems, Shenyang, China, 12–14 August 2009, pp. 336–340 (2009)

13. Yao, B., Viswanathan, R., Chang, F., Waddington, D.G.: Topology inference in the presence of anonymous routers. In: IEEE INFOCOM 2003, The 22nd Annual Joint Conference of the IEEE Computer and Communications Societies, San Franciso, CA, USA, March 30 - April 3 2003 (2003)

An Improved Robust Low Cost Approach for Real Time Vehicle Positioning in a Smart City

Ikram Belhajem[(✉)], Yann Ben Maissa, and Ahmed Tamtaoui

Laboratory of Telecommunications, Networks and Service Systems,
National Institute of Posts and Telecommunications, Rabat, Morocco
{belhajem,benmaissa,tamtaoui}@inpt.ac.ma

Abstract. The Global Positioning System (GPS) aided low cost Dead Reckoning (DR) system can provide without interruption the vehicle position for efficient fleet management solutions in smart cities. The Extended Kalman Filter (EKF) is generally applied for data fusion using the sensor's measures and the GPS position as a helper.

However, the EKF depends on the vehicle dynamic variations and may quickly diverge during periods of GPS signal loss.

In this paper, we present a robust low cost approach using EKF and neural networks (NN) with Particle Swarm Optimization (PSO) to reliably estimate the real time vehicle position. While GPS signals are available, we train the NN with PSO on different dynamics and outage times to learn the position errors so we can correct the future EKF predictions during GPS signal outages. We obtain empirically an improvement of up to 94% over the simple EKF predictions in case of GPS failures.

Keywords: Data fusion · Extended kalman filter · Global positioning system · Intelligent transportation systems · Smart cities · Dead reckoning · Low cost · Neural networks · Particle swarm optimization

1 Introduction

Context. In a smart city, traditional infrastructures are merged with information and communication technologies to face problems resulting from the rapid urban population growth, for a sustainable economic development and a high quality of life [1]. Based on wireless technologies, smart cities can establish intelligent transportation systems (ITS) capable of carrying out effective and energy sufficient transport services at an inexpensive cost. There are several applications of ITS including fleet management solutions that can achieve the route optimization and reduce the fuel consumption by giving a real time situational awareness of traffic conditions and the data for a flow of vehicles in the roads

This work was financially supported by the National Center of Scientific and Technical Research (CNRST), Morocco.

© ICST Institute for Computer Sciences, Social Informatics and Telecommunications Engineering 2017
L.A. Maglaras et al. (Eds.): INISCOM 2016, LNICST 188, pp. 77–89, 2017.
DOI: 10.1007/978-3-319-52569-3_7

(e.g., ambulances and police vehicles). This will certainly require a real time visibility of an accurate vehicle position to improve the driver safety and comfort.

Positioning systems often rely on the Global Positioning System (GPS) which provides, based on satellite signals received, the location, altitude and velocity at a low frequency. Unfortunately, GPS receivers perform badly within tall urban buildings or beneath dense foliage because of signal masking and multipath phenomenon (i.e., multiple copies of GPS signal reach a receiver's antenna by two or more different paths). The combination of GPS and Inertial Navigation Systems (INS) (i.e., autonomous systems that provide positioning, velocity, and attitude information at high update rates) can ensure a continuous position estimate and overcome the limitations of using each sensor individually [7,9,12]. Another possibility is the GPS enhanced with INS based on microelectromechanical systems (MEMS) [2] since the high performance inertial sensors are very expensive. The MEMS technology offers cost reduction coupled to small size and lower power consumption advantages.

Practically, multisensor data fusion is performed using the Kalman filter (KF) which is an optimal state estimator start from noisy and erroneous observations [3]. The application of the KF is restricted to linear systems; therefore the Extended Kalman Filter (EKF) is adopted through a first-order linearization procedure for non-linear systems.

Problem. The INS impose restrictions on the environments where they are implemented because of their computing *complexity* in addition to their high *cost* [2]. Furthermore, MEMS-based INS suffer from a rapid accumulation of errors when operating in a stand-alone mode during GPS outages.

The KF performance depends on how the stochastic models of the sensors are accurate, also it requires a priori information of system noises and measurement errors. For those reasons, the KF predicted position tends to quickly *diverge* when GPS outage occurs.

Contribution. In this paper, we suggest a new robust low cost approach using EKF and Evolutionary Machine Learning in order to yield an optimal real time vehicle positioning in a smart city. The sensors used are GPS enhanced with low cost Dead Reckoning (DR) system (composed of only an odometer and a gyrometer to measure angular velocity and displacement of a vehicle) which is easy to use and keep the calculations simple. During GPS signal presence, the EKF estimates the position while the neural networks (NN) learn the position errors. The NN compensate the additional EKF position errors when no GPS information exists, allowing the system to correct the EKF estimations and preventing it from divergence. The training phase of NN is achieved through evolutionary learning algorithms notably the Particle Swarm Optimization (PSO).

Contents. The remainder of this paper is organized as follows: In Sect. 2, we discuss some relevant works on this topic. We present the essential background on EKF, NN and PSO in Sect. 3. Then, we deal with the formulation of our proposed approach in Sect. 4. In Sect. 5, we detail the experimental results.

2   Related Works

In literature, several works related to vehicle positioning suggest the integration of GPS and DR sensors like odometers and gyrometers [4,6]. The odometer provides the distance travelled by the vehicle while the gyrometer measures the angular velocity. Both of these sensors are subject to time growing errors (e.g., bias drift and scale factor change) in spite of their autonomy and independency of any signal blockage. The combined system GPS/DR helps then to keep down the odometer and gyrometer errors when GPS is available; conversely, in urban areas where GPS signals are frequently blocked, the DR ensures a continuous positioning.

Domenico et al. [4] propose a hybrid strategy using the EKF for the GPS, odometer and gyrometer data fusion when GPS signal is available; inversely the algorithm switches to an open-loop model-based estimation when it is not available because its loss for long periods reduces the EKF accuracy and even causes its divergence.

In their work, Georgy et al. [5] compare the performance of the KF and the Particle Filter (PF) used as vehicle state estimators combining GPS with the vehicle odometer and low cost MEMS-based inertial sensors; they conclude according to empirical results that the PF outperforms KF in case of GPS masks. Nevertheless, the increased power of PF may require a large number of particles; this comes at the cost of higher computational complexity.

Ismaeel et al. [7] propose the use of multilayer feed-forward NN with Back-propagation Learning Algorithm (BPLA) to integrate data from INS and GPS for vehicular positioning and velocity information. Besides, the wavelet multi-resolution analysis is used to compare the INS and GPS position outputs at different resolution levels before processing them by the NN.

In [8], Hasan et al. introduce an adaptive neuro-fuzzy inference system (ANFIS) using PSO to combine data from MEMS grade INS and GPS for a reliable navigation solution. This network is trained during the availability of GPS signal so to estimate the INS position errors during GPS signal blockage.

Malleswaran et al. [9] present a performance analysis of GPS/INS integration based NN trained with weight optimization techniques namely the BPLA, Genetic Algorithm (GA), and PSO. Experimental tests indicate that the PSO training algorithm provides superior learning capability and is well adapted for intelligent navigation systems.

Unluckily, replacing the EKF completely by NN can be a non-optimal solution because their estimation quality can only be guaranteed if the trained data are sufficient. Belhajem et al. claim that the use of NN only [10] or coupled to Autoregressive Integrated Moving Average (ARIMA) models [11] can bridge the gap in the EKF prediction mode based on data from GPS and a low cost DR system. While GPS is available, the NN are trained on different samples to learn the position errors, so they can correct the additional EKF drifts during GPS signal loss.

3   Background

In this section, we cover the background of the EKF that estimates the vehicle position and the NN used for learning the EKF predicted position errors. Also, we describe the principle of the PSO metaheuristic.

3.1   Extended Kalman Filter

The EKF is a non-linear version of the KF that linearizes the process and measurement models about the current mean and covariance. The filter is a set of mathematical equations which uses the process model to estimate the current state of a system, then a correction of this estimate is performed using any available sensor measurements.

3.1.1 Modeling

Let us consider a car-like model of a front-wheel drive vehicle. The origin M of the body frame (rigidly attached to the vehicle) is located midway the rear axle while the x-axis is aligned with the vehicle longitudinal axis (see Fig. 1). For the vehicle dynamics analysis, the North-East-Down frame known also as a navigation frame is used; so any movement related to the body frame have to be converted to the navigation frame.

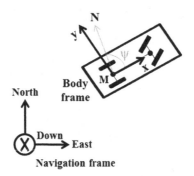

Fig. 1. Vehicle kinematic model

The kinematic equations mentioned below describe the vehicle position denoted by (N,E,ψ) where N and E denote the north and east components and ψ represents the heading [6]:

$$\begin{cases} N_{k+1} = N_k + ds_{k+1}.sinc(\frac{d\psi_{k+1}}{2}).cos(\psi_{k+1} + \frac{d\psi_{k+1}}{2}) \\ \quad -d\psi_{k+1}.(D_x.sin(\psi_k) + D_y.cos(\psi_k)). \\ E_{k+1} = E_k + ds_{k+1}.sinc(\frac{d\psi_{k+1}}{2}).sin(\psi_{k+1} + \frac{d\psi_{k+1}}{2}) \\ \quad +d\psi_{k+1}.(D_x.cos(\psi_k) - D_y.sin(\psi_k)). \\ \psi_{k+1} = \psi_k + d\psi_{k+1}. \end{cases} \quad (1)$$

where

- ds_{k+1} is the distance traveled by the vehicle between k and $k+1$;
- $d\psi_{k+1}$ represents the heading variation corresponding to the angular velocity between k and $k+1$;
- D_x and D_y are the distances in the body frame between the GPS antenna and the middle of the rear axle.

3.1.2 Prediction and Correction Phases

Figure 2 shows a scheme for the KF model. In our case, the state vector at time epoch k is $X_k = (N_k, E_k, \psi_k)$ and the measurement vector is $Z_k = (N_{GPS_k}, E_{GPS_k})$. Before the estimation process starts, values for the initial state $\hat{X}_0^+$ and the corresponding error covariance P_0^+ are assumed to be known. The prediction mode starts by projecting the state and error covariance ahead to estimate $\hat{X}_k^-$ and P_k^-. When new GPS measurements are available at time epoch k, the filter starts the update mode. At this stage, the Kalman gain K_k, updated state $\hat{X}_k^+$ and error covariance P_k^+ are computed.

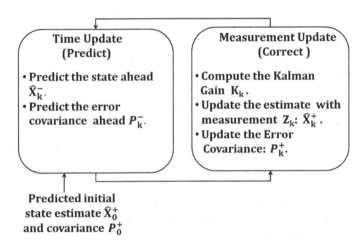

Fig. 2. Kalman filter model

3.2   Neural Networks

NN are a subset of Machine Learning methods acting as massively parallel distributed processors that have a natural propensity for storing experiential knowledge and making it available for use [13]. Inspired by the structure and functions of the human brain, NN are adaptive models that can map input patterns to output patterns without knowing the mathematical process involved. NN are composed of smaller units called neurons interconnected through synaptic weights.

The way a neural network links the input data into output data is defined by its architecture that refers to the arrangement of neurons into layers and the connection strengths within and between these layers [14]. In many practical applications, the most used model is the multilayer feed-forward NN in which all signals flow in one direction; from the input layer to the output layer passing by one or more hidden layers. In order to train the NN, weights of each unit are adjusted according to learning rules defined by weight optimization algorithms like PSO.

3.3 Particle Swarm Optimization

PSO is a robust stochastic evolutionary optimization technique developed by Kennedy and Eberhart [15]. The fundamental PSO inspiration is the social behavior of animals namely the movement and intelligence of swarms looking for the most fertile feeding location. In PSO, each problem to address is represented by a swarm of particles considered as candidate solutions which explore the search space looking for the best solution.

Since the strengths of the PSO include ease of implementation, computational efficiency, and fast convergence [16], it is used to optimize the NN connection weights during the training phase. For this, an initial swarm is generated randomly and the particles are the NN weights to learn. Each particle i moving around the search space is charcterized by a position vector x_i, a velocity vector v_i, and a position at which the best fitness $pbest_i$ is achieved by the particle. Besides, the global best position $gbest_i$ represents the position yielding the lowest error among all the $pbest_i$. At each iteration, the particles of the swarm are updated according to the following equations:

$$v_i(k+1) = wv_i(k) + c_1 r_1(k)(pbest_i - x_i(k)) + c_2 r_2(k)(gbest_i - x_i(k)). \quad (2)$$

$$x_i(k+1) = x_k(t) + v_i(k+1). \quad (3)$$

where c_1 and c_2 are the acceleration constants, $r_1(k)$ and $r_2(k)$ are random numbers uniformly distributed in [0,1], and w is the inertia weight employed to control the impact of the previous history of velocities on the current one. The update process is repeated until a maximum number of iterations is reached or an acceptable $gbest$ is achieved [16].

4   Formulation of the Hybrid EKF/NN Approach

In this section, we present a possible vehicle prototype and the formulation of our suggested approach in both the training and prediction phases. The prototype is not yet implemented, however we conducted extensive simulations on the Institut Pascal Data Sets [17] that were collected using VIPALAB, a platform equiped with multiple sensors. We have improvements over the EKF solution between 54 % and 94 %.

4.1   Possible Vehicle Prototype

Figure 3 illustrates the positions of the GPS and the odometer/gyrometer sensors in our possible vehicle prototype; each one of them is coupled to an Arduino nano and a Xbee module. The Arduino nano is dedicated for the treatement while Xbee module ensures a Zigbee communication for the wireless sensor networks. For the data treatment, a Raspberry with Xbee communication module is mounted on the car's dashboard. Our vision then is to support a real implementation of this prototype.

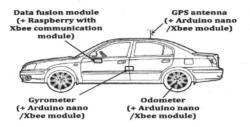

Fig. 3. Wireless sensor network

4.2   EKF/NN Combination

Practically, the EKF receives the speed V_{odom} and the heading ψ_{gyro}; then computes the vehicle predicted position (N_{pred}, E_{pred}). When new GPS measurements arrive, the EKF updates the predicted position (N_{cor}, E_{cor}) as presented in Fig. 4. However, when no GPS signal exists, the NN trained with PSO compensate the additional EKF predicted position errors.

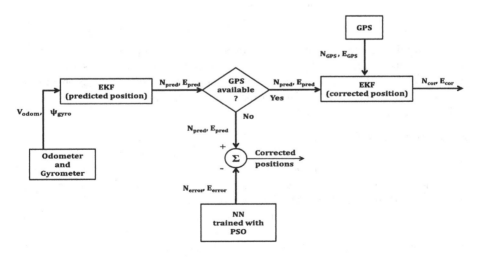

Fig. 4. EKF/NN combination

4.2.1 Training Phase

In general, the odometer bias or gyrometer drift consists of deterministic and stochastic parts. The former can be removed by calibration procedure while the latter is not easy to handle due to its random nature. Accordingly, the EKF performance depends on how the sensor components are correctly modeled; though a perfect tuning of the filter is rarely achieved since vehicle dynamic variations and environment changes occur oftenly. As a consequence, the EKF performs badly during GPS signal blockage which may result in its divergence.

To circumvent the EKF deficiencies, NN are a natural choice that require no calibration or modeling procedures. The networks are used to estimate the time-correlated position errors during the EKF prediction phase when no GPS signal is available. Two three-layer feed-forward NN are trained on different dynamics using PSO, so they can help to predict the north and east error drifts.

To fully represent the vehicle dynamics, the NN inputs consist of vehicle velocity, heading angle and time elapsed since last GPS measurement. The networks outputs are north and east errors which are compared to desired position errors. Figure 5 shows the north and east networks architecture.

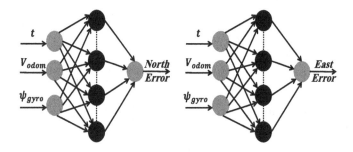

Fig. 5. North and east networks architecture

For training the NN, the target values used are computed as a difference between positions provided by two parallel EKFs. One filter provides a reference vehicle position while the other gives a predicted one by removing intentionally the GPS signals [12]. It should be noted that the training procedure presented in Fig. 6 is executed at the GPS sampling rate.

4.2.2 Prediction Stage

After training on different dynamics and outage times, the networks are used in prediction mode to help compensate for real GPS outages. The inputs are sent to the networks which provide estimates for the position errors along the north and the east directions. Since the EKF predictions without GPS measurements update contain errors, they are compensated by the networks outputs to form the corrected positions. The testing procedure is shown in Fig. 7.

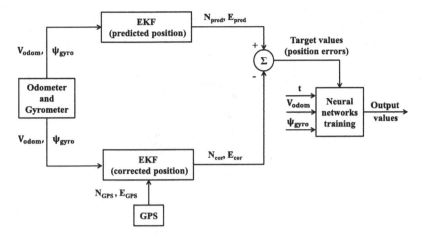

Fig. 6. NN training phase

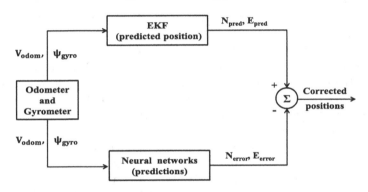

Fig. 7. NN testing phase

5   Experimental Tests and Results

In this section, we present the test vehicle prototype and the simulation results of our suggested hybrid approach.

5.1   Test Vehicle Prototype

The performance of the proposed hybrid technique was examined with the Institut Pascal Data Sets [17]. The field test data were collected using VIPALAB, a platform equiped with multiple sensors. In our case, the test system comprises three sets of an uBlox-6T-0-001 GPS receiver, an odometer and a Melexis MLX90609-N2 gyrometer. GPS values were collected at the frequency rate of 1 Hz while the odometer/gyrometer data at 50 Hz. The road test trajectory used is CEZEAUX-Heko (given in Fig. 8) which spans over a distance of 4.2 km during 28 min.

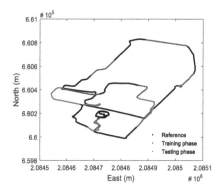

Fig. 8. Field test trajectory

5.2 Simulation Results

To examine the performance of the proposed approach, the field test data were divided into two parts. During the first 19 min, a total of seven GPS simulated outages (given in Fig. 8) are used to train the networks. Each outage lasts 60 s to leave the EKF position errors enough time to diverge. For the last 9 min, the NN run in the testing mode to generate predictions of the position drifts.

The NN are trained using batch-incremental approach. For every outage, a set of new inputs/targets are presented to train the NN using PSO to learn the network weight parameters. The objective is to reduce the mean squared error (MSE) between the networks outputs and the desired values. In our case study, the north and east networks architecture chosen emprically consist of 3 inputs, 5 hidden neurons and one output while the training goal is to reach MSE less than $2.10^{-4}\,\mathrm{m}^2$ given the real time constraints. Figure 9 shows the results of the training outages while the time intervals between them are masked. It appears clearly that the outputs of north and east networks are very close to the target values.

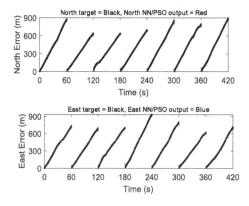

Fig. 9. North and east networks training results using PSO

To investigate the performance of this hybrid method, the GPS data were intentionally removed since there were no natural GPS outages in the field test. The networks can then be used to provide predictions of position drifts to correct the EKF predictions. For this purpose, they generate outputs based on dynamic inputs and latest estimated weight parameters. Relatively, results of the GPS test outages (presented in Fig. 8), with period lengths of 90 and 60 s, are given in Fig. 10.

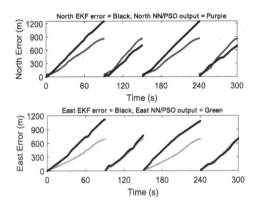

Fig. 10. North and east networks testing results using PSO

To compare the estimated position by our proposed approach and the one of EKF, two different evaluation indicators are calculated for each outage: the root mean square error (RMSE) and the mean absolute error (MAE). They are expressed by the following formulas:

$$RMSE = \sqrt{\frac{1}{n}\sum_{k=1}^{n}(A_k - F_k)^2}. \tag{4}$$

$$MAE = \frac{1}{n}\sum_{k=1}^{n}\left|A_k - F_k\right|. \tag{5}$$

where A_k is the actual EKF updated position by GPS measurements at time epoch k, F_k is either the EKF predicted position or the EKF corrected position by NN while n is the total number of predictions. These results are listed in Tables 1 and 2 for north and east position components. By combining EKF and NN together, the results show a significant decrease in RMSE and MAE over the EKF method. This hybrid approach enhances the vehicle position accuracy over the EKF predictions during GPS outages.

Table 1. GPS test outages north improvement

Outages	EKF		Our approach (EKF/NN)		Improvement (%)	
	RMSE (m)	MAE (m)	RMSE (m)	MAE (m)	RMSE (m)	MAE (m)
Outage 1	732.47	630.57	218.32	190.20	70	69
Outage 2	408.82	343.18	106.51	96.38	73	71
Outage 3	715.54	613.58	203.83	176.78	71	71
Outage 4	418.99	372.16	104.37	85.69	75	76

Table 2. GPS test outages east improvement

Outages	EKF		Our approach (EKF/NN)		Improvement (%)	
	RMSE (m)	MAE (m)	RMSE (m)	MAE (m)	RMSE (m)	MAE (m)
Outage 1	640.44	545.17	251.99	217.47	60	60
Outage 2	419.84	359.72	29.88	25.63	92	92
Outage 3	681.06	606.22	296.68	275.06	56	54
Outage 4	377.17	319.96	21.83	18.91	94	94

6   Conclusion

In this paper, we present an improved *robust* approach to estimate the real time vehicle positioning required by various fleet management applications in the context of a *smart city*. We propose the combination of EKF and NN based on PSO to fuse data coming from a GPS and *low cost* DR integrated sensors. After being trained on different dynamics and outage times, the NN are used to correct the EKF position errors when no GPS signal is detected. Experimental results with field test data demonstrate the ability of feed-forward NN trained with PSO to learn and make reasonable predictions of EKF drifts during different GPS blockage periods.

Future Work
Empirical results with simulated GPS outages showed very promising progress. Nonetheless, the GPS quality degradation in real GPS outages is more complex to handle. Further investigation is then needed to test and improve this hybrid solution during real GPS outages, that is why we intend to implement our vehicle prototype in future related works.

References

1. Caragliu, A., Del Bo, C., Nijkamp, P.: Smart cities in Europe. J. Urban Technol. **18**, 65–82 (2011). Routledge, England
2. Noureldin, A., Karamat, T.B., Eberts, M.D., El-Shafie, A.: Performance enhancement of MEMS-based INS/GPS integration for low-cost navigation applications. IEEE Trans. Veh. Technol. **58**, 1077–1096 (2009). IEEE

3. Grewal, M.S.: Kalman filtering. In: Lovric, M. (ed.) International Encyclopedia of Statistical Science, pp. 705–708. Springer, Heidelberg (2011)
4. Domenico, D.D., Fiengo, G., Glielmo, L.: On-board prototype of a vehicle localization system. In: 2007 IEEE International Conference on Control Applications, pp. 438–443. IEEE, USA (2007)
5. Georgy, J., Iqbal, U., Noureldin, A.: Quantitative comparison between Kalman filter and Particle filter for low cost INS/GPS integration. In: Proceedings of the 6th International Symposium on Mechatronics and Its Applications (ISMA 2009), pp. 1–7. IEEE, USA (2009)
6. Lucet, E., Betaille, D., Donnay Fleury, N., Ortiz, M., Salle, D., Canou, J.: Real-time 2D localization of a car-like mobile robot using dead reckoning and GPS, with satellite masking prediction. In: Accurate localization for land transportation Workshop, pp. 15–18. France (2009)
7. Ismaeel, S.A., Hasan, A.M.: GPS/INS system integratin based on neuro-wavelet techniques. In: Proceedings of the 2006 International Conference on Artificial Intelligence (ICAI 2006), vol. 2, pp. 446–452. CSREA Press, Las Vegas (2006)
8. Hasan, A.M., Samsudin, K., Ramli, A.R.: Optimizing of ANFIS for estimating INS error during GPS outages. J. Chin. Inst. Eng. **34**, 967–982 (2011). Taylor & Francis, London
9. Malleswaran, M., Vaidehi, V., Sivasankari, N.: A novel approach to the integration of GPS and INS using recurrent neural networks with evolutionary optimization techniques. In: Aerospace Science and Technology, vol. 32, pp. 169–179. Elsevier B.V., Netherlands (2014)
10. Belhajem, I., Ben Maissa, Y., Tamtaoui, A.: A hybrid low cost approach using Extended Kalman filter and neural networks for real time positioning. In: 2016 International Conference on Information Technology for Organizations Development (IT4OD), pp. 1–5. IEEE (2016)
11. Belhajem, I., Ben Maissa, Y., Tamtaoui, A.: A hybrid machine learning based low cost approach for real time vehicle position estimation in a smart city. In: El-Azouzi, R., Menasché, D.S., Sabir, E., Pellegrini, F.D., Benjillali, M. (eds.) Advances in Ubiquitous Networking 2. LNEE, vol. 397, pp. 559–572. Springer, Heidelberg (2017). doi:10.1007/978-981-10-1627-1_44
12. Goodall, C., Syed, Z., El-Sheimy, N.: Improving INS/GPS navigation accuracy through compensation of Kalman filter errors. In: Proceedings of the 64th IEEE Vehicular Technology Conference, VTC Fall 2006, pp. 1–5. IEEE (2006)
13. Haykin, S.: Neural Networks: A Comprehensive Foundation. Prentice Hall PTR, USA (1994)
14. Yegnanarayana, B.: Artificial Neural Networks. Prentice-Hall of India Pvt. Ltd., New Delhi (2004)
15. Kennedy, J., Eberhart, R.C.: Particle swarm optimization. In: Proceedings of the IEEE International Conference on Neural Networks, pp. 1942–1948. IEEE, USA (1995)
16. Kulkarni, R.V., Venayagamoorthy, G.K.: Particle swarm optimization in wireless-sensor networks a brief survey. IEEE Trans. Syst. Man Cybern. Part C (Appl. Rev.) **41**, 262–267 (2011). IEEE Press, Piscataway, NJ, USA
17. Korrapati, H., Courbon, J., Alizon, S., Marmoiton, F.: The Institut Pascal data sets: un jeu de données en extérieur, multicapteurs et datées avec réalité terrain, données d'étalonnage et outils logiciels. In: ORASIS 2013, Congrès des jeunes chercheurs en vision par ordinateur. France (2013)

Effect of Network Architecture Changes on OCSVM Based Intrusion Detection System

Barnaby Stewart[1], Luis Rosa[2], Leandros Maglaras[1(✉)], Tiago J. Cruz[2],
Paulo Simões[2], and Helge Janicke[1]

[1] De Montfort University, Leicester, UK
leandrosmag@gmail.com
[2] University of Coimbra, Coimbra, Portugal

Abstract. Intrusion Detection Systems are becoming an important defense mechanism for (supervisory control and data acquisition (SCADA) systems. SCADA systems are likely to become more dynamic leading to a need for research into how changes to the network architecture that is monitored, affect the performance of defense mechanisms. This article investigates how changes in the network architecture of the SCADA system affect the performance of an IDS that is based on the One class Support Vector Machine (OCSVM). Also the article proposes an adaptive mechanism that can cope with such changes and can work in real time situations.

Keywords: Intrusion Detection Systems · Support Vector Machines · Adaptive mechanisms

1 Introduction

Compared to Information Technology (IT) systems, Industrial Control (IC) systems have both a greater need for security and a more difficult environment in which that security can be implemented. This is becoming ever more critical as IC systems become increasingly connected to other systems (both IC and IT) and, inevitably, the internet. The term SCADA is traditionally associated with the subset of ICS known as Wide Area Control systems but more recently is being used as synonymously with ICS as a whole. For the purposes of this review we will be intending the traditional use of the term. Support Vector Machines (SVM) provide a viable method for very quickly analysing and classifying data in order to provide an intrusion detection function. The speed of SVMs is critical in SCADA systems due to their distributed nature and the need for high speed detection and response as well as the ability to have minimum impact on the performance of the system itself.

The need for security in SCADA systems is much higher than for the majority of computer systems due to the potential impact and consequences of service degradation or failure. Despite this, at the time when most older systems were developed, their isolation and extensive use of proprietary technologies was often

© ICST Institute for Computer Sciences, Social Informatics and Telecommunications Engineering 2017
L.A. Maglaras et al. (Eds.): INISCOM 2016, LNICST 188, pp. 90–100, 2017.
DOI: 10.1007/978-3-319-52569-3_8

considered sufficient safeguard from interference [1,2]. Additionally, security on the whole was a far lower priority for all computer systems, and the overriding priority for SCADA was reliability.

Now that these systems are becoming increasingly connected (both to other systems and to the internet) as recognised in Yang et al. [2], their security is becoming ever more important. In particular, Kim [1] notes that not only are SCADA systems more connected to the internet, but are also increasingly being implemented using shared Internet Protocol (IP) infrastructure and even the internet itself for communication links. While most research focuses on the increased risks associated with these developments it is important to note the importance of these changes to business in order to reduce costs and increase efficiency [3]. Many issues facing the implementation of security in SCADA have been identified by contemporary research:

- The need for reliability frequently overrides security considerations. This can make it very difficult to implement standard good practice, such as frequent patching.
- Lack of encryption in older communication protocols (plain text frequently used).
- Loss of obscurity caused by the adoption of widespread, well-documented protocols as well as the use of off the shelf SCADA systems [4]. Although obscurity is not a security mechanism in itself, its loss may facilitate attacks.
- The need for continuous operation again makes it very difficult to update, modify, and maintain components of the system.
- Significantly longer lifespan for systems, potentially taking both hardware and software beyond their supported lifespan.

Moreover, SCADA security has specific characteristics and constrains which require a domain-specific approach. In-line security mechanisms (such as certain network IDS deployments) or host-level security tools (such as anti-virus) are unadvised because of the potential latency impact or the introduction of single points of failure in the critical communications path. Moreover, the increased sophistication of attacks against ICS infrastructures means that cyber-security cannot solely rely on supervised, pattern-based detection algorithms to ensure ongoing security monitoring. This situation requires complementary approaches for dealing with rogue threats, providing an adequate balance between its maintenance effort and detection robustness.

2   Intrusion Detection Systems

Many techniques for implementing IDS in a SCADA environment have been proposed. The two primary approaches are model based and machine learning. The model based approach is the more traditional of the two and will tend to result in fewer false positives but are also more likely to miss unknown attacks [5,6]. The machine learning approach are more prone to generate false positives but are superior at detecting novel attack vectors.

2.1   Model Based

Model based systems use detailed knowledge of the protocols and behaviours used within a system as well as details of known attacks to formulate rules which can identify both unexpected behaviour and known bad behaviour. This type of system is unlikely to recognise unknown attacks and requires frequent updates to the signatures to remain viable. The system proposed by Yang et al. [2] comprises a number of model based methods including Access Control Whitelists; Protocol Based Whitelists and Behaviour Based Rules). The proposed system appears to have a greater capability for recognising unknown attacks than most model based system, but the study does not go into detail as to the time costs of properly setting up and maintaining such a system.

2.2   Neural Networks

Neural networks are a method of processing which mimics the manner in which biological systems, such as the brain, operate. This is generally implemented in the form of neurons (or nodes) which exchange data. Multiple input nodes can receive data, process and pass it on to further nodes until an output node is reached. By calculating the cost of paths and modifying the behaviour of individual nodes it is possible for the network to adapt and learn (back propagation). By modelling complex relationships between the inputs and outputs of the system it is possible to perform sophisticated pattern recognition. The main drawback of neural networks, as noted by both Pandit and Dudy [7] and Wang et al. [8] is that they can take a long time to train and are difficult to scale.

2.3   Genetic Algorithms

This is a method for determining the optimal solution to a problem from a pool of potential solutions. In an evolutionary manner, poorly performing solutions are eradicated, leaving the best performing solutions standing. Essentially survival of the fittest. This is not an ideal technique for providing an IDS solution on its own, but is an excellent method for complementing and refining other machine learning systems to improve their accuracy and performance. Kim et al. [9] propose a system for supplementing an SVM based IDS with a Genetic Algorithms (GA) to ensure that the system maintained the most optimal detection model. The GA is used to detect both the optimal feature set as well as the optimal kernel and parameters. This can improve both the accuracy and the speed of the IDS.

2.4   Hierarchical Clustering

This method involves generating a dendrogram, which is a tree like structure representing clusters of data as differentiated by a chosen metric. This is a rapid means of categorisation and can be used to augment other systems. An example of this is given in Maglaras and Jiang [10] where k-means clustering is used recursively to categorise the outliers detected by the SVM process in order to reduce the number of false positives (in the form of severe alerts).

3   Support Vector Machines - OCSVM

SVMs provide a method for rapidly categorising data. The initial stage is the creation of a model using training data which can then be used to categorise new data. A defining characteristic of SVMs is the use of a kernel function to map data into a higher dimensional feature space such that the categories can be separated by hyperplanes. The SVM process iteratively determines the optimal hyperplane for distinguishing categories. The optimal hyperplane will have the largest margin between itself and the nearest data points and those data points which coincide with the margin are the support vectors.

It is possible to have multiple categories into which the data can be allocated, however when labeling of data is not possible One Class SVMS (OCSVM) can be used, which has a single category and simply determine if new data belongs to that category or not. This allows OCSVMs to potentially detect new or unknown anomalies as it is not attempting to categorise any data as bad according to known attack profile, but simply to identify it as not good.

As there are no data points from a second class, the standard method for one class SVM is to treat the origin as the perfect class 1 vector and determine the optimal distance from the origin at which a data point no longer belongs to that class. Finding appropriate values for the calculation of this model is crucial in achieving the optimal result. This process is frequently improved by the use of other machine learning techniques to determine superior values for this algorithm.

3.1   Disadvantages

The main drawbacks of one class SVMs are false positives and over fitting, and as recognised by Maglaras and Jiang [10] and Wang et al. [8]. False positives can result from rare but legitimate traffic which may not have been represented in the training data. Over fitting is a problem with the generation of the model where the boundary for categorisation is too tightly constrained to the test data. This can cause valid outliers to register as out of class (i.e. bad).

3.2   Examples of Use

The CockpitCI Framework detailed in Cruz et al. [11] uses a number of separate OCSVMs which are individually modelled for different parts of the ICS. The output of these is aggregated by a Main Correlator before being reported to the Security Management Platform. It is of note that the framework uses the Intrusion Detection Message Exchange Format (IDMEF) for interchange of data (RFC 4765). This is a message format to standardise the exchange of Intrusion Detection related information based on plain Extensible Markup Language (XML). Security features such as integrity or confidentiality are achieved by exchanging those messages via a dedicated Event Bus.

3.3   Suitability of OCSVMs in IDS

These systems all demonstrate that OCSVM is not a sufficiently refined tool to implement an effective IDS on its own but is highly valuable when coupled with other methods, especially as an integrated part of a larger framework. It is likely that while anomaly detection provides opportunity to detect unknown attacks it will be necessary to combine them with signature and ruled based IDS components to achieve the greatest accuracy. Yang et al. [2] have shown that multiple techniques can be used to create a highly effective IDS and Maglaras et al. [5] argue that model based systems alone are insufficient. Wang et al. [8] crucially note that a greater understanding of the range of SCADA applications and protocols is required to achieve truly effective model based IDS components.

4   Effects of Network Architecture Changes

We have established that, relative to IT systems, IC systems (most notably SCADA), have both a greater need for security and a more difficult environment in which to provide it. Support Vector Machines have been shown to be an effective tool for providing intrusion detection, although they lack effectiveness in isolation and are far more powerful when used in conjunction with other methods. Maglaras et al. [5] argue that rule based IDS are ineffective, however the system proposed by Yang et al. [2] shows that they can be implemented very effectively, although the maintenance demands are likely to be very different.

None of the materials and research studied examines the adaptability or susceptibility of the proposed IDS systems to changes in the monitored architecture. This is almost certainly due to a large extent to the fact that SCADA systems tend to be relatively static. While Cheung et al. [12] argue that model based IDS are suited to SCADA due to their traditionally more stable environment, this stability is decreasing as SCADA systems evolve, undermining this argument.

5   Hybrid Testbed

The HEDVa (Hybrid Environment for Design and Validation) was developed by the Israeli Electric Company with the purpose of providing a flexible platform to support the creation and maintenance of multiple testbed environments, within a multi-tenant environment. It provides resources for component development, test and integration, which can be dynamically added and/or allocated to deployed scenarios, enabling flexible reconfiguration. The HEDVa provided the CI environment in which the development and validation of the CockpitCI concept was undertaken (see Fig. 1).

The CockpitCI validation effort leveraged the HEDVa resources to build a hybrid CI scenario, in the sense that it makes use of real/physical SCADA and network/telecom infrastructure components to implement a simulation model of an electric grid (see Fig. 2). It was developed using key performance indicators and data from production environments, also implementing standard operator

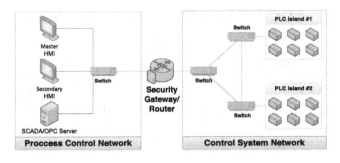

Fig. 1. Simplified HEDVa networking architecture

Fault Detection Isolation and Recovery procedures used for electric grid management.

In the CockpitCI testbed, grid elements (such as feeders and breakers) are emulated by real PLC devices, which take part in the simulation - moreover, all voltage and current values on critical points are dynamically calculated and updated accordingly with the mathematical model of the power grid. By emulating the cyber-physical parameters, this scenario allows to implement several different attacks and failure use cases for validation and interdependence analysis in a safe environment, while providing a realistic attack surface.

The topology depicted in Fig. 1 constitutes the CI that supports the simulated grid environment. The entire CockpitCI security detection components (in which the OCSVM IDS is included) were trained and deployed in this infrastructure, which also served as demonstrator vehicle.

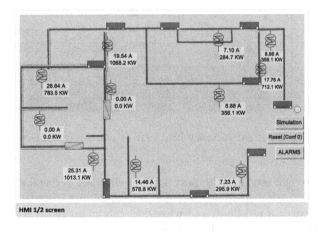

Fig. 2. HEDVa grid scenario, with breakers and substation feeders

6   Testing of OCSVM on Different Architectures

Six data sets were provided using the HEDVa. These sets represent network traffic from a SCADA network running in six different configurations. There are two groups of Programmable Logic Controllers (PLCs) and two Human Machine Interface (HMI) devices which may be active on the system (see Fig. 1). Table 1 shows the configuration of the network for each of the data sets:

Table 1. Configurations of the network

Data set	PLC group 1	PLC group 2	HMI 1	HMI 2
1	Active	-	Active	-
2	Active	-	Active	Active
3	Active	Active	Active	-
4	Active	Active	Active	Active
5	-	Active	Active	Active
6	-	Active	Active	-

While the accuracy for models when tested against themselves varied very little from the mean, the deviation for testing against other data sets was shown to be extreme. The results presented on Fig. 3 show that while there are some large deviations, these have occurred primarily in data set 4, which is later removed from the study.

		Test Data					
		part1	part2	part3	part4	part5	part6
Model	part1	98.76	96.99	94.21	6.36	96.66	98.77
	part2	98.93	99.5	94.45	13.67	99.23	98.92
	part3	99.66	98.98	99.31	24.48	98.89	99.56
	part4	68.92	75.02	61.66	98.64	75.09	70.87
	part5	95.38	98.32	89.57	10.82	98.53	97.2
	part6	97.92	96.91	94.2	6.35	96.84	99.15

Fig. 3. Initial accuracy heat map (Color figure online)

From this we can see that the part 4 of the data set is displaying significant variation from the other sets, both when other models are tested against its data (shown by the vertical red line), and where the model for part4 is tested against other data sets (the horizontal light green line).

To investigate the cause of this behaviour we inspected the meta data created for each PCAP file. We could see that all of the data sets exhibit a very high maximum rate value (in the region of 20 h). We then looked at the rates meta data file created at the same time. These files contain a list of every rate value calculated when processing a PCAP file, and the number of times it occurs in that file. We found out that there existed some big gaps between transmitted packets. These gaps clearly do not represent the true traffic rate feature we are attempting to extract and could, themselves, trigger an alert from the IDS. More importantly, these outlier values would affect the significance of the normal traffic rate values when scaling is applied. To eliminate this issue, the program was updated to filter out any rate value over 3 s, and to substitute the current average rate so far.

Next we investigated the IP addresses encountered in the traffic. We observed that for the majority of the data sets, all of the IPs are from the private address space 172.27.xx.xx. In the part 4 data set, however, we see that there are also 10 IP addresses from other, external networks. Another factor is the type of traffic detected in the captured data. For all sets other than part4, only TCP traffic is detected. The part4 data set, however, also shows UDP traffic as well as traffic which has not been successfully identified.

It seems clear from these indicators that the part 4 data set differs from the other data sets in a substantial way, and not merely in the architecture of the network and we decided to filter out the whole part 4 data set from the analysis. On the other hand we came to some useful conclusions about how different behavior of the system in terms of packet rate and number of sources affect the accuracy of the IDS. These findings will be used in the near future in order to create a real adaptive IDS.

Eliminating the data 4 set leaves us the following results (See Fig. 4).

		Test Data				
		part1	part2	part3	part5	part6
	part1	98.76	96.99	94.21	96.66	98.77
	part2	98.93	99.5	94.45	99.23	98.92
Model	part3	99.66	98.98	99.31	98.89	99.56
	part5	95.38	98.32	89.57	98.53	97.2
	part6	97.92	96.91	94.2	96.84	99.15

Fig. 4. Final accuracy heat map

With the anomalous results from part 4 eliminated we can aggregate the data to demonstrate the combined accuracy when testing against self vs other (See Fig. 5).

This does demonstrate a weak overall correlation between testing against other sets and accuracy. As the values approach 100%, any difference can be very significant, especially in an IDS where every percent of inaccuracy can represent false positives or negatives. This, in turn, can represent either missing malicious activity or generating a large number of spurious alerts which can consume monitoring resources and renders the system ineffective.

		Test Data	
		Self	Other
Model	part1	98.76	96.6575
	part2	99.5	97.8825
	part3	99.31	99.2725
	part5	98.53	95.1175
	part6	99.15	96.4675

	Mean	99.05	97.0795

Fig. 5. Final mean accuracy

7   Proposed Adaptive IDS

In order to cope with the drop of accuracy that the IDS demonstrates when the architecture of the system changes, we propose an adaptive mechanism that can be used in any system. The mechanism that is presented on Fig. 6 matches the current network traffic of the system to the traffic that the IDS was trained with. Based on the fact that the matching takes additional computation time, the proposed adaptive system imposes a delay on the performance of the IDS. The matching that is proposed on this article only takes into account the different IPs that exist on the network traffic and chooses the OCSVM that was trained to a similar network. This could be extended also to the overall traffic that exist inside the system, based on the fact that the volume of traffic changes between morning and evening and between working days and weekends, especially for a system that controls critical infrastructures that are directly related to human activity, e.g. traffic controls, smart grid e.t.c.

In the core of our adaptive IDS we have included Spearman's rank correlation coefficient. Spearman's rank is a non-parametric measure of correlation widely

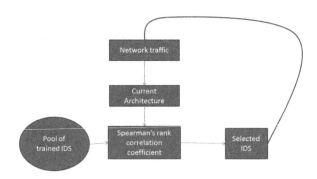

Fig. 6. Proposed Adaptive IDS

used to describe the relationship between two variables that is used to report the difference in ranking produced by two methods. Based on this metric we can find the most suitable IDS for the current architecture of the network with a notion of traffic in it, since the metric also ranks the sources based on the total traffic they induce in the system. One important parameter of the proposed Adaptive IDS is how frequent the comparison of the current traffic to the pool of the trained IDS will be and also the number of trained IDS that we have in order to better match the current situation of the network. These are issues that will be investigated in the near future and the trade off between accuracy and delay will be analyzed.

8 Conclusions

The current research on IDS for SCADA systems focuses on relatively static systems, and while this has been reasonable in the past when SCADA systems have remained unchanged for long periods, it is also clear that as SCADA systems adopt more of the technology and characteristics of IT systems they are likely to become more dynamic as a result leading to a need for research into how such changes will affect IDS. This article investigates how changes in the architecture of the SCADA system affect the performance of an IDS that is based on the OCSVM. Also the article proposes an adaptive mechanism that can cope with such changes and can work in real time situations. The proposed mechanism can be a basis for developing real time Adaptive IDS for other IT and IC systems and that are based on different classification mechanisms.

References

1. Kim, H.: Security and vulnerability of scada systems over ip-based wireless sensor networks. Int. J. Distrib. Sensor Netw. **2012**, 1–10 (2012)
2. Yang, Y., McLaughlin, K., Sezer, S., Littler, T., Im, E.G., Pranggono, B., Wang, H.: Multiattribute scada-specific intrusion detection system for power networks. IEEE Trans. Power Deliv. **29**(3), 1092–1102 (2014)
3. Igure, V.M., Laughter, S.A., Williams, R.D.: Security issues in scada networks. Comput. Secur. **25**(7), 498–506 (2006)
4. Nicholson, A., Webber, S., Dyer, S., Patel, T., Janicke, H.: Scada security in the light of cyber-warfare. Comput. Secur. **31**(4), 418–436 (2012)
5. Maglaras, L.A., Jiang, J., Cruz, T.: Integrated ocsvm mechanism for intrusion detection in scada systems. Electron. Lett. **50**(25), 1935–1936 (2014)
6. Maglaras, L.A., Jiang, J., Cruz, T.J.: Combining ensemble methods and social network metrics for improving accuracy of OCSVM on intrusion detection in SCADA systems. J. Inform. Secur. Appl. **30**, 15–26 (2016)
7. Pandit, T., Dudy, A.: An artificial neural network based approach for dos attacks detection in manet (2014)
8. Wang, Y., Wong, J., Miner, A.: Anomaly intrusion detection using one class svm. In: Information Assurance Workshop, 2004, Proceedings from the Fifth Annual IEEE SMC, pp. 358–364. IEEE (2004)

9. Kim, D.S., Nguyen, H.-N., Park, J.S.: Genetic algorithm to improve svm based network intrusion detection system. In: 19th International Conference on Advanced Information Networking and Applications, AINA 2005, vol. 2, pp. 155–158. IEEE (2005)

10. Maglaras, L.A., Jiang, J.: Ocsvm model combined with k-means recursive clustering for intrusion detection in scada systems. In: 2014 10th International Conference on Heterogeneous Networking for Quality, Reliability, Security and Robustness (QShine), pp. 133–134. IEEE (2014)

11. Cruz, T., Proença, J., Simões, P., Aubigny, M., Ouedraogo, M., Graziano, A., Yasakhetu, L.: Improving cyber-security awareness on industrial control systems: the cockpitci approach. In: 13th European Conference on Cyber Warfare and Security ECCWS-2014 The University of Piraeus Piraeus, Greece, p. 59 (2014)

12. Cheung, S., Dutertre, B., Fong, M., Lindqvist, U., Skinner, K., Valdes, A.: Using model-based intrusion detection for scada networks. In: Proceedings of the SCADA Security Scientific Symposium, vol. 46, pp. 1–12. Citeseer (2007)

Smart Behavioural Filter for SCADA Network

Giovanni Corbò, Chiara Foglietta$^{(\boxtimes)}$, Cosimo Palazzo, and Stefano Panzieri

University "Roma TRE", Via della Vasca Navale 79, 00146 Rome, Italy
`corbo.giovanni@gmail.com,`
`{chiara.foglietta,cosimo.palazzo,stefano.panzieri}@uniroma3.it`

Abstract. Industrial Control Systems (ICS) are jeopardized from a large set of threat vectors, which exploit their vulnerabilities in order to impact the physical Critical Infrastructures they control. The Information Technology (IT) classical approach to cyber attacks can not be applied to ICS due to their extreme differences from main priorities to resource constrains. Therefore, innovative approaches and equipment must be developed in order to suit with ICS world.

In this paper, a Smart Behavioural Filter (SBF) for the PLCs/RTUs is proposed aiming to secure the PLC/RTU itself against logic attacks, that are stealth for other more classical security approaches. Those logic attacks are usually anomaly behaviours, for instance a large number of open/close commands towards a valve. This smart field equipment can communicate with other equipment like itself in order to react in short time to cyber attacks and increase the resilience of the physical system. It can also generate alarms for the local Intrusion Detection System (IDS) The proposed equipment has been developed and validated in a real test-bed within the FP7 CockpitCI project. The results are promising.

Keywords: Industrial control systems · Security · Logic filtering · Redundancy

1 Introduction

Geographically distributed physical processes are continuously monitored and controlled by means of a SCADA system. An important set of those physical systems is usually defined as critical infrastructures, e.g., power grids, water pipelines and transport networks. Nowadays, the SCADA systems faced new challenges due to the increase of interconnected devices and due to the use of standard hardware, software and network.

SCADA systems are usually composed of a set of networked devices, such as sensors, actuators, controllers and communication equipment. The SCADA server (also called Master Terminal Unit - MTU) gathers real-time data from Remote Terminal Units (RTUs) and issues control commands (i.e., open or close electrical switches) towards field devices to control the physical process. Due to the cyber-physical interaction, a cyber incidence can have a direct effect on the physical world, as demonstrated by the Stuxnet worm attack that turned

© ICST Institute for Computer Sciences, Social Informatics and Telecommunications Engineering 2017
L.A. Maglaras et al. (Eds.): INISCOM 2016, LNICST 188, pp. 101–110, 2017.
DOI: 10.1007/978-3-319-52569-3_9

off a centrifuges' control system in a nuclear plant [1]. Stuxnet provided proof-of-concept and demonstrated the feasibility of a cyber attack to change the physical processes. Highly-skilled attackers have the potential to be the most harmful, causing a loss of observability, controllability or eventually the loss of power in the physical system. In this paper, a highly-skilled attacker is a person with multiple capabilities: the ability to stealthy penetrate within a telecommunication network and the ability to discover the physical process controlled by the network.

In [2], the various type of attacks on SCADA systems have been grouped into network protocol and application protocol attacks. In the network protocol attacks, the hacker exploits weak points of network protocols, such as Modbus TCP/IP, that have a number of serious vulnerabilities [3]. The common types of those attacks are Denial of Service (DoS), scan and host discovery. Application protocol attacks can cause damage to field devices by sending out improper commands, because authentication or cryptographic mechanisms are not supported. In general, application protocol attacks use unconventional commands at irregular interval, substituting the regular and predictable sets of commands used for communication between SCADA servers and field devices. In both cases, these attacks are preceded by some steps of information gathering devoted to finding vulnerability security flaws in the network.

In this paper, we consider a highly-skilled attacker able to gain the access of a SCADA network and to disrupt the physical process before the intrusion is detected. A false logic attack, as in [4,5], is invisible to Intrusion Detection System (IDS) for SCADA networks, because it uses well-formed packets with a content that is allowed even if a logic constraint is violated.

1.1 Contributions

The contribution of this paper is twofold. Although an host-based intrusion detection system for anomaly behaviour is not new, its use within a SCADA network is still a research area that is far from being completely explored. The appliance presented in this paper is a behavioural filter that has to be inserted between each Remote Terminal Unit (RTU) or Programmable Logic Controller (PLC) and the field network in order to intercept packets carrying incorrect or dangerous commands.

Second, the appliance (Smart Behavioural Filter - SBF) communicates with other similar appliances and with a possible local Intrusion Detection System (IDS) through an additional secure channel in order to generate another invisible network for transmitting/receiving alert messages.

1.2 Paper Organization

The paper is organized as follows: Sect. 2 surveys the literature of the appliances for anomaly behaviour; in Sect. 3 the ecosystem made of several smart appliances in a SCADA network is described in order to provide an overall picture of the main functionalities; in Sect. 4 the Smart Behavioural Filter (SBF) is detailed in terms of functionalities and design; the implementation and the first results are presented in Sect. 5; finally, conclusions and future works are in Sect. 6.

2 Related Works

A SCADA system is considered a critical control system since it monitors and controls the performance and availability of other critical infrastructures, such as transport systems, energy suppliers, water treatment systems or communication systems.

SCADA networks are vulnerable to threats as the traditional IT networks. Moreover, SCADA networks have different risk management priorities: in SCADA network, availability is preferred to confidentiality, while in IT systems the priorities are turned around. This makes difficult implement traditional IT solutions for security within SCADA networks [6].

During the last years, several defence approaches have been studied. One of the first recommendation is to segment the SCADA network from the enterprise one using suitable firewalls in order to protect PLCs/RTUs from unauthorized requests that originate from outside the field. [7] In time-critical systems, firewalls must be carefully introduced for reducing additional packet latency. Filtering unwanted traffic by means of a firewall can increase the network performances [8].

Firewall are classified into two categories: Packet filtering and application firewall. Packet filtering has been recommended as an effective way to protect field devices from network protocol attacks. This appliance monitors incoming and outgoing packets and allows them to route or drop based on filtering rules using layer three and four on OSI model [2].

An application firewall (or proxy server) is placed between a client application and a server, acting as an intermediary never allowing a direct connection between them. [9] The application firewall adds the capability of examining specific application traffic, such as FTP services, OPC servers or others. Coverage for SCADA applications is limited and performance impact is typically greater than other firewall types. The benefits of using this method are important because the application firewall is the only thing exposed to untrusted traffic. The disadvantage of the approach is that it must be tuned to each application allowed [10].

In this paper, we present an advanced filter for detecting false logic attacks. A false attack [4] takes into account two different approaches:

– False data values, where the attacker changes the data coming from sensors, see the literature related to false data injection [11];
– False logic commands, where the attacker changes the logic of the control commands. This type of attack is the main focus of this paper.

In [4,5], the feasibility of a false logic attack is modelled considering the case of two valves that can be opened or closed. Two logic constrains are considered: (1) they cannot be both in open state, and (2) valve 1 should be opened before valve 2. The results of this paper demonstrates how a traditional Intrusion

Detection System (IDS) is not able to effectively protect the physical process. The Smart Behavioural Filter (SBF) is able to detect the violation of a logic constraint that can been implemented as a rule.

In the following Section, the ecosystem is detailed. The smart ecosystem is realized using a set of Smart Behavioural Filters (SBFs) placed just in front of the PLCs that can interact between them and with a local IDS using an additional radio-frequency channel.

3   Smart Ecosystem

In Fig. 1, the architecture of the smart ecosystem is depicted. The Smart Behavioural Filter filters the commands coming from the SCADA system through a set of rules and also the information coming from the other elements of the smart ecosystems. The SBF has three channel:

1. A legacy channel for receiving/sending command packets from and to the SCADA system;
2. An additional channel for communicating with the PLC/RTU in order to send authorized commands;
3. An additional channel for exchanging messages with the other SBFs or with an IDS. This channel has been realised using radio-frequency module.

The aim of this ecosystem is a local and fast reaction to advanced cyber attacks. The SBF that intercepts a false logic attack can block the commands and then is able to send an alarm to the IDS and to other near SBFs using the radio frequency. In this way, the SBF can increase the alert level and therefore augment the security controls in event of cyber attacks to other near facilities.

4   Smart Behavioural Filter (SBF)

Traditional RTUs/PLCs send to the SCADA server the actual data coming from sensors, receive commands to be translated for the actuators and execute fast and real time control strategies related to the physical process. The difference between a PLC and an RTU is usually hard to find especially because their functionalities overlap with each other. In this paper we use both the terms RTU and PLC for identifying a remote controller which communicate with the SCADA server. The PLC is able to detect the disconnection of a sensor or an actuators.

The Smart Behavioural Filter (SBF) wants to add a new class of logical errors, detected directly by the PLC. Those errors are usually malicious cyber attacks but can also be generated from unintentional commands coming from an operator. These false logic errors are, among the others: contradictory instructions, dangerous or out of the normal operating cycle, or abnormal sequence of operations.

The Smart Behavioural Filter (SBF) intends to create a further security element for industrial control systems. This new appliance element was created

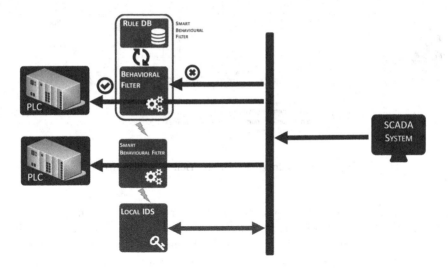

Fig. 1. System diagram of the smart ecosystem, where blue icons represent the legacy SCADA system and the red ones represent the elements of the smart ecosystem.Color figure online

as a security system at application level which is able to work on industrial communication protocols. The technological solutions implemented in the SBF are mostly known and simple to apply but the smart combination allows us to get a very interesting and innovative element in the context of industrial security.

The SBF, in Fig. 2, is made of two main modes: the passive and the reactive one. The first concept is related to the filtering action, mainly related to logical constraints. The second one is related to the response and mitigation action: an SBF can cooperate with other SBFs in event of an external attacks, and can eventually change its operating mode until the complete isolation from the external world.

In order to filter packets, PLC registers and coils have been mirrored within the SBF in order to understand the impact of the received commands. The first important cyber security feature of SBF concerns the capability to create a kind of SandBox (a virtual controlled environment) that replicates the information system of a PLC. In those circumstances, an hypothetical intruder, which enters into the SCADA network, believes he is changing the registers/coils value into the PLC performing successfully the cyber attack but without have any effect on system thanks to the SBF. The Ethernet module of the PLC is securely connected to the Ethernet module of the SBF, that substitute the PLC port. In this way, the SBF can guarantee to be undetectable to an intruder, who beliefs to communicate with the original PLC.

SBF implements a rule-based filtering, able to understand the effects of specific commands thanks to a set of rules. Those rules have been hard-wired into the SBF starting from the knowledge of the physical processes. For a Medium

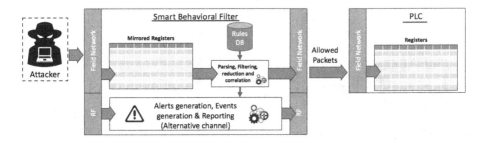

Fig. 2. Diagram of the Smart Behavioural Filter

Voltage power grid, the SCADA system reconfigures the physical network after a permanent failure, in well-define scheme. Therefore, the reconfiguration is a sequence of commands sent from the SCADA control system to the PLCs connecting the electrical switches. The possible reconfiguration procedures are modelled within the set of possible rules inside the SBF. The SBF is an application-level behavioural filtering performing an anomaly detection highly specialized in its own operative context.

In order to be an active appliance, each SBF is equipped with its own Radio Frequency (RF) Module able to create a mesh-network between all the PLCs/RTUs with SBFs and with a possible local IDS. The radio frequency module has a limit due to the distance of the transmission channel. This RF element, in combination with the SBF, establishes a redundant wireless network between PLCs/RTUs of the same system and then a further preferential (or alternative) communication channel where transmits system alerts.

The system alerts can eventually activate specific rules that increase the security status of the PLC. The security status can require an higher level of authentication in performing specific commands. In the worst case, the PLC can be isolated from outside world for a limited amount of time in order to avoid a more dangerous situation and preserve the physical process actuators.

The additional radio frequency channel creates a new security issue, but it is invisible to a hacker which penetrates in the classical telecommunication network. The additional channel can exploit secure communications, such as encryption, due to the small dimension of the exchanged messages.

Briefly summarizing, an SBF is able to:

1. Mirror the PLC registers to deceive the intruder;
2. Recognize false logic events or sequence of events;
3. Alert the other closest SBFs and the eventual local IDS;
4. Change its security status in accordance with a pre-set strategy.

Another feature of the SBF is the undetectability and the transparency at the communication level and for a malicious attacker. In the following section the implementation and some results are explained.

5   Implementation and First Results

In order to implement the features described in the previous section, we need a platform that could:

- Receive commands from the field network
- Reconstruct the instructions received
- Filter through the rules' instructions
- Send the filtered commands to the connected PLC
- Send and receive alarm messages to/from the other SBFs
- React to cyber attacks through a set of fixed rules

A standard RTU/PLC has a modular design, and usually consists of a Power Supply, a CPU, and an Input/output card. The actual and initial implementation of the SBF is realized on hardware using a microcomputer such as Raspberry PI, as in Fig. 3.

In order to test the SBF, we consider as PLC a Schneider Electric Modicon M340 [12] with Modbus TCP/IP interface. The SBF receives packets and it is invisible to the downstream PLC and also to the rest of the control network. The SBF is advanced network card with additional processing capabilities.

Fig. 3. Implementation of the SBF using a Raspberry Pi microcomputer. Two USB ports are used for exchanging commands with the PLC (with a network adapter) and the other SBF, using an USB radio frequency module.

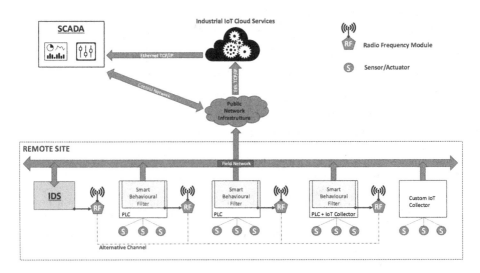

Fig. 4. Future development and possible integration with Internet of Things (IoTs)

The SBF has been integrated within the existing Roma TRE testbed [13]. The testbed is made of a SCADA server, a PLC and an IDS. Specifically, the IDS has been given the ability to communicate through the radio frequency (RF) protocol with the mesh network created by SBFs. This feature improves globally and locally the situational awareness. A soon as the IDS recognizes a potential threat it warns the control room and sends a broadcast alert message to the radio frequency network. Depending on the danger degree, the SBF can automatically reconfigure themselves in an attempt to mitigate the threat.

The results are promising: the Smart PLC (PLC and SBF, together) succeeds to recognize the dangerous instructions and sends an alert message to the control room. At the same time provides information on the incident to the other reachable Smart PLC that are reconfigured in an appropriate way and, in case it is required, turn over the alert message to the control room. The IDS is able to communicate the details of an attack to the network of Smart PLC which reconfigures itself, thus obtaining an automatic response to the ongoing threat.

Depending on the type of attack will also change response policies. Smart PLCs will then be able to decide and implement the best strategy in each case.

The SBF has been implemented and validated within the FP7 European CockpitCI project (www.cockpitci.eu).

6   Conclusions and Ongoing Works

In this paper, we present a Smart Behavioural Filter (SBF) able to detect and block commands that are anomalous from a logic point of view. This anomalous behaviour can be interpreted as a very specific cyber attack performed by a high-skilled attacker.

The SBF is a passive firewall and is also a local reaction module for mitigating risk of cyber attacks. In order to exchange securely information, the SBF has an additional and invisible radio frequency channel among SBFs and the IDS.

The SBF can be improved considering rules that can be modified or generated through an on-line training of the physical system.

Actual works are more related to the industrial Internet of Things (IoTs), see Fig. 4. The SBF can also be applied in the modern industrial system. This is possible integrating a further module which is entrusted with the task of IoT Connector. This connector enables the outsourcing of the data coming from industrial sensors to collect and analyse them thanks to Industrial Cloud IoT. Therefore, the SCADA system transfers some functionalities to the Industrial Cloud IoT to improve performances, decrease start-up plant costs and enhance data mining.

Acknowledgement. The research paper is partially supported by the European Union's Horizon 2020 research and innovation programme under Grant Agreement No. 700581 (ATENA - Advanced Tools to Assess and Mitigate the Criticality of ICT Components and Their Dependencies over Critical Infrastructures)

References

1. Kushner, D.: The real story of stuxnet. IEEE Spectr. **50**, 48–53 (2013)
2. Kang, D.H., Kim, B.K., Na, J.C.: Cyber threats and defence approaches in SCADA systems. In: 16th International Conference on Advanced Communication Technology, pp. 324–327, February 2014
3. Huitsing, P., Chandia, R., Papa, M., Shenoi, S.: Attack taxonomies for the modbus protocols. Int. J. Crit. Infrastruct. Prot. **1**, 37–44 (2008)
4. Li, W., Xie, L., Liu, D., Wang, Z.: False logic attacks on SCADA control system. In: Services Computing Conference (APSCC), 2014 Asia-Pacific, pp. 136–140, December 2014
5. Li, W., Xie, L., Deng, Z., Wang, Z.: False sequential logic attack on SCADA system and its physical impact analysis. Comput. Secur. **58**, 149–159 (2016)
6. Alcaraz, C., Fernandez, G., Roman, R., Balastegui, A., Lopez, J.: Secure management of SCADA networks. Novatica, New Trends Netw. Manage. **9**, 22–28 (2008)
7. Nivethan, J., Papa, M.: On the use of open-source firewalls in ICS/SCADA systems. Inf. Secur. J. A Global Perspect. **25**, 1–11 (2016)
8. Sheth, C., Thakker, R.: Performance evaluation and comparative analysis of network firewalls. In: 2011 International Conference on Devices and Communications (ICDeCom), pp. 1–5, February 2011
9. Aziz, M.Z.A., Ibrahim, M.Y., Omar, A.M., Rahman, R.A., Zan, M.M.M., Yusof, M.I.: Performance analysis of application layer firewall. In: 2012 IEEE Symposium on Wireless Technology and Applications (ISWTA), pp. 182–186, September 2012
10. Mahan, R.E., Fluckiger, J.D., Clements, S.L., Tews, C.W., Burnette, J.R., Goranson, C.A., Kirkham, H.: Secure data transfer guidance for industrial control and SCADA systems. Pacific Northwest National Laboratory (2011)
11. Hug, G., Giampapa, J.A.: Vulnerability assessment of AC state estimation with respect to false data injection cyber-attacks. IEEE Trans. Smart Grid **3**, 1362–1370 (2012)

12. Modicon M340 - Schneider Electric
13. Di Pietro, A., Foglietta, C., Palmieri, S., Panzieri, S.: Assessing the impact of cyber attacks on interdependent physical systems. In: Butts, J., Shenoi, S. (eds.) ICCIP 2013. IAICT, vol. 417, pp. 215–227. Springer, Heidelberg (2013). doi:10.1007/978-3-642-45330-4_15

Adaptive Down-Sampling and Super-Resolution for Additional Video Compression

Bin Zhao[1] and Jianmin Jiang[2(✉)]

[1] School of Computer Science and Technology, Tianjin University, Tianjin, China
woxintaoxiang@outlook.com
[2] Research Institute of Future Media Computing, Shenzhen University, Shenzhen, China
jianmin.jiang@szu.edu.cn

Abstract. While almost all down-sampling based video codecs gain additional compression at the expense of image degradation, we set a good example of achieving both large compression and even better reconstruction quality. Such progress is realized by: (i) minimizing the introduction of information loss with a proposed decomposition-based adaptive down-sampling method so that more reserved pixels can be allocated to image details where human visual perception is more sensitive. Specifically, a modified content complexity measurement is put forward and the optimum down-sampling rate is adaptively selected with a customized formula; (ii) maximizing the information compensation via a content-adaptive super-resolution algorithm, which is accelerated and optimized by two stages of pruning to select the closest correlated dictionary pairs. Extensive experiments support that, by using prevailing H.264 codec as benchmark, the proposed scheme achieves 5 times more of additional compression and the reconstruction quality outperforms other state-of-the-art approaches, and even better than decoded non-shrunken frames in human visual perception.

Keywords: Video compression · Decomposition · Super resolution · Sparse representation

1 Introduction

Currently, the ubiquitous application of digital mobile video and high-definition (HD) visual enjoyment suffer severe bottleneck due to limited bandwidth. Though off-the-shelf codecs, such as the prevailing H.264/MPEG-4 AVC [1] and one of its potential successors, the H.265/HEVC (High Efficiency Video Coding) [2] have provided sharp compression, further shrinkage is still required. Accordingly, the scaling based coding schemes, which down- and up-sample video frames respectively prior and posterior to generic codecs, stand out as a feasible division of ongoing research for compression improvement [3–6]. However, for pertinent literature, the up-sampling or essentially the super resolution methods have been actively researched to compensate the discarded high frequency details while little efforts were made to optimize the information loss that the down-sampling process introduced. Most approaches simply applied a fixed down-sampling rate to the whole frames and neglected the heterogeneity of human visual system

© ICST Institute for Computer Sciences, Social Informatics and Telecommunications Engineering 2017
L.A. Maglaras et al. (Eds.): INISCOM 2016, LNICST 188, pp. 111–121, 2017.
DOI: 10.1007/978-3-319-52569-3_10

in the tolerance of content information loss. As [7] suggested, to complex regions with more details, human visual perception is more susceptible, thus less pixel loss should be brought in. For this purpose, we proposed a decomposition-based adaptive down-sampling scheme, which initially executes two successive decomposition, temporal and spatial, to divide the input video into a number of fragment sequences. Each of them contains a certain level of complexity and is appropriate to adopt diverse down-sampling rate. Specifically, to achieve the best possible trade-off between compression effectiveness (reconstruction quality at the decoder end) and compression efficiency (additional compression ratios), we developed a local-homogeneity-based global metric (LHGM) as decomposition criterion and paved the way for the selection of optimum down-sampling rate. The resulting decomposed and down-sampled sub-sequences can be encoded separately by any existing codecs. And the decoded counterparts will then be up-sampled and pasted together with the along coded side information.

At the decoder, resolution enhancement and detail compensation critically count on super-resolution (SR) reconstruction techniques, among which the dictionary- or example-based learning methods protrude as the most active area over recent years. By using learned co-occurrence prior knowledge between low resolution (LR) and high resolution (HR) image patches, the learning-based methods effectively overcome a variety of deficits in other SR techniques, for instance, the over-smoothness or ringing and jagged artifacts of interpolation-based methods [8] and the requirement of multiple aliasing frames of the same scene in multi-frame methods [9]. A typical dictionary-based example is the Neighbor Embedding (NE) method, which utilizes the local geometry similarity between LR image patches and their HR counterparts [10]. Recent Nonnegative Neighbor Embedding (NNE) [11] and Anchored Neighborhood Regression (ANR) [12] both stemmed from this hypothesis. Sparse Coding (SC) represents another major direction of dictionary-based learning methods. Yang et al. [13] exploited joint sparse representation for the input LR and expecting HR image patches based on a pair of over-complete dictionaries and produced better SR images with fine details. Zeyde et al. [14] built upon his framework and improved the execution speed by modifying the training approaches. However, from extensive investigation, we found that the majority of dictionary-based algorithms primarily focused on the selection of the nearest neighbors in NE or the representation of sparse signals in SC, while the preparation for the dictionaries was often ignored, which make space for our exploration in this aspect.

Besides, due to the fact that receivers at the decoder end tend to evaluate video quality based on direct visual impact rather than computed signal-to-noise ratio that compared with the pre-encoding references, it' s more reasonable to assess reconstructed image quality according to human visual system [7]. Given that, we adopted the blind/no-reference image quality assessment model (BRISQUE) [23] in reconstruction evaluation, which was demonstrated statistically better than the full-reference peak signal-to-noise-ratio (PSNR) and structural similarity index (SSIM) in both computational efficiency and the correlation with human visual characteristics.

The rest of the paper proceeds as follows: Sect. 2 is a fine description of the proposed quadtree-based decomposition and adaptive down-sampling methods. Section 3 theoratically formulized the content-adaptive sparse representation of super-resolution. Section 4 reports our experimental results and Sect. 5 provides concluding remarks and some ideas for future work.

2 Decomposition-Based Down-Sampling

The design of our decomposition-based down-sampling scheme was in view of the non-uniform distribution of video content and the benefit of applying flexible down-scaling rates to complexity-varied regions. Meanwhile, considering the computational cost, we assumed that content distribution across video frames like color, texture and motion remains relatively stable within one scene and appropriate to apply a unified decomposition pattern in accordance with the first frame or Intra-frame.

To achieve above ideas, we first utilized a content change detection similar to shot cut technique [15] to temporally divide the input video into several scenes, or so called V-units [16] (shown as Fig. 1 Temporal Decomposition). In each V-unit, the frame number was limited (not more than twenty in our case) to make sure that a certain level of content-consistency is maintained. Then we implemented a quad-tree decomposition on the first frame of each V-unit. In this process, a content complexity measurement is required for determining whether a frame patch should be divided.

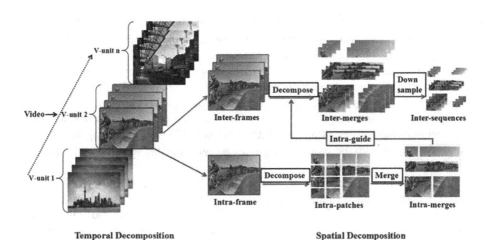

Fig. 1. Illustration of decomposition-based adaptive down-sampling

Existing complexity measurements [17–20], such as the variance-based [17] and edge-based approaches [20], were primarily designed for the selection of partition mode, which made them only suitable for the calculation of coding blocks. In that, directly applying these formula to large frame patches would lead to astronomical figures. On the contrary, MSE (mean square error) calculation was free of scale limitation while its result value lack reliability on discrepant content characteristics and lack stability on the change of luminance or chrominance even when the image textures remain consistent. To solve the dilemma, we proposed a local-homogeneity-based global metric (LHGM) in formula (1) to accurately reflect image details. Importantly, our algorithm is unconstrained by image scales. At the same time, the result is unaffected by the variation of image size.

$$LHGM(p) = \frac{1}{m \times n} \sum_{i=1}^{m} \sum_{j=1}^{n} \left[g(i,j) - g^s(i,j) \right]^2 \tag{1}$$

Here p represents a frame patch with the size of $m \times n$, $g(i,j)$ is the gray-level at pixel (i,j), and $g^s(i,j)$ is the averaged gray-level in an $s \times s$ window centered at (i,j). The size of s depends on the requirement of detail levels (in our application, it is empirically set at 5 pixel).

To illustrate our quadtree-based hierarchical decomposition, we use p (Lp, Ip, Dp) to represent a patch node in the tree structure. Here Lp indicates the decomposition level of p, Ip indexes p at that level, and Dp gives the down-sampling rate that to be applied at the current patch. By this definition, the original version of each first frame, like the Intra-frame in V-unit 2 (Fig. 1 Spatial Decomposition) is labeled as a root node ($Lp = 0$). Next, we decompose it into four equal parts via a quad-tree decomposition and calculate each of their content complexity with formula (1). If any resulting LHGM value exceeds a predefined threshold (70 db), indicating the existence of detailed fragment(s), it will be replaced by the four partitions. Otherwise, the Intra-frame will be treated as a leaf node and processed as a whole. Similarly, each partition with an over-threshold LHGM value will be further decomposed iteratively until either its four sub-patches are all smaller than the threshold or the highest level K (limited to video resolution and minimum coding size) is reached. For implementation efficiency, adjacent leaf patches of the final partitions (the Intra-patches in Fig. 1.) that belong to the same complexity range (with the same Dp value) are merged together so that down-sampling can be operated integratedly later. The Intra-merges in Fig. 1 displays the final decomposition pattern of V-unit 2 and succeeding Inter-frames can just follow this pattern. Such process is named as Intra-Guide.

In general, patches at deeper tree levels contains more details and ought to be compressed with larger down-sampling rates. Exception exist when a smooth area is separated out due to the high LHGM value of its brother nodes. So during the selection of adaptive down-sampling rate Dp, we synthetically considered both the quad-tree level Lp and the the patch's content complexity. Exact formula is given below:

$$D_p = \begin{cases} \partial^{K-L_p+1} & LHGM(p) < threshold \\ \partial^{K-L_p} & LHGM(p) > threshold \end{cases} \tag{2}$$

Where ∂ is a base number, deciding the scaling extent and can be adjusted according to the limitation of bandwidth or the requirement of reconstruction quality.

3   Content-Adaptive Sparse Representation of Super-Resolution

Based on sparse signal representation, research on image statistics suggested that image patches can be well-represented as a sparse linear combination of elements from an appropriately chosen over-complete dictionary [13] as expressed below:

$$I = D\alpha \qquad (3)$$

Where $I \in R^n$ is a given image, $\alpha \in R^k$ is a sparse vector with very few ($<< k$) nonzero elements, and $D \in R^{n \times k}$ is an over-complete dictionary of k prototype signal-atoms. Later, theoretical results from compressed sensing [21] demonstrated that under mild conditions, the sparse representation of a HR patch can be correctly recovered from its down-sampled version. Inspired by above facts, Yang et al. [13] designed their SR approach in following steps: (i) given a set of HR images, jointly train two dictionaries D_H and D_L for original patches and their down-sampled version; (ii) represent a LR input patch I_L by:

$$\min\|\alpha\|_1 \quad s.t. \|F(D_L\alpha) - F(I_L)\|_2^2 \leq \varepsilon \qquad (4)$$

Where F is a feature extraction operator, which provides a constraint on how closely the α approximates D_L; (iii) apply the LR sparse representation α with D_H to generate a super resolved image patch.:

$$I_H = D_H\alpha \qquad (5)$$

Since the reconstruction of I_H is based on those HR training images, whose content has the highest level of similarity to I_H, it is crucial that the two training dictionaries D_H and D_L be optimized. To this end, we proposed to analyze the input LR image I_L and extract its content features to select corresponding HR training images in the dictionary preparation. In this way, the super-resolution process can be made adaptive to the content of input video frames, and hence achieve the advantage that their reconstruction quality can be further improved. The problem of training the two dictionaries D_H and D_L can be formulated as:

$$D_H = \arg\min_{\{D_H, C\}} \left\| f_H(T, I_L) - D_H C \right\|^2 + \lambda\|C\|_1 \qquad (6)$$

$$D_L = \arg\min_{\{D_L, C\}} \left\| f_L(T, I_L) - D_L C \right\|^2 + \lambda\|C\|_1 \qquad (7)$$

Where $C \in R^{r \times m}$ is a coefficient matrix, r is determined by the dimension of selected content features, the l_1 norm $\| C \|_1$ is used to enforce the extent of sparse, and T is the set of training image candidates. Finally, $f_H(T, I_L)$ and $f_L(T, I_L)$ are the sets of optimized HR and LR image patches, the elements of which are derived through two stages of pruning process.

For the first stage of pruning, we applied a texture descriptor [22], which is based on three edge patterns, to facilitate the similarity based selection. The basic principle is to examine two DCT coefficients $X(0, 1)$ and $X(1, 0)$ for every block of 8×8 pixels with any DCT-based video compression technology and produce the following block-edge patterns (BEP), Where λ is a threshold to control the number of edge patterns:

$$BEP = \begin{cases} no\_edge & if \max(|X(1,0)|, |X(0,1)|) < \lambda \\ vertical\_edge & if \ |X(0,1)| \geq |X(1,0)|) \\ horizontal\_edge & otherwise \end{cases} \quad (8)$$

The texture descriptor is then constructed via a histogram-based approach to pre-select those training images in compressed domain, that are likely to produce good match for training dictionaries [22].

The second stage of pruning is carried out at the image patch level, where direct match among detailed content features out of SIFT is implemented. Specific process is described as follows:

$$e_H(T, I_L) = P_H \left(\arg\min_{x_i \in T} \{ d[SIFT(x_i), SIFT(I_H)] \} \right) \quad (9)$$

$$e_L(T, I_L) = P_L \left(\arg\min_{x_i \in T} \{ d[SIFT(x_i), SIFT(I_L)] \} \right) \quad (10)$$

Where $P_H(.)$ and $P_L(.)$ are two operators that segment the image into HR patches and LR patches, respectively. $d(.)$ is the Euclidean distance, which is used to measure the similarity between the SIFT descriptors of the training image candidate x_i and the input image patches I_L or I_H.

4   Experimental Results

To evaluate the proposed additional compression algorithm, we carried out extensive experiments on video sequences with various sizes, mostly VGA ($640 \times 480p$), SD ($1280 \times 720p$) and HD ($1920 \times 1080p$). The down-sampling rates that we adopted ranged from 2 to 8, depending on the level of content complexity. For each video frame, both of their original and down-sampled versions were encoded by JM codecs with 5 QP parameters (12, 18, 24, 30, 36). After the decoder, those down-scaled frame patches were enlarged with proposed SR method and 4 additional state-of-the-art SR methods that we mentioned in Introduction. Their eventual recovery quality were compared together with h.264 directly reconstructed, non-downsampled frames in terms of BRISQUE value.

Table 1. summarized the experiment results from 3 video samples with the size of VGA, SD and HD separately. And each BRISQUE value was an average of 120 video frames. As shown in Table 1, all of the super resolution methods provide competitive performance, among which our proposed is obviously the best, even outperforms the h.264 directly decoded non-shrinked ones. Especially in case of large QP values where transformation coefficients are quantified with coarse parameters, our super resolution method exhibits remarkable compensation effect for high frequency information loss. To more clearly demonstrate the promotion of restoration quality with our method, we appended the multiple spline curves of QP vs. BRISQUE value for the listed methods in Fig. 2.

Table 1. BRISQUE value of control methods and our proposed.

BRISQUE	QP	h.264	Proposed	Zeyde	ANR	NE	NNLS
VGA	12	0.8697	0.8379	0.7690	0.7647	0.7641	0.7669
	18	0.8380	0.8389	0.7528	0.7519	0.7500	0.7531
	24	0.7965	0.8241	0.7301	0.7269	0.7258	0.7294
	30	0.7539	0.8064	0.7073	0.7039	0.7023	0.7060
	36	0.6460	0.7301	0.6176	0.6161	0.6162	0.6185
SD	12	0.5773	0.6130	0.5294	0.526	0.5341	0.5282
	18	0.6037	0.6128	0.5358	0.5335	0.535	0.5345
	24	0.5824	0.6095	0.5296	0.5289	0.5298	0.5296
	30	0.5295	0.5887	0.5064	0.5053	0.5070	0.5067
	36	0.4671	0.5413	0.4507	0.4512	0.4504	0.4514
HD	12	0.6375	0.6877	0.6053	0.6007	0.6042	0.6138
	18	0.6425	0.6859	0.6072	0.6035	0.6087	0.6180
	24	0.6101	0.6805	0.5993	0.5947	0.6005	0.6086
	30	0.5560	0.6526	0.5699	0.5648	0.5705	0.5779
	36	0.4839	0.5897	0.5041	0.4995	0.5034	0.5096

Besides above quantitive valuation, figurate examples (the original frame, h.264 decoded, proposed reconstructed and one best example of other four contrast methods reconstructed frame) are presented in Fig. 3. It can be seen that our proposed is obviously the clearest.

The original size of 3 video sequences and the size of their bitstream that respectively compressed by h.264 codec and our scheme are listed in Table 2. Compared with h.264, our proposed gain an add-on compression of over 5 times in average, indicating that if our proposed codec is applied to telecommunication, the transfer speed will be improved by more than five times. In terms of storage, application of the proposed codec will give us additional savings of about five sixths of the overall storage space.

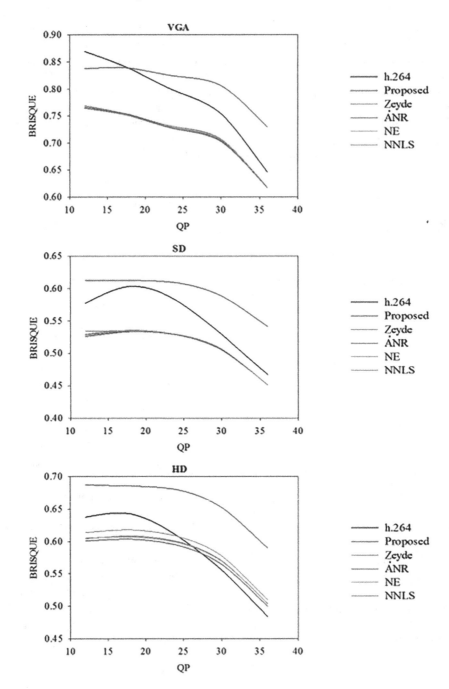

Fig. 2. BRISQUE vs. QP value of h.264, our proposed and 4 control methods

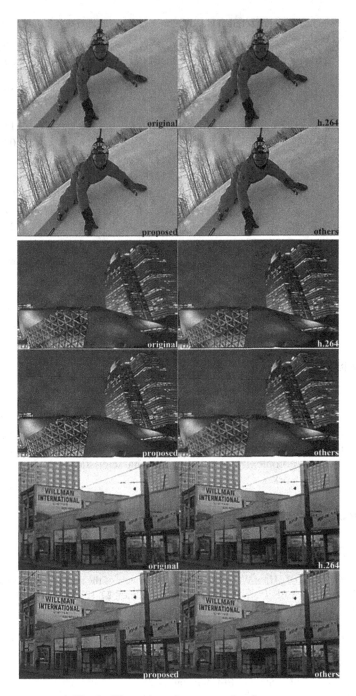

Fig. 3. Illustration of reconstruction frames

Table 2. Averaged data size of original video, compressed bitstream via h.264 and our proposed scheme, as well as the add-on compression ratio.

Data size	Original (KB)	QP	h.264 (KB)	Proposed (KB)	Add-on
VGA	20172	12	700	217	3.23
		18	389	120	3.24
		24	190	61	3.14
		30	86	28	3.01
		36	37	12	3.00
SD	37800	12	1132	126	8.98
		18	623	72	8.65
		24	315	37	8.51
		30	148	18	8.22
		36	64	8	8.00
HD	60723	12	2632	542	4.86
		18	1229	284	4.33
		24	548	139	3.95
		30	220	70	3.15
		36	107	36	2.99

5   Conclusion

In this paper, we designed an adaptive video compression technique on top of existing codecs for achieving additional contraction, accelerated transformation and also excellent reconstruction quality. The performance discrepancies in aspects of additional compression ratio and reconstruction quality may be associated with differential video resolutions, content complexity or other video characteristics, which remain to be researched in future work.

References

1. Schwarz, H., Marpe, D., Wiegand, T.: Overview of the scalable video coding extension of the h.264/avc standard. IEEE Trans Circ. Syst. Video Technol. **17**(9), 1103–1120 (2007)
2. Sullivan, G.J., Ohm, J., Han, W.J., Wiegand, T.: Overview of the high efficiency video coding (HEVC) standard. IEEE Trans Circ. Syst. Video Technol. **22**(12), 1649–1668 (2012)
3. Shen, M., Xue, P., Wang, C.: Down-sampling based video coding using super-resolution technique. IEEE Trans Circ. Syst. Video Technol. **21**(6), 755–765 (2011)
4. Chang, P.C.: Adaptive down-sampling video coding. In: Proceedings of SPIE - The International Society for Optical Engineering, vol. 24(11), pp. 1957–1968 (2010)
5. Nguyen, V.A., Tan, Y.P. Lin, W.: Adaptive downsampling/upsampling for better video compression at low bit rate. In: IEEE International Symposium on Circuits and Systems, pp. 1624–1627 (2008)
6. Alfred, M.B., Elad, M., Kimmel, R.: Down-scaling for better transform compression. IEEE Trans. Image Process. **12**(9), 1132–1144 (2003)

7. Jiang, J.: A low-cost content-adaptive and rate-controllable near-lossless image codec in dpcm domain. IEEE Trans. Image Process. **9**(4), 543–554 (2000)
8. Li, X., Orchard, M.T.: New edge directed interpolation. IEEE Trans. Image Process. **10**(10), 1521–1527 (2001). A Publication of the IEEE Signal Processing Society
9. Farsiu, S., Robinson, M.D., Elad, M., Milanfar, P.: Fast and robust multiframe super resolution. IEEE Trans. Image Process. **13**(10), 1327–1344 (2004)
10. Chang, H., Yeung, D.Y., Xiong, Y.: Super-resolution through neighbor embedding. In: IEEE Computer Society Conference on Computer Vision & Pattern Recognition, pp. 275–282. IEEE Computer Society (2004)
11. Bevilacqua, M., Roumy, A., Guillemot, C., Alberi-Morel, M.L.: Low-complexity single-image super-resolution based on nonnegative neighbor embedding. In: BMVC (2012)
12. Timofte, R., De Smet, V., Van Gool, L.: Anchored neighborhood regression for fast example-based super-resolution. In: IEEE International Conference on Computer Vision (ICCV), pp. 1920–1927 (2013)
13. Yang, J., Wright, J., Huang, T.S., Ma, Y.: Image super-resolution via sparse representation. IEEE Trans. Image Process. **19**(11), 2861–2873 (2010). A Publication of the IEEE Signal Processing Society
14. Zeyde, R., Elad, M., Protter, M.: On single image scale-up using sparse-representations. In: Boissonnat, J.-D., Chenin, P., Cohen, A., Gout, C., Lyche, T., Mazure, M.-L., Schumaker, L. (eds.) Curves and Surfaces 2010. LNCS, vol. 6920, pp. 711–730. Springer, Heidelberg (2012). doi:10.1007/978-3-642-27413-8_47
15. Ren, J., Jiang, J., Chen, J.: Shot boundary detection in MPEG videos using local and global indicators. IEEE Trans. Circ. Syst. Video Technol. **19**(19), 1234–1238 (2009)
16. Ren, J., Jiang, J.: Hierarchical modelling and adaptive clustering for real-time summarization of rush videos. IEEE Trans. Multimed. **11**(5), 906–917 (2009)
17. Min, B., Cheung, R.C.C.: A fast cu size decision algorithm for the HEVC intra encoder. IEEE Trans. Circ. Syst. Video Technol. **25**(5), 892–896 (2015)
18. Zhao, T., Wang, Z., Kwong, S.: Flexible mode selection and complexity allocation in high efficiency video coding. IEEE J. Sel. Topics Signal Process. **7**(6), 1135–1144 (2013)
19. Cho, S., Kim, M.: Fast cu splitting and pruning for suboptimal cu partitioning in HEVC intra coding. IEEE Trans. Circ. Syst. Video Technol. **23**(9), 1555–1564 (2013)
20. Dai, S., Han, M., Xu, W., Wu, Y., Gong, Y.: Soft edge smoothness prior for alpha channel super resolution. In: IEEE Conference on Computer Vision & Pattern Recognition, pp. 1–8 (2007)
21. Kondo, S.: Compressed sensing and redundant dictionaries. IEEE Trans. Inf. Theor. **54**(5), 2210–2219 (2008)
22. Jiang, J., Armstrong, A., Feng, G.C.: Direct content access and extraction from JPEG compressed images. Pattern Recogn. **35**(11), 2511–2519 (2002)
23. Saad, M.A., Bovik, A.C., Charrier, C.: Blind image quality assessment: a natural scene statistics approach in the DCT domain. IEEE Trans. Image Process. **21**(8), 3339–3352 (2012)

Improving Classification of Tweets Using Linguistic Information from a Large External Corpus

Hugo Lewi Hammer$^{(\boxtimes)}$, Anis Yazidi, Aleksander Bai, and Paal Engelstad

Department of Computer Science,
Oslo and Akershus University College of Applied Sciences, Oslo, Norway
{hugo.hammer,anis.yazidi,aleksander.bai,paal.engelstad}@hioa.no

Abstract. The bag of words representation of documents is often unsatisfactory as it ignores relationships between important terms that do not co-occur literally. Improvements might be achieved by expanding the vocabulary with other relevant word, like synonyms.

In this paper we use word-word co-occurence information from a large corpus to expand the vocabulary of another corpus consisting of tweets. Several different methods on how to include the co-occurence information are constructed and tested out on the classification of real twitter data. Our results show that we are able to reduce the number of erroneous classifications by 14% using co-occurence information.

Keywords: Classification · Co-occurrence information · Text mining · Tweets

1 Introduction

Founded in 2006, Twitter (www.twitter.com) has grown to become one of the most popular social media services, known for its 140-character restriction on each post. In addition to a large general user base, Twitter is used extensively by celebrities, politicians, and news services to entertain, engage, or inform their followers. With over 500 million users, Twitter sees a daily stream of more than 400 million tweets a day [1].

Twitter is known to be an important source for early detecting of important events like breaking news, changes in the stock market, spread of diseases, earthquakes etc. or analyzing different trends in politics, fashion, entertainment etc., see e.g. [2–6]. Such approaches are typically based on training a machine learner on a bag-of-words representation of the tweets, maybe in addition to other features like number of words, publication time etc. The bag of words representation is often unsatisfactory as it ignores relationships between important terms that do not co-occur literally. Many important words and phrases for correct classification may never occur in the training material, but only show up in the test material (e.g. future tweets). A bag-of-words approach will not be able to detect such tweets since the important words never occurred in the

© ICST Institute for Computer Sciences, Social Informatics and Telecommunications Engineering 2017
L.A. Maglaras et al. (Eds.): INISCOM 2016, LNICST 188, pp. 122–134, 2017.
DOI: 10.1007/978-3-319-52569-3_11

training set. For example, suppose we want to detect tweets about the war in Syria. In the manually annotated training material we may have good predictors like "al-Assad", "Syria", "Homs" etc., but may miss other relevant phrases like "Damascus", "gas attack", "Baath party", "ISIL" which potentially could improve the classifications since such words are likely to occur in future tweets about the Syrian war.

In this paper we suggest to "enrich" the vocabulary in the training material with other potentially relevant phrases by using word-word co-occurrence information from an other large news corpus (1.1 billion words). Computing words that tend to co-occur with "al-assad" in the news corpus, we find among the top ten words "bashar", "al-sharaa" (vice president in Syria), "negotiations" and "syria" which seem like other relevant words to detect tweets about the Syrian war. It's not obvious what's the best way to incorporate such external co-occurrence information in the training material of tweets. We suggest a large set of different approaches and test them extensively on real twitter data.

The paper is extention of the preliminary results in the paper [7].

2   Related Work

Techniques for enriching text fall under two main categories: those who use intrinsic information contained in the current corpus and those who use extern resources. A representative example of intrinsic techniques is the Self-Term Expansion Methodology due to Pinto et al. [8] for clustering tweets. The method compromises two main steps: the Self-Term Enriching step, and a Term Selection step. The Self-Term Enriching procedure enriches the text representation of the tweets by exploiting the current tweets corpus and without the need of any external corpus, that is why the technique is called Self-Term Enriching. Terms of a documents are represented with a set of co-related terms. A co-occurrence list is calculated from the target data set by applying Pointwise Mutual Information (PMI). The Term Selection step identifies the most important features and tries to reduce the noise introduced by the Self-Term Enriching phase.

The second category of techniques for enriching text representation uses external resources other than the current text materials to be clustered or classified. It is worth mentioning that the later techniques have received most attention in the literature compared to techniques that resort to intrinstic information for the enriching task. For example in [9–12], the authors enrich the text representation using WordNet [13] where terms of the documents are replaces with their hypernym and synonym.

Similarly, the seminal work of Gabrilovich et al. [14] leverages knowledge bases from Wikipedia and Open Directory Project (ODP) in order to enhance the textual representation of short messages. The authors concluded that augmented knowledge based features generated from ODP and Wikipedia improved the text categorization task.

Alahmadi et al. [15] use an approach based on supplementing the bag-of-words representational scheme with a concept-based representation that utilises Wikipedia as a knowledge base.

In [16] Wikipedia semantic knowledge are used to tackle data sparseness in a question answering task. Experiments show that the approach significantly outperforms the baseline method (with error reductions of 23.21%).

Chen et al. [17] propose a word-word co-occurrence matrix based method for improved relevance feedback in information retrieval. Unlike other studies about word association, the authors consider the influence of the inter word distance and co-windows ratio. Experiments with TREC dataset demonstrate the effectiveness of the method.

3   Word-Word Co-occurrence Matrix and Document Term Matrix

In this section we represent relevant background information for the rest of the paper. More specifically we define the word-word co-occurrence matrix (COM) and the document term matrices (DTM).

3.1   Word-Word Co-occurrence Matrix

Suppose we have a large corpus consisting of a total of N words and let $w_1, w_2, \ldots, w_{N_w}$ denote the different unique words in the corpus. Further let N_i, $i \in \{1, 2, \ldots, N_w\}$ denote the number of times w_i occurs in the corpus and let N_{ij}, $i, j \in \{1, 2, \ldots, N_w\}$ denote the number of times w_i occurs in the neighbourhood of w_j in the corpus. The neighbourhood of a word, w_j, is typically those words closest to w_j in front and behind in the text. We assume symmetry such that $N_{ji} = N_{ij}$. A COM is the matrix with the element N_{ij} in position (i, j), $i, j = 1, 2, \ldots, N_w$. A COM computed from a large corpus is a highly valuable tool to analyze semantic relations between words, see e.g. [18,19].

Suppose we want to use COM to compute the semantic relation between w_i and w_j. There are typically three main approaches.

Correlation. The empirical correlation in occurrence with other words

$$\text{Corr}(w_i, w_j) = \frac{\text{Cov}(w_i, w_j)}{\sqrt{\text{Var}(w_i)\text{Var}(w_j)}}$$

where

$$\text{Var}(w_i) = \frac{1}{N_w - 1} \sum_{k=1}^{N_w} (N_{ik} - \overline{N_{i\cdot}})^2$$

$$\text{Cov}(w_i, w_j) = \sum_{k=1}^{N_w} (N_{ik} - \overline{N_{i\cdot}})(N_{jk} - \overline{N_{j\cdot}})$$

where

$$\overline{N_{i\cdot}} = \frac{1}{N_w} \sum_{k=1}^{N_w} N_{ik}$$

Angle. The angle between the co-occurrence vectors for w_i and w_j given as $[N_{i1}, N_{i2}, \ldots, N_{i\,N_w}]$ and $[N_{j1}, N_{j2}, \ldots, N_{j\,N_w}]$.

PMI.   The Pointwise Mutual Information between w_i and w_j defined as

$$PMI(w_i, w_j) = \log_2 \frac{P(w_i, w_j)}{P(w_i)P(w_j)} = \log_2 \frac{P(w_i \,|\, w_j)}{P(w_i)} = \log_2 \frac{P(w_j \,|\, w_i)}{P(w_j)} \quad (1)$$

Looking at the rightmost expression the numerator denotes the probability that w_j occurs in the neighborhood of w_i and the denominator the probability that a randomly selected word from the corpus is w_j. If w_i and w_j tend to co-occur, we expect that $P(w_j \,|\, w_i) > P(w_j)$.

The PMI can be estimated as follows based on the rightmost expression in (1)

$$\widehat{PMI}(w_i, w_j) = \frac{N_{ji}/N_i}{N_j/N}$$

Because of the symmetry, $N_{ji} = N_{ij}$, we get the same expression for $\widehat{PMI}(w_i, w_j)$ estimating based on the leftmost and middle expression in (1). Also note that $\widehat{PMI}$ are just simple reweightings of the entries in COM and thus very fast to compute.

In our experiments the PMI performed better than the two other approaches and the descriptions below therefore are based on PMI.

3.2   Document Term Matrix

Other words for a document term matrix (DTM) are bag-of-words and n-grams. Suppose that a corpus consist of D tweets (more generally documents). Let n_{di} denote the number of times word w_i occur in tweet $d \in \{1, 2, \ldots, D\}$ and n_w the total number of unique words in the D tweets. A DTM is the matrix with the elements n_{di} in positions (d, i), $d = 1, 2, \ldots, D, i = 1, 2, \ldots, n_w$. A natural generalization is to not only use words, but all phrases of subsequent words in the corpus called n-grams. In this paper we only resort to single words (unigram). Reweightings of the pure term frequencies in a DTM is also very common, e.g. the TF-IDF ([18], Chap. 15).

4   Incorporating Co-occurrence Information from a Large External Corpus in a Document Term Matrix

In this section we present different methods to incorporate COM information from a large external corpus to a DTM. We start by expanding the vocabulary

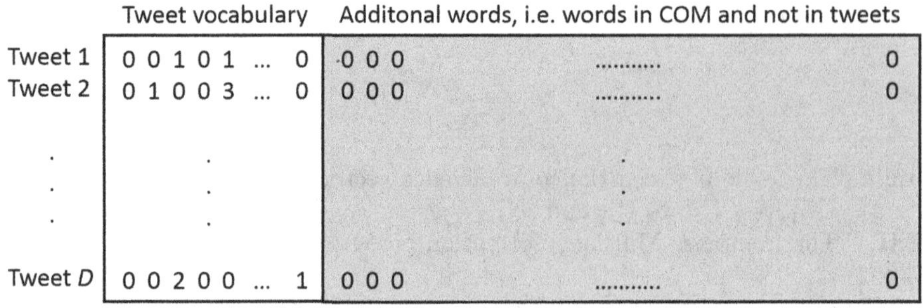

	Tweet vocabulary	Additonal words, i.e. words in COM and not in tweets		
Tweet 1	0 0 1 0 1 ... 0	0 0 0	....	0
Tweet 2	0 1 0 0 3 ... 0	0 0 0	....	0
.	.			
.	.		.	
.	.		.	
			.	
Tweet D	0 0 2 0 0 ... 1	0 0 0	....	0

Fig. 1. Illustration of the expansion (shown in gray) of the original tweet DTM shown in white.

of DTM from all the unique words in the tweets to the union of the unique words in the tweets and the words in COM. See Fig. 1 for a simple visualization of the expansion. The gray part shows the additional words added to the original DTM shown as the white part of the matrix. Our goal is to add reasonable values in the gray part of the matrix and adjust values in the white part of the matrix to improve classification. To simplify the notation below, let r_{ij} refer to $\widehat{PMI}(w_i, w_j)$. Also assume that all words in the tweet vocabulary are part of the COM vocabulary. In practice we obtained this by letting words that is in the tweet vocabulary and not in the COM vocabulary, are added to COM with all co-occurence frequencies with other words equal to zero.

Suppose a tweet $d \in \{1, 2, \ldots, D\}$ consists of the η_d unique words $w_{d(1)}, \ldots, w_{d(\eta_d)}$ and recall that we assume that all being part of the COM vocabulary $w_1, w_2, \ldots, w_{N_w}$. Further let $n_{d,d(1)}, \ldots, n_{d,d(\eta_d)}$ denote the frequency (or some reweighting like TF-IDF) of $w_{d(1)}, \ldots, w_{d(\eta_d)}$. Define the matrix $\text{PMI}_{\text{tweet}}$ consisting of the entries $r_{d(i),j}$, $i = 1, 2, \ldots, \eta_d$, $j = 1, 2, \ldots, N_w$ containing the PMI scores between the words in the tweet and all the words in COM. Figure 2 illustrates this matrix. Based on $\text{PMI}_{\text{tweet}}$ we can expand the vocabulary of the tweet d in different ways. Maybe the most natural is for each word in COM to compute the sum of PMI scores for the words in the tweet and add this values to the expanded DTM shown in Fig. 1

$$\widetilde{n}_{d,j} = \frac{1}{\eta_d} \sum_{i=1}^{\eta_d} r_{d(i),j}, \quad j = 1, 2, \ldots, N_w \tag{2}$$

where $\widetilde{n}_{d,j}$ refers to the scores to add to the expanded DTM in position (d, j). We can interpret this as adding the (pointwise mutual) information from all the tweet words together and thus the approach intuitively seem reasonable.

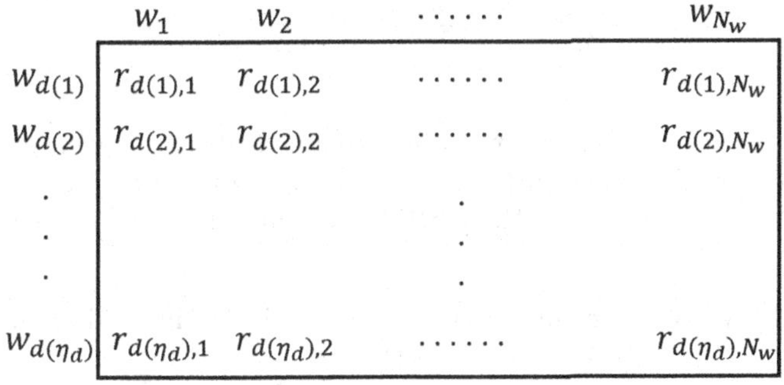

	w_1	w_2	$\cdots\cdots$	w_{N_w}
$w_{d(1)}$	$r_{d(1),1}$	$r_{d(1),2}$	$\cdots\cdots$	$r_{d(1),N_w}$
$w_{d(2)}$	$r_{d(2),1}$	$r_{d(2),2}$	$\cdots\cdots$	$r_{d(2),N_w}$
$\vdots$		$\vdots$		
$w_{d(\eta_d)}$	$r_{d(\eta_d),1}$	$r_{d(\eta_d),2}$	$\cdots\cdots$	$r_{d(\eta_d),N_w}$

Fig. 2. Illustration of the of the matrix $\text{PMI}_{\text{tweet}}$.

A natural modification of (2) is to weight with the occurrences of the tweet words

$$\widetilde{n}_{d,j} = \frac{1}{\eta_d} \sum_{i=1}^{\eta_d} n_{d,d(i)}\, r_{d(i),j} \tag{3}$$

For words being part of the original tweet vocabulary, we update the values from $n_{d,d(i)}$ to $n_{d,d(i)} + \alpha\widetilde{n}_{d,d(i)}$ for $i \in 1,2,\ldots,\eta_d$ where α is a rescaling parameter since we have no reason to believe that $n_{d,d(i)}$ and $\widetilde{n}_{d,d(i)}$ are on the same scale. For the other words we substitute zero with $\alpha\widetilde{n}_{d,j}, j \in \{1,2,\ldots,N_w\}\backslash\{d(1),d(2),\ldots,d(\eta_d)\}$ where $A\backslash B$ refers to all the elements in A except those that are in B. Below we describe different alternatives to (3).

A challenging part of including PMI-information is that large amounts of noise may be included. Consider the following fictive tweet about the Syrian war: "President al-Assad agrees to negotiate". Using the method in (3), we add the PMI scores for all the words together, but words like "agrees" and "to" are not at all relevant for the classification to Syrian war and may introduce unfortunate noise. Intuitively we expect that words that have high PMI score for two or more words in the tweet are more likely to be relevant words, while words with only one high PMI value are less likely to be relevant. For example, the word "al-Sharaa" (vice president in Syria) has high PMI score with *all* the three words "President", "al-Assad" and "negotiate" and thus is most likely be a relevant word. We can achieve this property by doing transformation with monotonically increasing concave functions like the logarithm and $r^\gamma, \gamma < 1$. The following simple example motivates such transformations. Suppose a word w_i has a PMI score of 8 with two of the words in the tweet (and zero to the other words) and suppose that another word w_j has a PMI score of 16 to one word in the tweet (and zero to the other words). Using (3), the two words will get equal score, but transforming with the logarithm w_i gets the score $\log_2 8 + \log_2 8 = 3+3 = 6$ and w_j gets the $\log_2 16 = 4$. We see that w_i now gets a higher score then w_j after the transformation. Therefore we generalize (3) to

$$\widetilde{n}_{d,j} = \frac{1}{\eta_d} \sum_{i=1}^{\eta_d} n_{d,d(i)} (r_{d(i),j})^\gamma \tag{4}$$

and setting $\gamma < 1$ we achieve what is explained above. If $r_{d(i),j} < 0$ in (4), we replace $(r_{d(i),j})^\gamma$ with $-(|r_{d(i),j}|)^\gamma$. In the rest of the paper we denote the approach based on (4) for method SPMI. The methods below are variants of this.

– Method RAW: We take sum of the raw ratios in (1) instead of the PMIs

$$\widetilde{n}_{d,j} = \frac{1}{\eta_d} \sum_{i=1}^{\eta_d} n_{d,d(i)} (2^{r_{d(i),j}})^\gamma = \frac{1}{\eta_d} \sum_{i=1}^{\eta_d} n_{d,d(i)} 2^{\gamma\, r_{d(i),j}} \tag{5}$$

– Method RAWL: We take the logarithm of the scores $\widetilde{n}_{d,j}$ from method RAW.
– Method MAXL: In stead of taking the sum over PMI values as for the methods SPMI, RAW and RAWL, we just use the maximal PMI score. Let $\hat{i} = \arg\max_{i \in 1,2,\ldots \eta_d} \{r_{d(i),j}\}$ and compute the scores as

$$\widetilde{n}_{d,j} = n_{d,d(\hat{i})} r_{d(\hat{i}),j}$$

– Method MAX: The same as method MAX except that we use the raw ratios

$$\widetilde{n}_{d,j} = n_{d,d(\hat{i})} 2^{r_{d(\hat{i}),j}}$$

– Method GEOM: The geometric mean. If we compute $\widetilde{n}_{d,j}$ from (3), the geometric mean can be computed as

$$2^{\widetilde{n}_{d,j}}$$

While method SPMI with a low value for γ ends up with many scores $\widetilde{n}_{d,j}$ with almost the same values, method RAW combined with a high value of γ ends up with only a few scores $\hat{n}_{d,j}$ with high values and all the other close to zero (after proper rescaling with the parameter α). The other methods above are different variants which lies between these extremes.

4.1 Only Important Words

As mentioned above, a potential challenge with the idea of using COM information is that the scores $\widetilde{n}_{d,j}$ from the methods above may be disturbed by PMI information from irrelevant words like "agree" and "to" from the example tweet above. Another approach to reduce the possible noise is to only include PMI information for words with a positive correlation with the response. For the example tweet we expect that words like "al-Assad", "president" and "negotiate" are positively correlated with tweets about the Syrian war compared to tweets about other topics while words like "agree" and "to" are less correlated with the Syrian war. A more detailed description of how to achieve this is as follows. Assume we have a multiclass classification problem with classes $C_1, C_2, \ldots, C_K$

and let $Y_{dk}, d = 1, 2, \ldots, D, k = 1, 2, \ldots, K$ be equal to one if tweet d belong to class k and zero else. Further let $Y_k = [Y_{1k}, Y_{2k}, \ldots, Y_{Dk}]$. We now compute the correlation between the Y_k and word frequencies of a word w_i being part of the tweet vocabulary

$$\text{Corr}(Y_k, w_i) = \frac{\text{Cov}(Y_k, w_i)}{\sqrt{\text{Var}(Y_k)\text{Var}(w_i)}}$$

where

$$\text{Cov}(Y_k, w_i) = \sum_{d=1}^{D}(Y_{dk} - \overline{Y_k})(n_{di} - \overline{n_{\cdot i}})$$

We now only include PMI information for tweet words where the maximal correlation to $Y_1, Y_2, \ldots, Y_K$ is above some threshold τ. This result in the following rewriting of Eq. (4)

$$\tilde{n}_{d,j} = \frac{1}{\eta_d} \sum_{i=1}^{\eta_d} I\left(\max_{k=1,2,\ldots,K}\{\text{Corr}(Y_k, w_{d(i)})\} > \tau\right) n_{d,d(i)}(r_{d(i),j})^{\gamma} \qquad (6)$$

and similar for the other methods above. $I(\cdot)$ is the indicator function.

5 Linguistic Resources

In this section we present the resources necessary to evaluate the methods above. All the analyzes are done for the Norwegian language.

The COM are computed from a huge corpus that is made openly available by the National Library of Norway (NLN). The corpus consists of news articles collected from Norwegian newspapers from 1998 until 2011. This corresponds to roughly 1.1 billion Norwegian words distributed over 4 million articles. To compute N_{ij}, we used a neighborhood of six words in front and behind of w_j (recall Sect. 3.1). We only used words that occurred at least 50 times in the news corpus ending up with a vocabulary with 287904 unique words.

The Twitter corpus is selected from all tweets published in Norwegian on Twitter from 20th of July to 8th of August 2011 a total of about two million tweets. We selected a subset of tweets as follows:

1. We counted the number of times different hashtags were used.
2. Among the most frequently used hashtags we manually picked hashtags related to six topics as summarized in Table 1 and selected all the tweet consisting at least one of these hashtags.

The resulting corpus consists of a total of 21270 tweets. Since the tweets are from the time span around the tragic 22th July terror it is as expected that we observe many tweet related to this. The classification task is to classify the correct topic of these tweets when all the hashtags are removed from the tweets.

Table 1. Details of the six topics. Columns from left to right: Description of cluster, number of tweets for the different topics and hashtags representing the topics.

Topic	No.	Hashtags
The 22th July 2011 terror	11519	#Utøya #PrayForOslo etc.
Justin Beiber	3409	#Bieber #Bieberlove etc.
Norwegian national elections	2218	#Valg #Valg11 etc. (valg = election)
Tour de France	1668	#TdF #2dF etc.
TheØya music festival	1311	#Øya
Libya	879	#Libya

6 Experiments

In this section we compare the classification performance of the different extended DTMs described above. We base our classifications on multinomial LASSO regression [20]. Multinomial LASSO regression can document excellent classification performances, and is at least as effective as Support vector Machine [21]. Another advantage of the LASSO is that the estimated parameter space is sparse, i.e. only a little handful of the hundreds of thousands of words in the vocabulary are used by the classifier. This gives us the possibility to inspect which words are used by the classifier and interpret the results. We return to this in Sect. 6.2.

In all the experiments we sat the rescaling parameter $\alpha = 1$ (recall Sect. 4). Our results show that expanding the tweet vocabulary using only important words (Sect. 4.1) in stead of all the words, improved classification performance. Thus in Sect. 6.1, we only present results based on the important words method in Sect. 4.1. In the experiments we sat $\tau = 0.08$ in (6) ending up with a total of 316 important words fairly evenly spread over the six classes in Table 1.

We expect that incorporating external information is particularly useful if the number of documents (tweets) in the annotated training material are few. Then many important predictors (words) are missing in the training material and thus not being part of the classifier. Our results is in accordance with this. Using 30% or more of the tweet corpus to train the classifier (more than 6381 tweets), the reduction in erroneous classifications is below 5% compared to not using external information. Using less than 30% of the tweets to train the classifier, the reduction in erroneous classifications is between 5 and 15%.

6.1 Classification performance

Above we summarized the main results from the experiments. In this section we look closer at the cases which gave the best result, i.e. we expanded only by important words (Sect. 4.1) and used less than 30 % of the tweet corpus in the training set. Table 2 shows classification results using 5% (1064 tweets) and 10% (2127 tweets) of the tweets for training. To reduce the uncertainty in our

Table 2. The values represent the percentage of tweets classified to the correct class. Columns two to four show results using 5% of the tweets as a training set, while the last three columns show results for 10% training. NOEXT refers to classification using the tweet DTM (no additional words included).

Method	5% training			10% training		
	$\gamma = 0.1$	$\gamma = 1$	$\gamma = 10$	$\gamma = 0.1$	$\gamma = 1$	$\gamma = 10$
NOEXT	–	69.0	–	–	73.1	–
SPMI	73.1	68.9	73.4	75.8	72.4	75.5
RAW	72.9	68.3	72.9	75.8	72.4	75.5
RAWL	72.6	73.3	73.3	75.6	75.8	75.9
MAX	–	72.9	–	–	75.5	–
MAXL	–	73.3	–	–	75.9	–
GEOM	–	72.2	–	–	75.1	–

results in Table 2, we used cross validation repeatedly using different parts of the tweets as training and test corpus. The results in Table 2 are the average classification performance for the different cross validation runs. The width of confidence intervals based on the cross validation runs where about 0.1, i.e. in practice it is no uncertainty in the values in Table 2.

As expected a higher percentage of the tweets are classified correctly when 10% of the tweets are used for training compared to only 5%. For 10% training the highest reduction in erroneous classifications were

$$\frac{(100 - 73.1) - (100 - 75.9)}{100 - 73.1} \cdot 100\% = 10.4\%$$

For 5% training the highest reduction is

$$\frac{(100 - 69.0) - (100 - 73.4)}{100 - 69.0} \cdot 100\% = 14.2\%$$

We see, as expected, that when the training set is small inclusion of external co-occurence information have a larger positive effect on the classification performance. An other interesting observation is that NOEXT using 10% training performs poorer (73.1%) than using 5% training and external information (73.4%). In other words it is better to include external co-occurence information than increasing the number of annotated tweets from 5% (1064 tweets) to 10% (2127 tweets). Having in mind that manual annotation of documents are very resource demanding, this is quite an impressive result and documents the usefulness of the methods in this paper.

From Table 2 we see that the most natural choice of using external information, SPMI with $\gamma = 1$ (which is equivalent to (3)) do not document any improvements. It seems that better results are achieved by either using a few words with high values (e.g. RAW and $\gamma = 10$ and MAX) or many words with almost the same value (e.g. SPMI and $\gamma = 0.1$), not the alternatives in between.

Table 3. The table shows the words that are the best predictors (translated from Norwegian to English) for the different topics. The words in the second column (tweet words) were part of the original vocabulary of the tweets in the training set. Third column shows words that are good predictors but were not part of the original tweet vocabulary but added using some of the methods in Sect. 4.

Topic	Tweet words	Added words
The 22th July 2011 terror	auf, dead, killed, people, norway, people, police, together, thoughts, sad, utøya	arrested, armed, bomb
Justin Beiber	album, bieber, love, follow, hope, justin, culture, 4ever, aloooot, follower, lookin	dream, teenagers, brands, selena, girls, loves
Norwegian national elections	frp, nrk, political, jensen, vote, tv2, election, voting machine	argument, conservative, industry, vice chairman, prime minister
Tour de France	schleck, boasson, edwald, stage, france, paris, tdf, jersey	meters, astana, eneco, stages, french, prestigious, overall lead, fell
TheØya music festival	fleet foxes, håkan, kanye, consert, music, sunshine, plays	winehouse, gitarist, linkin, mayhem, acquired, surferosa, equalized
Libya	gaddafi, jail, hell, hotel, fire, libya, libyan, nightmare, tripoli	attacks, continued, kaim, coastal, town, sirte, officer, nato, regime, soldiers

6.2 Words used in the Classifier

In this section we inspect which words are the best predictors of the different classes in Table 1. Using the multinomial LASSO model with a higher value of the regularization parameter than the optimal value, classification is performed using only a few words. Naturally the classification performance is reduces using such a sparse classifier, but on the other hand interpretation is very easy. Table 3 shows the results for the case with 5% of the tweets in the training set and method SPMI with $\gamma = 10$ and a high value of the regularization parameter. We see that both the tweet words (second column) and the added words (third column) are very relevant words for the different topics. E.g for the Justin Bieber topic, words like his ex girlfriend Selena are not part of the original training vocabulary, but added using the methods in Sect. 4. Selena occurred several times in the test set and thus improved classification were achieved by including Selena. For the Øya music festival, we see that several other relevant artists are added as extra words like (Amy) Winehouse, Mayhem and Surferosa. For the Libya topic words like the Deputy Foreign Minister (Khaled) Kaim and references to the battle of Sirte also were good predictors resulting in improved classification performance.

7   Closing Remarks

In this paper we show how external information from a word-word co-occurrence matrix can be used to improve the classification of tweets. The methods in this paper are particularly useful if the number of tweets in the training set is small. E.g. if the number of tweets is about a thousand, our results show a reduction in erroneous classifications with about 15%.

There are several interesting directions for further research using word-word co-occurrence information. We believe that the constructed methods in this paper are useful also for other sorts of documents and could be interesting to investigate further. It could also be interesting to evaluate the methods above for unsupervised tasks like clustering and topic modeling [22].

References

1. Zubiaga, A., Spina, D., Martinez, R., Fresno, V.: Real-time classification of twitter trends. J. Am. Soc. Inform. Sci. Technol. **66**(3), 462–473 (2015)
2. Petrović, S., Osborne, M., Lavrenko, V.: Using paraphrases for improving first story detection in news and twitter. In: Proceedings of the 2012 Conference of the North American Chapter of the Association for Computational Linguistics: Human Language Technologies. NAACL HLT 2012, Stroudsburg, PA, USA, Association for Computational Linguistics, pp. 338–346 (2012)
3. Zhang, X., Fuehres, H., Gloor, P.A.: Predicting stock market indicators through twitter I hope it is not as bad as I fear. Procedia Soc. Behav. Sci. **26**, 55–62 (2011)
4. Lampos, V., Bie, T., Cristianini, N.: Flu detector - tracking epidemics on twitter. In: Balcázar, J.L., Bonchi, F., Gionis, A., Sebag, M. (eds.) ECML PKDD 2010. LNCS (LNAI), vol. 6323, pp. 599–602. Springer, Heidelberg (2010). doi:10.1007/978-3-642-15939-8_42
5. Lee, K., Palsetia, D., Narayanan, R., Patwary, M.M.A., Agrawal, A., Choudhary, A.: Twitter trending topic classification. In: Proceedings of the 2011 IEEE 11th International Conference on Data Mining Workshops, ICDMW 2011, Computer Society, pp. 251–258. IEEE, Washington, DC (2011)
6. Sakaki, T., Okazaki, M., Matsuo, Y.: Earthquake shakes twitter users: real-time event detection by social sensors. In: Proceedings of the 19th International Conference on World Wide Web. WWW 2010, pp. 851–860. ACM, New York (2010)
7. Hammer, H.L., Yazidi, A., Bai, A., Engelstad, P., et al.: Improving classification of tweets using word-word co-occurrence information from a large external corpus. In: Proceedings of the 31st Annual ACM Symposium on Applied Computing, pp. 1174–1177. ACM (2016)
8. Pinto, D., Rosso, P., Jiménez-Salazar, H.: A self-enriching methodology for clustering narrow domain short texts. Comput. J. **54**(7), 1148–1165 (2011)
9. Hotho, A., Staab, S., Stumme, G.: Ontologies improve text document clustering. In: Third IEEE International Conference on Data Mining, ICDM 2003, pp. 541–544. IEEE (2003)
10. Hotho, A., Staab, S., Stumme, G.: Wordnet improves text document clustering. In: Proceedings of the SIGIR Semantic Web Workshop (2003)

11. Rodriguez, M., Hidalgo, J., Agudo, B.: Using wordnet to complement training information in text categorization. In: Proceedings of 2nd International Conference on Recent Advances in Natural Language Processing II: Selected Papers from RANLP, vol. 97, pp. 353–364 (2000)

12. Dave, K., Lawrence, S., Pennock, D.M.: Mining the peanut gallery: opinion extraction and semantic classification of product reviews. In: Proceedings of the 12th international conference on World Wide Web, pp. 519–528. ACM (2003)

13. Miller, G.A.: Wordnet: a lexical database for english. Commun. ACM **38**(11), 39–41 (1995)

14. Gabrilovich, E., Markovitch, S.: Overcoming the brittleness bottleneck using wikipedia: Enhancing text categorization with encyclopedic knowledge. In: AAAI, vol. 6, pp. 1301–1306 (2006)

15. Alahmadi, A., Joorabchi, A., Mahdi, A.: A new text representation scheme combining bag-of-words and bag-of-concepts approaches for automatic text classification. In: 2013 7th IEEE GCC Conference and Exhibition (GCC). IEEE Press (2013)

16. Cai, L., Zhou, G., Liu, K., Zhao, J.: Large-scale question classification in CQA by leveraging wikipedia semantic knowledge. In: Proceedings of the 20th ACM International Conference on Information and Knowledge Management. CIKM 2011, pp. 1321–1330. ACM, New York (2011)

17. Chen, Z., Lu, Y.: A word co-occurrence matrix based method for relevance feedback. J. Comput. Inf. Syst. **7**(1), 17–24 (2011)

18. Manning, C.D., Schütze, H.: Foundations of Statistical Natural Language Processing. MIT Press, Cambridge (1999)

19. Pennington, J., Socher, R., Manning, C.D.: Glove: Global vectors forword representation (2015). http://nlp.stanford.edu/projects/glove/glove.pdf. Accessed 27 July 2015

20. Friedman, J., Hastie, T., Tibshirani, R.: Regularization Paths for Generalized Linear Models via Coordinate Descent. J. Stat. Softw. **33**(1), 1–22 (2010)

21. Genkin, A., Lewis, D.D., Madigan, D.: Large-scale bayesian logistic regression for text categorization. Technometrics **49**(14), 291–304 (2007)

22. Blei, D.M.: Probabilistic topic models. Commun. ACM **55**(4), 77–84 (2012)

Walking into Panoramic and Immersive 3D Video

Yingbin Nie and Jianmin Jiang[✉]

Research Institute for Future Media Computing, School of Computer Science
and Software Engineering, Shenzhen University, Shenzhen 518060, China
nybl992@gmail.com, jianmin.jiang@szu.edu.cn

Abstract. To enable viewers to perceive the video content as if he or she is
walking inside the video scenes, we need to have two essential video technologies. One is to present the audience with panoramic videos with 360°, and
the other is view-adaptive video playback, i.e. presenting video scenes in
accordance with the change of viewing angles. For the first technology, we
propose a fast video stitching algorithm via exploiting the audio information for
frame synchronization, and for the second, we propose a Fake-3D and True-3D
mix method to immerse viewers inside the video scene via its dynamic playback
of panoramic videos, adaptive to multi-view changes. Our proposed technologies have great potential in practical applications, such as virtual reality gaming
and new concept movie shows etc.

Keywords: Panoramic 3D videos · Free-view video processing · Dynamic
video playback · Video stitching · Fake-3D · True-3D · Virtual reality

1 Introduction

At present, video production and consumption is limited to the principle that video
content is processed and produced for people to watch. In other words, video capture of
live events is limited to camera views, and most of the video entertainment only
provides people with one single view, facilitated by one or more cameras [7, 8]. As a
result, the viewing experience achieved by such a see-what-camera-captures is not
comparable with those on-spot views with our naked eyes. On spot, we can move our
head and change the viewing angle to enjoy free-view of the event. We could even
walk around to select the best possible viewing position, including the adjustment of
viewing angles and distance to achieve the most effective viewing experience. An
illustrative scenario is watching a show inside an opera house, where somebody may
wish to walk onto the stage and enjoy watching the show from the back. In addition,
on-spot view also provides the advantage that the audience can interact with relevant
people to experience the event rather than watch. This is not achievable with current
video technology, although research and technology innovation is active around areas
of immersive video, multi-view video, and virtual reality [9, 10]. In this paper, we
describe a new 3D panoramic and immersive video processing tool, which pioneers the
concept to allow viewers not only watch the video content, but also walking into the
video and experience the scene, the event, and the atmosphere as if he or she is on spot.

© ICST Institute for Computer Sciences, Social Informatics and Telecommunications Engineering 2017
L.A. Maglaras et al. (Eds.): INISCOM 2016, LNICST 188, pp. 135–142, 2017.
DOI: 10.1007/978-3-319-52569-3_12

2   Panoramic and Immersive 3D Video Constructions

To pioneer the concept of allowing viewers to walk into videos and perceive the content on real-time basis, we need to develop a number of new technologies and overcome three fundamental hurdles. These include: (i) creating panoramic video via capture of the scene with 360° along both horizontal and vertical directions; (ii) presenting and playback the video content in accordance with the change of viewing angles and body movements; (iii) interacting with video objects and participating in activities with instant and natural responses. To overcome the first hurdle, we configured one row of multi video cameras to ensure sufficient video capture for 360° along the horizontal direction. To overcome the second hurdle, we use VR helmet display unit and exploit its accelerometer sensor and magnetic sensor output to control the video playback corresponding to the view or pose changes.

2.1   Multi-camera Synchronization

Panoramic video need multi-camera to capture multi angle perspective, we can't promise all cameras to start recording in the same time, so that these videos captured by multi cameras need to be synchronized. We use the Chroma feature [1] as a descriptor for the audio content of multi video streams in different views, which gives a 12-dimensional representation of the tonal content of an audio signal derived by combining bands belonging to twelve pitch classes (C, C#, D, D#, E, F, F#, G, G#, A, A#, B), corresponding to the same distinct semitones, and use method [11] to synchronization.

Firstly, decompose the audio signals from the multi-camera captured videos and cut a segment starting from the pth frame to the qth frame for all audios and every audio has overlap in this segment. Then compute Chroma features for each segment, where C_n is used to represent the nth camera's audio, F_n the nth camera's audio segment, and v_n the Chroma feature of F_n.

To compute the time-shifts between pairs of recorded videos, we calculate the Euclidean distance, $d_{ij} = E(v_i, v_j)$, between their Chroma features F_i and F_j [2] to derive a distance matrix. Figure 1(a) shows the distance matrix d_{ij} for two feature vectors obtained from two camera recorded segments, each of them has 2 s duration. The distance matrix d_{ij} contains information about the feature matching of the two audios. In order to interpret this information, the point of minimum distance across each row of the distance matrix d_{ij} is calculated. As seen in Fig. 1(a), the distance matrix d_{ij} is a rectangular matrix, in which the main diagonal corresponds to zero time-shift, and the diagonal above or below the main diagonal correspond to positive and negative time-shifts, respectively. We calculate the matching histogram $v_{ij}(\Delta t)$ for C_i and C_j from the distance matrix d_{ij} for the count of the number of minimum distances along each diagonal as shown in Fig. 1(b). As seen, while $\Delta t = 1.00$ s, the count reached the maximum, and hence F_i starts one second earlier than F_j, which mean that C_i starts one second earlier than C_j. This is also shown as the sub-diagonal in the 1 s position in Fig. 1(a).

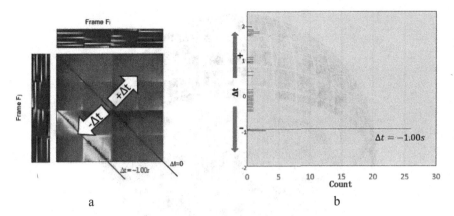

a   b

Fig. 1. Illustration of Chroma feature matching for computing the time-shifts between pairs of recorded videos: (a) Using the distance matrix for two camera recorded segments with the duration of 2 s. (b) The minimum across each row is calculated and the count of minimum distances is accumulated across each diagonal to give the histogram, and its peak corresponds to the time-shift.

For each video, this method can find time-shift and adjusting to the same point in time to start stitching video frames.

2.2   Panoramic Video Creation

While image stitching has been extensively researched for the past decades [2–6], our investigation reveals that dedicated design of the technique and new elements are still needed for video stitching since: (i) video stitching requires synchronization of frames to guarantee that right frame pairs are stitched together across the entire sequence; (ii) video frame stitching requires low computing cost and high speed, and thus a number of video-unique features need to be exploited. To this end, we introduced two changes into the image stitching method reported by Brown and Lowe [2], which include: (i) considering the calibration of video cameras beforehand, we limit the SIFT extraction and correspondence within the half frame area as shown in Fig. 2; (ii) to improve the stitching effectiveness, we introduce an additional alignment procedure by exploiting the coordinate transformation between the left and right frames to be stitched.

Specifically, given the perspective transformation as follows:

$$[x', y', w'] = [u, v, w] \begin{bmatrix} a_{11} & a_{12} & a_{13} \\ a_{21} & a_{22} & a_{23} \\ a_{31} & a_{32} & a_{33} \end{bmatrix} \tag{1}$$

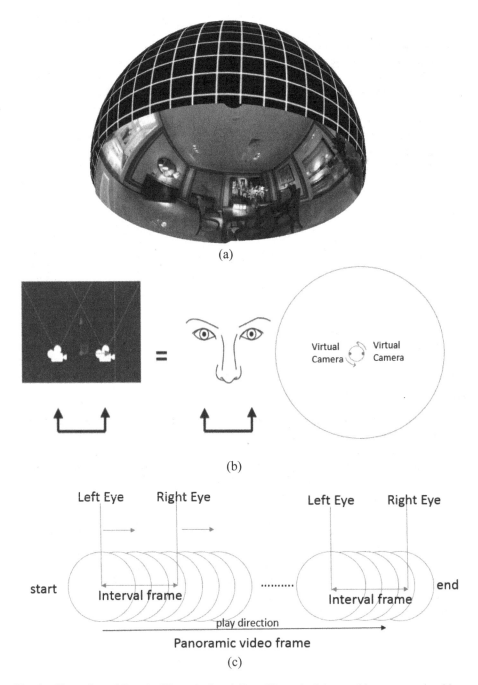

(a)

(b)

(c)

Fig. 2. Illustration of Pseudo-3D method and True-3D method in watching panoramic video: (b) Pseudo-3D method using distance of virtual camera in OpenGL to simulate pupillary distance and change virtual camera location according viewer head orientation; (c) True-3D using the tth frame from panoramic video to replace scene of left eye and right eye in fixed angle.

and the transformed coordinates:

$$x = \frac{x'}{w'} = \frac{a_{11}u + a_{21}v + a_{31}}{a_{13}u + a_{23}v + a_{33}} \tag{2}$$

$$y = \frac{y'}{w'} = \frac{a_{12}u + a_{22}v + a_{32}}{a_{13}u + a_{23}v + a_{33}} \tag{3}$$

We select a group of N registered pair of SIFT points, $\{(x_L^1, x_R^1),$ $(y_L^1, y_R^1); \dots (x_L^N, x_R^N), (y_L^N, y_R^N)\}$, to verify the perspective transformed coordinates via the following:

$$\Delta_x = \frac{\sum_{i=1}^{N} (x_L^i - x_R^i)}{N} \tag{4}$$

$$\Delta_y = \frac{\sum_{i=1}^{N} (y_L^i - y_R^i)}{N} \tag{5}$$

and the additional alignment is done by:

$$(x, y) = \begin{cases} (x + \Delta_x, y + \Delta_y) & \text{if } |\Delta_x| \geq T \cap |\Delta_y| \geq T \\ (x, y + \Delta_y) & \text{if } |\Delta_x| < T \cap |\Delta_y| \geq T \\ (x + \Delta_x, y) & \text{if } |\Delta_x| \geq T \cap |\Delta_y| < T \\ (x, y) & \text{if } |\Delta_x| < T \cap |\Delta_y| < T \end{cases} \tag{6}$$

Where T stands for a threshold, which is determined empirically.

2.3 View-Change Adaptive Playback of Videos

Panoramic video playback needs special treatment in order to simulate the on-spot view changes. Using OpenGL, making panoramic video as a texture, and stick it to a sphere model as shown in Fig. 2(a), and in this way, we are able to create 360° panoramic video effect via the video stitching algorithm described earlier.

It is proved difficult to create 360° 3D panoramic videos due to the fact that (i) the requirement on video frame resolutions leads to processing of huge information quantity; (ii) 3D video stitching requires excessive computing cost. To this end, we propose a pseudo-3D approach to complete the creation of 3D panoramic 360° videos, details of which are described below.

Set two virtual cameras to simulate the viewer's position inside the Sphere as shown in Fig. 2(b). As the viewing point changes, the distance between the virtual left eye and the right virtual right eye will change depending on the value of yaw. Correspondingly, we use this changing distance to select the tth frame for the right eye and the current frame (the 1st frame) for the left eye. The specific algorithm is given as follows:

Algorithm:

I. Using d to represent the distance of virtual cameras (eyes), d dynamically changes according to the viewer's head position, and its initial value is $d = d_{max}$. As the view changes, the distance between the two virtual cameras can be derived by:

$$d = abs(\cos(yaw)) \cdot d_{max} \quad yaw \in [0, 2\pi] \tag{7}$$

II. In True-3D, let t represents the number of frames controling the selection of the frame for the right eye, we have:

$$t = \text{int}(\sin(yaw) \cdot t_{max}) \quad yaw \in [0, 2\pi] \tag{8}$$

Where t_{max} is the initial value, which can be determined as zero when yaw = 0. In the proposed algorithm as described above, the value of yaw can be obtained from the orientation sensor in VR helmet such as oculus, or the mouse position etc.

3 Experiments

To evaluate the proposed system, we carried out extensive experiments in two phases. While the first phase of experiments is to test the performance of creating the panoramic videos, the second phase of experiments is to evaluate the effectiveness of VR-helmet adaptive display of the panoramic video and the experience of walking into

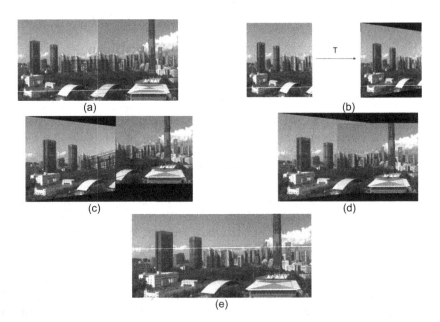

Fig. 3. Illustration of experimental results for creating panoramic videos

the video scene. Figure 3 illustrates the experimental results and the sequence of the panoramic 3D video creation process. As seen, part (a) illustrates the SIFT point extraction and matching process, Part (b) illustrates the effectiveness of perspective transformation, part (c) and (d) illustrate the SIFT point verification and additional alignment, which shows that better stitching quality is achieved by such additional alignments, especially after the fusion as shown in (e). As the value of yaw changes from 0 to 360°, the video frame will be adaptively presented to the viewer (Fig. 4).

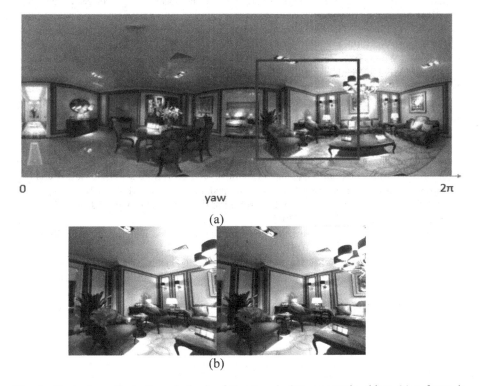

Fig. 4. Illustration of adaptive playback of the Pseudo-3D panoramic video: (a) a frame in panoramic video (b) when yaw = 1.4π, the scene mix True-3D and Pseudo-3D method to present video content to the viewers adaptively.

4   Conclusions

In this paper, we introduced a new concept of creating 3D panoramic videos via a fast video stitching algorithm to enable viewers to "walk into video content". We also described our proposed algorithm design for implementing such a new concept. Extensive experiments support that (i) our video stitching is fast and fit the purpose based on the simplifications introduced; (ii) our proposed adaptive pseudo-3D panoramic video playback achieves good 3D and immersive effect, pioneering the concept of immersive, panoramic, multi-view.

The authors wish to acknowledge the financial support for the work from CNSF (Chinese Natural Science Foundation) under the grant number 61373103.

References

1. McVicar, M., Santos-Rodríguez, R., Ni, Y., De Bie, T.: Automatic chord estimation from audio: a review of the state of the art. IEEE Trans. Audio Speech Lang. Process. **22**, 556–573 (2014)
2. Brown, M., Lowe, D.G.: Automatic panoramic image stitching using invariant features. Int. J. Comput. Vis. (2007)
3. Tang, W., Wong, T.T., Heng, P.: A system for real-time panorama generation and display in tele-immersive applications. IEEE Trans. Mult. **7**, 280–292 (2005)
4. Burt, P., Adelson, E.: A multiresolution spline with application to image mosaics. ACM Trans. Graphics **2**, 217–236 (1983)
5. Xu, W., Mulligan, J.: Panoramic video stitching from commodity HDTV cameras. Multimedia Syst. **19**, 407–426 (2013)
6. Molina, E., Zhu, Z.: Persistent aerial video registration and fast multi-view mosaicking. IEEE Trans. Image Process. **23**, 2184–2192 (2014)
7. Song, X., Zhang, J., Han, Y., Jiang, J.: Semi-supervised feature selection via hierarchical regression for web image classification. Multimedia Syst. **22**(1), 41–49 (2016)
8. Zhang, J., Han, Y., Jiang, J.: Tensor rank selection for multimedia analysis. J. Vis. Commun. Image Represent. **30**, 376–392 (2015)
9. Li, J.Y., Jiang, J.: Nonrigid structure from motion via sparse representation. IEEE Trans. Cybern. **45**(8), 1401–1413 (2015)
10. Pan, Z.L., Ming, Z., Zhong, H., Wang, X., Xu, C.: Compressed knowledge transfer via factorization machine for heterogeneous collaborative recommendation. Knowl. Based Syst. **85**, 234–244 (2015)
11. Bano, S., Cavallaro, A.: Discovery and organization of multi-camera user-generated videos of the same event. Inf. Sci. **302**, 108–121 (2015)

Mobile Agent Itinerary Planning Approaches in Wireless Sensor Networks- State of the Art and Current Challenges

Tariq Alsboui$^{(\boxtimes)}$, Mustafa Alrifaee, Rami Etaywi,
and Mohammad Abdul Jawad

Faculty of Science and Information Technology,
Al-Zaytoonah University, Amman, Jordan
{tariq.alsboui,rami.etaywi}@sandsacademy.edu.jo,
{m.rifaee,CouncilsSec}@zuj.edu.jo

Abstract. A ubiquitous embedded network, such as wireless sensor net-work (WSN), is characterised by its capability to carry out common tasks by sharing resources that are placed in-node or in-network domains. One of the most critical properties of mobile agent (MA) based wireless sensor network is how to design the itinerary through the WSN for mobile agent. In addition to that, a huge amount of redundant data is generated by sensors due to node density and placement. This consumes network resources such as bandwidth and energy, thus decreasing the life time of sensor network. Several studies have demonstrated the benefits of using mobile agent technology as an effective technique to overcome these limitations. MA itinerary planning techniques can be classified into three categories depending on the factors that define the route of the MA: static-itinerary, dynamic-itinerary, and hybrid-based. This paper presents a survey of the state-of-the-art MA itinerary planning techniques in WSN. The benefits and shortcomings of different MA itinerary planning approaches are pre-sented as motivation for future work into energy efficient MA itinerary planning mechanism.

Keywords: Wireless sensor networks (WSN) · Mobile agent (MA) · Itinerary planning · Static-itinerary · Dynamic-itinerary · Hybrid-itinerary

1 Introduction

The main purpose of a wireless sensor networks (WSN) is to provide users with access to the information of interest from data collected by spatially distributed sensors. In real-world applications, sensors are often deployed in high numbers to ensure a full exposure of the monitored physical environment. Consequently, such networks are expected to generate enormous amount of data [1]. The desire to define and route mobile agents in an energy efficient manner makes the success of WSNs applications, largely, determined by the methods used for mobile

© ICST Institute for Computer Sciences, Social Informatics and Telecommunications Engineering 2017
L.A. Maglaras et al. (Eds.): INISCOM 2016, LNICST 188, pp. 143–153, 2017.
DOI: 10.1007/978-3-319-52569-3_13

agent itinerary planning. The principal concerns when dispatching a mobile agent include the selection, determination, and migration cost of the mobile agent itinerary planning and the methods used for defining such a plan. Practical constraints on sensor node implementation such as power consumption (battery limits), computational capability, and maximum memory storage, make MA itinerary planning a challenging distributed task [2].

One of the most important features of WSN is collaborative information processing i.e. exploiting the relationship between the data of spatially correlated nodes so as to reduce the total data transmitted to the sink [3].

There has been sustained research into Mobile agent technology (MA) for WSNs over the last few years [4–7]. For a comprehensive literature review, we refer the interested readers to [8] and the references therein. Such research efforts focused on itinerary planning based on specific architectures, data dissemination, data collection and data fusion. However, there has been little attention on grouping sensor nodes, such that the efficiency of the itinerary planning and the quality of the returned information is maximized. MA brings a relatively new trend in distributed computing, which mainly comes in response to enable flexibility and scalability problems of centralised models. The term mobile agent refers to a piece of software that performs data processing autonomously while migrating between nodes [9].

Mobile Agents (MAs) are primarily used in the field of WSNs for data collection and in-network processing. They can perform data aggregation and make local decisions autonomously without human cooperation. Consequently, most of the works are applied towards the optimization of energy consumption in nodes through planning of mobile agent itinerary. The itinerary followed during the migration of the mobile agent can have a significant impact on energy consumption. Finding an optimal sequence of visited sources is a difficult problem to solve (NP-hard problem) [4]. Itinerary planning is defined as the route followed during MA migration [10]. It determines the order of source nodes to be visited during agent migration.

In terms of dispatching Mobile Agents to collect information that is required by an application, itinerary planning of MA in WSNs can be classified into three broad categories: static, dynamic, and hybrid. In a static itinerary, the route is computed at the dispatcher prior to the MA migration. In a dynamic itinerary, the route of MA is determined by the MA on the fly. In a hybrid itinerary, the sensor nodes to be visited by the MA are selected by the dispatcher, but the visiting sequence is determined by the MA on the fly.

The rest of this paper is organised as follows: Sect. 2 describes the Anatomy of Mobile Agent. Section 3 looks at static Itinerary planning approaches and presents sample developments. Section 4, describes dynamic itinerary planning and recent successful deployments. Section 5, describes and identify recent advances in hybrid itinerary planning and present some of the recent approaches. In Sect. 6, a summary on future research direction for MA Itinerary planning is discussed. In Sect. 6.1 an energy efficient itinerary planning mechanism is introduced. Section 7 concludes this paper.

2   Anatomy of Mobile Agent

Mobile Agent technology has the capability of performing data aggregation and ability to make local decisions autonomously without user input. MA consists of four components as shown in Fig. 1.

- Identification: is a number used to uniquely identify a MA as well as the dispatcher. Identification comes in the format of a 2-tuple (i : j) where i represents the IP address of the dispatcher, and j is a serial number the dispatcher assigns to each MA. However, due to the sheer number of sensor nodes in WSNs it is infeasible to assign individual nodes with a unique identification, e.g. IP address. Instead of addressing nodes with ID, it is natural to access data directly via content, attribute, e.g., location of node.
- Data space: The agent's data buffer, which is responsible for carrying results of data integration. The results should provide a progressive accuracy as the agent migrates from node to another.
- Itinerary: is defined as the route followed during mobile agent migration. In general, itinerary planning can be classified into three categories: static, dynamic, hybrid.
- Method: is the execution code that is carried by the agent.

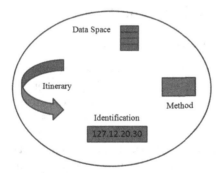

Fig. 1. Components of mobile agent.

Nodes organisation plays an important role in MA Itinerary planning because it defines, among other factors, the cost (amount of energy), accuracy (level of coverage), reliability (e.g. timeliness) of Itinerary planning [2]. The organisation of nodes can be either centralised or hierarchical. In the centralized approach, data collected by all nodes are sent towards a sink node using single or multi-hop communication [11]. However, this approach does not provide scalability, which is a main design factor for WSN. Also, it causes communication bottlenecks and transmission delays due to congestions especially in areas around the sink [12]. To overcome the problems in the centralised approaches, hierarchical techniques have been proposed as an effective solution for achieving longer network lifetime and better scalability.

Since the number of existing MA Itinerary planning approaches is significantly large, it will not be feasible to provide a detailed description of each approach. Instead, we have selected recent approaches that particularly represent directions of future research without focusing on the details of these approaches. However, characteristics of various approaches that are common for the approach they apply will be presented. Table 1 lists the reviewed approaches for mobile agent itienray planning techniques. In Sects. 3, 4 and 5 the approaches are presented based on the categorisation so as related sub-categories are discussed in the common context. To make the analysis of different approaches more logical and to set up a common base for their comparison and connection we consider some qualitative criteria.

Table 1. Overview of the selected approaches to MA Itienrary Planning

Static-itinerary	[13–16]
Dynamic-itinerary	[17–20]
Hybrid-itinerary	[13, 21–23]

3   Static Itinerary Planning to MA

3.1   Description and Operation

In static itinerary planning of MA approaches in WSN, the global information of the network is used in identifying an efficient agent route at the dispatcher prior to mobile agent dissemination. In the simplest form, a dispatcher (gateway, sink) determines the route, and the number of nodes to be visited before agents are sent.

Static itinerary planning approaches uses a single MA that introduces long itinerary distance and increases the packet length. This leads to longer task duration and consumes energy. Among the benefits of this class of approaches are: they are efficient in computing, in an environment as dynamic as the sensor network, in which connections between nodes can be lost or the sensor node may be malfunctioning, they may not respond to the changes in real time; they are easy to implement and configure; they have satisfactory performance for small WSNs; and they are suitable for monitoring applications, e.g. environmental monitoring. However, there are a number of limitations to Static itinerary planning. First, they do not respond to the changes in real time. Second, increased MA state size, leads to energy consumption.

3.2   Static Itinerary Planning Approaches to MA

In earlier studies, MA itinerary planning solution was based on the use of single MA [13,14], the authors in [24] proposed two heuristics algorithms for MA itinerary. It is assumed that both algorithms start at the same sensor node closest to the dispatcher. In Local Closest First (LCF) algorithm, MA searches for the next destination with the shortest distance to the current location. In Global closest First (GCF) algorithm, MA searches for the next node closest to the sink. The two algorithms are mainly associated with low computational complexity. However, both LCF and GCF involves the use of a single MA that sequentially visits all sensor nodes and do not scale acceptably when thousands or millions of sensor nodes are to be visited by a single MA. This indicates that they are suitable for small WSNs. Also, when the agent migrates between sensor nodes the size of a MA increases continuously. The growing size of the MAs results in increased consumption of the limited wireless bandwidth, and also consumes the limited energy supplies of sensor nodes.

To overcome some of the inherent problems in the use of a single MA, [16] introduced a source grouping scheme and an iterative algorithm for multi-agent-based itinerary planning. The idea of their work is to divide source nodes into several sets and minimize the number of agents while achieving the required coverage of source nodes. However, their idea of selecting the centre of area with a high source node density is similar to that of clustering-based method, so a different set of source nodes may cause great difference in numbers. The unbalanced set numbers will lead to the unbalanced task duration of agents and unbalanced energy consumption.

Another MA itinerary planning approach based on genetic algorithm is proposed by [15], which uses the global information of sensor detection signal levels and link power consumption. The algorithm main components include an encoding mechanism, crossover and mutation operations, and an evaluation function. It assumes that each node cannot be visited repeatedly to shorten the search space. Although global optimization can be achieved using the genetic algorithm, it is not a lightweight solution that is suitable for sensor nodes constrained in energy supply.

4   Dynamic Itinerary Planning to MA

4.1   Description and Operation

In a dynamic- itinerary planning approaches of MA in WSN, the mobile agent has no prior path knowledge. A special node dispatches a MA after the route is designed and the sequence of nodes to be visited is determined on the fly during MA migration.

Dynamic- Itinerary planning approaches reduces the long route caused by utilising a single-MA and maximise the aggregation ratio during MA migration, they have the ability to respond to faults that might occur during its migration by changing its itinerary on the fly, they scale to handle millions of nodes, they are suitable for time critical applications such as, target tracking application, in which the trajectory of a moving object is initially unknown, they explicitly incorporate resource capacity, and highlights unused resources. However, there are a number of limitations to the Dynamic- Itinerary planning approaches.

First, they are limited to specific set of applications where consistent changes occur across the network, e.g. agricultural applications. Second, they are more difficult to design and complex to execute, as they need to group sensor nodes at first into subsets in a way that will create itineraries of approximately equal cost. Third, they require more time due to the fact that the decision about the next node to be visited is taken at each sensor node. Finally, they require a careful selection of the number of MAs and the number of nodes in a different groups to achieve an optimised task duration.

4.2   Dynamic Itinerary Planning Approaches to MA

In Dynamic-itinerary planning for MA in WSN, most of the published work in the literature considers MA has no prior knowledge of their path. Additionally, they use multi-agent that dispatches a multiple agent to collect data. For example, the authors in [17] applied the directed acyclic graph to model referral process in which node stands for agent, edge denotes relationship. The weights on nodes and edges represent the social ability and referral strength of agent respectively. Since it needs knowledge of the whole system structure prior to give weights, this method cannot adapt to the open environment. To overcome these limitation, [25] proposed a dynamic building method of mobile agent path with minimum payment based on referral. By referral, the next workplace (host) of mobile agent can be recommended by the current workplace provider based on his acquaintance knowledge. They claim that their proposed techniques do not require pre-fixed system, thus, it can adapt to open environment.

Similar approaches have been suggested in [18,19]. In [18] the authors build upon their previous work by introducing a dynamic planning method for mobile agent path based on the Markov Decision Process (MDP) and social acquaintance recommendation variable decision space. The path planning model is described with MDP, and social acquaintance recommendation, assuming that every social member can provide workplace and service recommendation for mobile agent in a cooperative work manner. However, their technique is time consuming and complicated to apply in practice.

Recently, [16] presented an itinerary planning scheme using multi-agent by building a spanning tree of WSN nodes. They have introduced an itinerary algorithm called disjoint multi-Agent Itinerary planning (DMAIP). Simply, the algorithm builds a network topology graph based on WSN, and then it generates a spanning tree of the connected graph to increase weigh and traverse the spanning tree recursively to find disjoint paths of all the sub trees.

Another approach proposed in [20] in which the authors concentrate on the computation side of an itinerary planning to enable an agent to achieve its mission while respecting a time deadline. The mission is characterized by a subset of resources that the agent should collect from the network servers while respecting a partial order. Resource is an abstract concept that could mean processing capacity, a data base, and a device, among other things. The network servers provide resources of varying kinds and qualities, giving rise to the problem of deciding which servers and the order in which they should be visited to maximize mission quality, while meeting the deadline. The work presented in [19] takes the computation itinerary work one step further by developing a graph theoretic model for itinerary computation under time constraints that enables the design of provably optimal, dynamic-programming (DP) algorithms and approximation algorithms.

5   Hybrid-Based Itinerary Planning to MA

5.1   Description and Operation

A hybrid approach is an approach that combines the functionality of two or more algorithms from different MA itinerary planning. The selection of the sensor visiting set is static, whereas the decision of the sequence for nodes to be visited is dynamic.

Hybrid approaches aims to minimise the effect of the disadvantages of individual MA itinerary planning categories described above.

5.2   Hybrid Approaches Itinerary Planning to MA

Many hybrid approaches for MA itinerary planning in WSN have been recently proposed in the literature. In [13], a hybrid planning mechanism called mobile agent-based directed diffusion (MADD) is proposed. In MADD, if the sources in the target region detect an event of interest, they flood exploratory packets to the sink individually. Based on these exploratory packets, the sink statically selects the sources that will be visited by a mobile agent, which autonomously decides on the source-visiting sequence as it migrates among the nodes in the source-visiting set. As a result, the mobile agent follows a cost-efficient path among target sensors in MADD.

The work presented in [21] uses an Angle Gap-based MIP (AGMIP), this approach provides a new way of grouping source nodes that do not use the circle shape. In AG-MIP the nodes within a particular angle gap threshold around one central location should be included in the same group. The idea of AG-MIP is to connect the sink and all source nodes with beelines and the angle gaps between beelines become a critical factor to describe the relevant degree among the source nodes. The importance of AG-MIP is their way of grouping; it uses angle gap to divide the network into sectors, which lead to a contention and interferences potentially reduced among mobile agent. However, the open interrogation in this approach is to find an optimal angle gap threshold remains a challenge.

The authors in [22], applied a tree structure with branches for planning the itineraries (CBID). The main idea of CBID is to include the node that makes the total cost minimal. The MAs are dispatched in parallel a number of MAs that sequentially visit sensor nodes arranged in tree structures. The proposed work has a significant result to reduce the overall energy consumption and response time. However, their work lacks scalability with the increasing number of nodes.

In [23], a Genetic Algorithm for Multi agents Itinerary Planning (GA-MIP) is proposed. The main idea is to encode the Source Node Sequence and the

Source Node Group into numbers as genes in the genetic evolution with randomly selection. After a number of evolution iterations, the solution corresponding to an efficient strategy of itinerary planning will be obtained. Although, extensive simulations were performed to show the performance of the GA-PMI in terms of time and energy consumption. However, the complexity of higher GA-PMI calculation makes the implementation of GA-MIP still debatable.

6   Discussion and Possible Future Directions

Before concluding this paper, this section provides a discussion about research issues, and future directions in the area of MA itinerary planning in WSNs. This short survey revealed that most of the existing approaches to MA itinerary planning suffer from inherent problems that limit their applications including: they are application specific [19,24]; some approaches indicate that they are suitable for small WSNs [24]; most algorithms assume that high redundancy exists among sensor data, which requires the use of a perfect data aggregation model [16]; they introduce overhead due to imperfect migrations, and access to legacy systems [21,23]; consume high power [16,25]; some techniques assume a constant size for the MA [24]. This is unrealistic due to the fact that MA grows in size while collecting data from sensor nodes. Furthermore, they mostly limit the MAs technology to a particular architecture. This restricts the use of the MAs on anything other than the architecture it was designed for.

Leading directly from the discussion above, we intend to investigate the usefulness of the watershed gradients to define the itinerary planning of the mobile agents. The order in which sensor nodes are visited by the mobile agent and the number of nodes it migrates to can have a significant impact on energy consumption. Furthermore, to select an optimal subset of sensor nodes and to decide on an optimal order of how to allow the MA to visit these nodes can be equally well supported by the Watershed gradients [26], and a Self Stabilizing algorithm [27].

6.1   An Energy Efficient Itinerary Planning Mechanism

The benefits of restricting the number of nodes that the MA will visit in a task are to reduce energy consumption, MA migration cost, and improve information accuracy by removing task-irrelevant nodes readings from a task computation. For instance, allowing a MA to collect temperature data over the whole network might end up getting the amount of data that is linked with the density of sensors but not necessarily pertinent to the monitored phenomena. The combination of the MA and Watershed algorithm will help answering the following questions:

1. How is a MA routed from node to node in an efficient way?
2. How does a MA decide a sequence to visit multiple nodes?
3. How the integration of the MA and the watershed reduces the cost of migration?

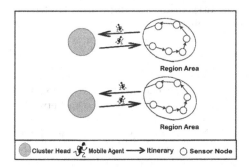

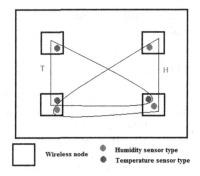

Fig. 2. MA Itinerary planning technique for WSNs.

Fig. 3. Heterogeneous grouping scheme.

The Watershed Segmentation approach [26] groups nodes sharing some common group state into segments. A segment is described as a collection of spatially distributed nodes with an example being the set of nodes in a geographic area with sensor readings in a specific range. A network segment formed with a logical notion of proximity determined by applicative information is, therefore, capable to return specified information with high confidence.

A key contribution of the work presented in this research paper is the creation of logical groups of nodes, called segments (region), within the network. These segments are used as a scoping mechanism that is used for defining the itinerary planning of the MA. The user can exploit segments to be used by the system to autonomously make decisions on where a MA should be disseminated efficiently.

Figure 2 shows an illustration of the described MA itinerary planning scheme utilising watershed segmentation approach. It shows how MAs will be directed to only to a subset of the networks and the sequence of the nodes to be visited during migration. Figure 3 shows the grouping scheme based on heterogeneous sensor type.

7   Conclusion

To conclude, the main objective of this paper is to provide an understanding of the current issues in this area for better future academic research and industrial practice of MA Itinerary planning. We have presented a review of the state of the art for MA Itinerary planning approaches in WSNs. We discussed various approaches to Mobile Agent Itinerary planning. We also discussed the challenges as well as future research directions in developing a complete MA Itinerary planning mechanism.

The majority of MA Itinerary planning techniques focus on a particular architecture type. In the authors opinion, the next step is to integrate the mobile agent with the gradients of the watershed algorithm to generate an energy efficient itinerary planning mechanism. The group is a key concept for defining MAs itinerary planning. When implementing this integration it is important that new vulnerabilities are not introduced into the system.

References

1. Hammoudeh, M., Newman, R. and Mount, S.: An approach to data extraction and visualisation for wireless sensor networks. In: International Conference on Networking, pp. 156–161 (2009)
2. Alsbou'i, T., Hammoudeh, M., Bandar, Z., Nisbet, A.: An overview and classification of approaches to information extraction in wireless sensor networks. In: SENSORCOMM 2011: Proceedings of the 2011 Fifth International Conference on Sensor Technologies and Applications, pp. 1–4, April 2011
3. Alsboui, T., Hammoudeh, M., Abuarqoub, A.: A service-centric stack for collaborative data sharing and processing. In: Green and Smart Technology with Sensor Applications: International Conferences, GST and SIA 2012, Proceedings, Jeju Island, Korea, 28 November–2 December 2012, pp. 320–327. Springer, Heidelberg (2012)
4. Aloui, I., Kazar, O., Kahloul, L., Servigne, S.: A new itinerary planning approach among multiple mobile agents in wireless sensor networks (WSN) to reduce energy consumption. IJCNIS **7**(2), 116 (2015)
5. Rasheed, A., Mahapatra, R.: An energy-efficient hybrid data collection scheme in wireless sensor networks. In: 3rd International Conference on Intelligent Sensors, Sensor Networks and Information, ISSNIP 2007, pp. 703–708, December 2007
6. Qi, H., Xu, Y., Wang, X.: Mobile-agent-based collaborative signal and information processing in sensor networks. Proc. IEEE **91**(8), 1172–1183 (2003)
7. Chen, M., Kwon, T., Choi, Y.: Data dissemination based on mobile agent in wireless sensor networks. In: Proceedings of the IEEE Conference on Local Computer Networks 30th Anniversary, LCN 2005, Washington, DC, USA, pp. 527–529. IEEE Computer Society (2005)
8. Pranesh, V., Kallapur, G., Article, V.: Research challenges in using mobile agents for data aggregation in wireless sensor networks with dynamic deadlines. Int. J. Comput. Appl. **30**(5), 34–38 (2011)
9. Kakkasageri, M.S., Manvi, S.S., Soragavi, G.D.: Mobile agent based event discovery in wireless sensor networks. In: Proceedings of the 5th WSEAS International Conference on Applied Computer Science, ACOS06, pp. 731–735, Stevens Point, Wisconsin, USA. World Scientific and Engineering Academy and Society (WSEAS) (2006)
10. Chen, G., Wu, S., Zhou, J., Tung, A.K.H.: Automatic itinerary planning for traveling services. IEEE Trans. Knowl. Data Eng. **26**(3), 514–527 (2014)
11. Iranli, A., Maleki, M. and Pedram, M.: Energy efficient strategies for deployment of a two-level wireless sensor network. In: Proceedings of the 2005 International Symposium on Low Power Electronics and Design, pp. 233–238 (2005)
12. Akkaya, K., Younis, M.: A survey on routing protocols for wireless sensor networks. Ad Hoc Netw. **3**(3), 325–349 (2005)
13. Chen, M., Kwon, T., Yuan, Y., Choi, Y., Leung, V.: Mobile agent-based directed diffusion in wireless sensor networks. EURASIP J. Appl. Signal Process. **2007**(1), 219 (2007)
14. Chen, M., Leung, V., Mao, S., Kwon, T., Li, M.: Energy-efficient itinerary planning for mobile agents in wireless sensor networks. In: 2009 IEEE International Conference on Communications, pp. 1–5, June 2009

15. Wu, Q., Rao, N.S.V., Barhen, J., Iyenger, S.S., Vaishnavi, V.K., Qi, H., Chakrabarty, K.: On computing mobile agent routes for data fusion in distributed sensor networks. IEEE Trans. Knowl. Data Eng. **16**(6), 740–753 (2004)

16. Liu, B., Cao, J., Yin, J., Yu, W., Liu, B., Fu, X.: Disjoint multi mobile agent itinerary planning for big data analytics. EURASIP J. Wirel. Commun. Netw. **2016**(1), 1–12 (2016)

17. Ramchurn, S.D., Huynh, D., Jennings, N.R.: Trust in multi-agent systems. Knowl. Eng. Rev. **19**(1), 1–25 (2004)

18. Zeng, G., Wang, X.: A dynamic building method of mobile agent path based on referral networks. Appl. Math. Inf. Sci. **19**, 1–5 (2014)

19. Camponogara, E., Shima, R.B.: Mobile agent routing with time constraints: a resource constrained longest-path approach. J. JUCS **16**(3), 372–401 (2010)

20. Rech, L., de Oliveira, R.S., Montez, C.: Dynamic determination of the itinerary of mobile agents with timing constraints. In: IEEE/WIC/ACM International Conference on Intelligent Agent Technology, pp. 45–50, September 2005

21. Chen, M., Gonzalez-Valenzuela, S., Leung, V.C.M.: Directional source grouping for multi-agent itinerary planning in wireless sensor networks. In: 2010 International Conference on Information and Communication Technology Convergence (ICTC), pp. 207–212, November 2010

22. Konstantopoulos, C., Mpitziopoulos, A., Gavalas, D., Pantziou, G.: CBID: a scalable method for distributed data aggregation in wsns. Int. J. Distrib. Sens. Netw. **2010**, 219 (2010)

23. Cai, W., Chen, M., Hara, T., Shu, L.: GA-MIP: Genetic algorithm based multiple mobile agents itinerary planning in wireless sensor networks. In: The 5th Annual ICST Wireless Internet Conference (WICON), pp. 1–8, March 2010

24. Qi, H., Wang, F.: Optimal itinerary analysis for mobile agents in ad hoc wireless sensor networks. In: Proceedings of the IEEE, pp. 147–153 (2001)

25. Xu, X., Wang, X., Zeng, G.: A dynamic building method of mobile agent path based on referral networks. Int. J. Innov. Comput. Inf. Control **19**, 1–5 (2014)

26. Hammoudeh, M., Alsboui, T.A.A.: Building programming abstractions for wireless sensor networks using watershed segmentation. In: Balandin, S., Koucheryavy, Y., Hu, H. (eds.) NEW2AN/ruSMART - 2011. LNCS, vol. 6869, pp. 587–597. Springer, Heidelberg (2011). doi:10.1007/978-3-642-22875-9_53

27. Abuarqoub, A., Hammoudeh, M.: Self-stabilizing algorithm for information extraction from mobile wireless sensor networks. In: 2013 6th Joint IFIP Wireless and Mobile Networking Conference (WMNC), pp. 1–4, April 2013

Mood-Based On-Car Music Recommendations

Erion Çano[1]([✉]), Riccardo Coppola[1], Eleonora Gargiulo[2], Marco Marengo[2], and Maurizio Morisio[1]

[1] Department of Control and Computer Engineering,
Polytechnic University of Turin,
Corso Duca degli Abruzzi, 24, 10129 Torino, Italy
`erion.cano@polito.it`
[2] Joint Open Lab MobiLAB, Torino, Italy

Abstract. Driving and music listening are two inseparable everyday activities for millions of people today in the world. Considering the high correlation between music, mood and driving comfort and safety, it makes sense to use appropriate and intelligent music recommendations based on the mood of drivers and songs in the context of car driving. The objective of this paper is to present the project of a contextual mood-based music recommender system capable of regulating the driver's mood and trying to have a positive influence on her driving behaviour. Here we present the proof of concept of the system and describe the techniques and technologies that are part of it. Further possible future improvements on each of the building blocks are also presented.

Keywords: Contextual music recommendations · Car based computing · Music mood recommendations · Connected car · Car mobile apps

1 Introduction

Since the advent of the first car radios, listening to music has always been one of the favorite activities carried out by people while driving their cars: as reported in [4], about 70% of the drivers do so. Driven by their tastes, attitudes and moods and by the nature of the trips, people have always selected the most adequate songs from their libraries creating their own customized playlists. In [19] the authors attempt to answer the question "Why do people listen to music?". Their finding is that the three most common motivations for listening to music are *Self awareness*, *Social relatedness* and *Arousal and mood regulation*. These findings reveal a strong correlation between listening to music and self regulation of mood. Thus, people may want to confirm the mood state they are in by listening to music in accordance with it; conversely, they may want to get out of a bad mood by listening to songs capable of encouraging opposite feelings. In the automotive domain there are many psychological studies that reveal connections between the played music and the actual behavior, concentration or performance of people driving their cars. Obviously, an appropriate background music stimulus may be an useful instrument to enhance the human performance and comfort in driving [15,21].

© ICST Institute for Computer Sciences, Social Informatics and Telecommunications Engineering 2017
L.A. Maglaras et al. (Eds.): INISCOM 2016, LNICST 188, pp. 154–163, 2017.
DOI: 10.1007/978-3-319-52569-3_14

On the other hand, the evolution of music recommender systems in the last decade has encouraged a high percentage of music listeners to rely on suggestions given by such applications. Music mood recommendations are embedded in many music social communities such as *Last.fm*, *TIMmusic* or *Spotify*. This article presents the proof of concept of a Mood-Based On Car Music Recommender System that uses various sources of information for tuning the recommendations: physiological information about the heart rate dynamics of the driver obtained from wearable sensors; user's saved musical preferences to take into account his/her musical tastes; telemetry of the current drive to consider the actual driving style of the user; location and time information to adapt the chosen playlists to the driving context. Using a tag-based folksonomy we classify the musical tracks in four categories: *Happy, Tender, Sad, Angry*. Four sets of tracks are fed inside the recommendation module together with the other data and the most convenient playlist is generated and recommended to the user. The rest of the paper is organized as follows: Sect. 2 provides the necessary background about the principal building blocks of the project; Sect. 3 illustrates the design of our project, with the choices we have made for each building block and the motivation behind them; finally, Sect. 4 gives some hints for future extensions of the project.

2 Background

In this section we give insights about the state of the art of the components of this project. First we present some models for mood representation, both for people and songs. We continue providing some relations between mood, music and driving safety. Then we describe what recommender systems are, and identify what contextual data can be utilized by them and how. Finally we give some information about in-car music infotainment systems, where our project of mood-based music recommendations will eventually be deployed.

2.1 Modeling Emotions

There are various definitions of mood in the works of psychiatrists that have relevance to this project. For example, while trying to point out the differences between *Affect*, *Emotion* and *Mood* (which seem to be highly interrelated), the author in [6] provides the following:

- **Affect** - a neurophysiology state consciously accessible as a simple primitive non-reflective feeling most evident in mood and emotion but always available to consciousness;
- **Emotional episode** a complex set of interrelated sub-events concerned with a specific object;
- **Mood** - the appropriate designation for affective states that are about nothing specific or about everything - about the world in general.

Angry	Sad	Tender	Happy
angry	sad	tender	happy
aggressive	bittersweet	soothing	joyous
visceral	sentimental	sleepy	bright
rousing	tragic	tranquil	cheerful
intense	depressing	good natured	happiness
confident	sadness	quiet	Quirky
anger	spooky	calm	gay
exciting	gloomy	serene	amiable
martial	sweet	relax	merry
tense	mysterious	dreamy	rollicking
anxious	mournful	delicate	campy
passionate	poignant	longing	light
quirky	lyrical	spiritual	Silly
wry	miserable	wistful	boisterous
fiery	yearning	relaxed	fun

Fig. 1. Circumplex model of mood   **Fig. 2.** Representation of Folksonomy

Obviously a key difference between Moods and Emotions is the fact that moods usually last longer. What matters from our perspective is to use well-defined models which represent the mood states of a person and the mood categories of songs. One of most used in literature is Russel's planar model [17] shown in Fig. 1. This model is based on two dimensions: *Valence* (pleasant-unpleasant) and *Arousal* (aroused-sleepy). Valence represents how much an emotion is perceived as positive or negative whereas Arousal indicates how strongly the emotion is felt. A prominent categorical model for the mood of songs is [8], which uses 66 descriptors categorized in 8 groups. A more recent approach we found is a folksonomy with four clusters of social community tags described in [12]. It is the one we use in this project.

2.2   Mood Recognition and Context

Psychologists evaluate the impact of music listening in one's mood using a standard method called Musical Mood Induction Process (MMIP). It consists of replaying mood-eliciting music to research participants. In [23] the authors outline several MMIP techniques for estimating the effects on mood given by music. Some of the most important ones are *Self-reports*, *Behavioral measures* and *Physiological measures*. For this project we base the driver's mood recognition in physiological measures obtained from wearable sensors. The physiological parameters provided by wearables can be combined and used as valuable emotion-related data sources. For example, in [16] the authors present one such system capable of recognizing emotions which is based on heart rate, skin conductivity, and skin temperature. In this project we utilize heart rate dynamics to assess the arousal and valence the driver perceives when listening to the recommended songs. His/Her mood can be considered as a contextual parameter. In context-aware systems research, one of the definitions of context-aware computing is the ability of a mobile user's application to discover and react to changes in the environment (i.e. driver's mood state) they are situated in [20]. Context is defined by different concepts or factors such as time and/or date, weather conditions and user's emotional state.

One approach used to consider the contextual factors in providing recommendations is the multidimensional model which considers dimensions as Cartesian products of some attributes and the recommendation space as Cartesian product of the dimensions [1]. In a music recommender based on mood the dimensions could be **User** $\subseteq$ *Uname x Age x Proffession*, **Item** $\subseteq$ *SongTitle x Artist x Genre x MoodLabel*, **Context** $\subseteq$ *Time x Location*, **Mood** $\subseteq$ *DrivingStyle x HeartRate x SkinConductance*. The other side of the coin is to detect or recognize mood categories inside musical tracks. In the literature this problem is addressed using the following approaches:

- **Social Tags** - many tags (such as *passionate, autumnal, witty, cool*) may be useful for mood or genre recognition in songs;
- **Lyrics** - song lyrics can also be used to classify music tracks into mood categories [10,25];
- **Audio** - audio processing techniques were the earliest employed to recognize mood in music using features like timbre, harmony, register, rhythm;
- **Multimodal** - to attain better predictive accuracy many studies combine the above three approaches in different ways building multi-modal algorithms [9,26].

There are also several studies which try to shed light on the moods that different structural properties of music induce to people. According to [5] *mode* is the highest important music property followed by *tempo, register, dynamics, articulation* and *timbre*. All these properties of music exhibit certain correlations with mood categories.

2.3   Mood and Driving Style

Several studies show correlations between a driver's mood and his/her behavior while driving: for instance, [7] shows the influence on driving cautiousness given by moods like anger or depression; [22] shows the outcomes of an experiment conducted on drivers in which the sad and relaxed moods were found as connected to a safer driving; conversely, [15] highlights the correlation between an angry mood and an aggressive style of driving. Regulative efforts should take place when the current driver's mood is not safe for driving: [22] shows the effectiveness of changing the mood of the listened songs in doing so and underlines that gradual shifts can obtain such result more efficiently. In general, the actions that can be performed on the driver's mood through music recommendations are:

- **Mood Regulation** - a target desired mood, different from the current one, is set as goal;
- **Mood Maintenance** - the driver is already in a suitable mood, thus actions have to be taken to try to maintain it.

Driving style can be retrieved dynamically gathering telemetrics from the car. To do so, the OBD-II technology can be leveraged, since it provides access to a set of diagnostic information about the car functioning. Recently, a vast assortment of OBD-II adapters (the so-called *dongles*) has been made available in the market. They may provide APIs to mobile applications, so they can telemetrics service and keep track of the driver's behavior. An alternative to the use of OBD-II adaptors, as discussed in [13], is the use of approximations done by the smarphones themselves, leveraging data collected from GPS, accelerometers and gyroscopes. Such measures, however, are vulnerable to external interference and provide little accuracy in short time windows. Once telemetric data are extracted and used to characterize the driver's behavior, they can be used to check whether the playlists recommended by the system have accomplished the objective of making the driving style shift to a safer one.

2.4   On-Car Infotainment Technology

Lately, a rapid growth and diffusion of on-car infotainment platforms [24] has been witnessed. Car dashboards are now being connected to the Internet and/or integrated with driver's hand held devices, thus enabling finer music listening experiences than just the plain classic radio playback. What follows is a quick overview on some available solutions for the access to music streaming on car:

- *Direct use of the smartphone* - The simplest solution is to connect the smartphone to the car speakers (via AUX or Bluetooth cables), and make use of it to provide the only human-machine interface with which the users will interact. "Auto" versions of renowned streaming music players (e.g., Spotify or Pandora), car-oriented music players accessing playlists stored in the smartphone, as well as prototypes of music recommendation apps [2] are available in the market.
- *Android Auto Integration* - Once a device is connected via a USB cable or bluetooth to a compatible car dashboard, it allows the use of applications installed on it as providers of music playlists to be played from the car speakers. The connectivity of the smartphone can be used to stream playlists. Once connected, the smartphone screen goes black and user interactions are performed with the car dashboard only. Android Auto mandates a common very minimal user interface for all the applications working with it.
- *Proprietary applications installed on dashboards* - Some automakers have signed partnerships with music streaming services provider, thus native streaming applications are installed on their dashboards.
- *Mirrorlink* - It performs a mirroring of compatible applications installed on the smartphone. All human-machine interaction is performed through the car dashboard. The guidelines for the application graphics are really strict, and both the smartphone and the car must be MirrorLink-enabled.

3   System Description

The architecture of the system is presented in Fig. 3. The main module is the Music Mood RS, which is responsible for providing the appropriate playlist

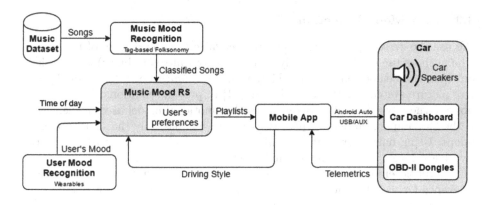

Fig. 3. Schematic view of the system.

of songs recommended for the driver. This module analyzes many data such as driving style patterns, contextual factors, mood labeled musical tracks and driver's mood state. User Mood Detection is the module responsible for providing the driver's mood representation. It takes in mood related physiological data provided by wearable sensors (e.g., heart rate dynamics), computes the *Valence* and *Arousal* values and feeds the driver's mood state in the RS module. The OBD-II module is responsible for providing car telemetry data from which driving style patterns are extracted. Music Mood Recognition module adds mood labels to the musical track the system uses. The Mobile App module is an Android application which shows up the user interface and enables media playback. The application may be used on the smartphone itself or may be integrated with the car-dashboard after having connected the smartphone to it.

3.1   Music Mood Recognition

This module works on the many songs obtained from public music datasets such as last.fm, Yahoo Music Ratings, or Million Song Dataset. These datasets are very important for training and testing purposes and are further described in [3]. We use a classifier that is based on a semantic mood model described in [12]. The model was derived from social tags of songs collected from last.fm music community. It is in consonance with many other existing mood models. The four categories *angry*, *sad*, *tender* and *happy* can be seen as the representative mood categories of each of the four subplanes in the planar model of Russell. Other studies such as [18] also confirm that tag based semantic mood models are effective to predict perceived mood of the songs. The top tags of each category are presented in Fig. 2.

3.2   User Mood Detection

We use the system presented in [21] to recognize the mood state of the driver. The authors use cardiovascular dynamics (Heart Rate Variability) observations on short-time emotional stimuli. They utilize the images of International affective picture system (IAPS) described in [11] to provoke emotional stimulus and observe the physiological consequences. The emotional model used in their work is the Circumplex Model of Affect (CMA) which is basically the same model we adopt. Using only heartbeat dynamics they effectively distinguish between the two basic levels of both arousal and valence, thus allowing for the assessment of four basic emotions. An important advantage of their framework that has relevance for us is the fact that it is fully personalized and does not require data from a representative population of subjects.

3.3   Driving Style Recognition

To track user's driving style, we have chosen to rely on the OBD-II adapter approach. In particular, we do a simple estimation of the driver's aggression in his/her driving style by calculating the jerkiness of the speed and acceleration profile of the car. To obtain the necessary telemetry data we leverage the *stats* API provided by Dash: the call provides the average speed in a finite time interval so the acceleration can be computed based on two subsequent measurements. A heuristic threshold is utilized to discriminate between calm and aggressive driving style, based on estimations of the jerk (the first-order derivative of acceleration). We consider the thresholds provided by [14], obtained as the average jerk values on a number of drive cycles in typical scenarios. The driving style is tagged *aggressive* if the actual jerk is greater than the threshold correspondent to the scenario where the drive is having place. The derived driving style is computed by the mobile application that is running the player and is then used as a flag inside the recommender to confirm or dissent the mood estimation of the wearables endorsed by the user (since an aggressive driving style is related to a high level of arousal, and in particular to an angry mood). Moreover, the driving style itself is used as a direct proof of the effectiveness of the recommendations, as they are used with the aim of relieving the driver from stress and aggression.

3.4   Music Mood RS

The recommendation module collects the different contextual, user and song data, analyzes them and generates the most appropriate playlist. Time of day is a contextual parameter related to the rate of arousal the driver needs. We assume that during the day there is no need for extra stimulation of the driver. For this reason the default recommended mood category is *tender* which based on the driving literature background (2.3) is the most favorable to a comfortable and safe driving. On the contrary, during a night drive it is usually better to avoid a sleepy state of mood and keep the driver more alerted, thus recommending *happy* music.

Fig. 4. Mobile Application interface.

Fig. 5. Android Auto interface.

We use the two values (arousal and valence) provided by the wearable sensors to identify the mood category the driver is in. The objective is to keep the driver in a relaxed state of mood by recommending music of his/her tastes. When the user is already in relaxed mood the recommender gives more priority to his/her past musical preferences. The driving style is obtained from the telemetric data of the OBD-II module and provides insights about how safe the car being driven. It falls in two categories, *aggressive* and *non aggressive*. The last data that goes in the recommendation module are the musical tracks which have already been classified in the four mood categories by the tag-based classifier. The recommender considers the contextual data and the user's past preferences to generate the playlist. The driver is free to chose which song to play. If no selection is made the top ranked song is played automatically.

3.5   Mobile App

The main outcome of the project is an Android application providing a music player Service. Since the intended use of the app is inside an in-car environment, we made the application compatible with the Android Auto platform. However, full functionalities are also available if the car dashboard is not compatible to Android Auto. The phone should anyhow be connected via AUX/USB-cable to the car dashboard to enable music playback through the car speakers The mobile app is targeted to Android 5.0 Lollipop and presents a simple landscape interface through which the user can give traditional music playback inputs and express his/her approval about the recommended songs. The application also shows information about the user's estimated mood. The user interface (see Fig. 4) is designed to provide minimum distraction to the driver.

The app is compatible with the Android Auto platform for the in-car streaming. To the standard interface, a button allowing to express appreciation for a recommended song has been added. The interface of the application can be seen in Fig. 5.

4   Discussion

A great amount of the music streamed from the Internet today is suggested by intelligent recommender systems embedded in popular music portals such as

TIMmusic, last.fm or Spotify. We have considered using a music recommender system also in a car environment, using the driver's mood and other contextual data to recommend musical tracks able to adjust the driver's mood for a comfortable and safe drive. In this work we presented the proof of concept of the system and its building blocks. The work is still in progress and we expect to have improvements or module extensions in the near future. We are working to adopt a finer grained mood representation model with more categories. Also the driver's mood recognition can be based on more than just heart rate dynamics (for instance, facial expressions and skin conductance can be additional alternatives) and can take into account external factors, like the speed of the vehicle compared to the speed limits of the road percurred (with a higher speed taken as a consequence of an excited mood, and a lower speed as a possible proof of drowsiness). Moreover, we are experimenting with multi-modal music mood classifiers which consider audio and textual feature of songs for better predictive and recommendation accuracy.

Acknowledgments. This work was done at the Joint Open Lab MobiLAB and was supported by a fellowship from TIM.

References

1. Adomavicius, G., Sankaranarayanan, R., Sen, S., Tuzhilin, A.: Incorporating contextual information in recommender systems using a multidimensional approach. ACM Trans. Inf. Syst. **23**(1), 103–145 (2005)
2. Baltrunas, L., Kaminskas, M., Ludwig, B., Moling, O., Ricci, F., Aydin, A., Lüke, K.-H., Schwaiger, R.: InCarMusic: context-aware music recommendations in a car. In: Huemer, C., Setzer, T. (eds.) EC-Web 2011. LNBIP, vol. 85, pp. 89–100. Springer, Heidelberg (2011). doi:10.1007/978-3-642-23014-1_8
3. Çano, E., Morisio, M.: Characterization of public datasets for recommender systems. In: 2015 IEEE 1st International Forum on Research and Technologies for Society and Industry Leveraging a Better Tomorrow (RTSI), pp. 249–257, September 2015
4. Dibben, N., Williamson, V.: An exploratory survey of in-vehicle music listening. Psychol. Music **35**(4), 571 (2007)
5. Eerola, T., Friberg, A., Bresin, R.: Emotional expression in music: contribution, linearity, and additivity of primary musical cues. Frontiers Psychol. **4**(487), 1–12 (2013)
6. Ekkekakis, P.: Affect, mood, and emotion. In: Measurement in Sport and Exercise Psychology. Human Kinetics (2012)
7. Garrity, R.D., Demick, J.: Relations among personality traits, mood states, and driving behaviors. J. Adult Dev. **8**(2), 109–118 (2001)
8. Hevner, K.: Experimental studies of the elements of expression in music. Am. J. Psychol. **48**, 246–268 (1936)
9. Hu, X.: Improving music mood classification using lyrics, audio and social tags. Ph.D. thesis, Citeseer (2010)
10. Hu, Y., Chen, X., Yang, D.: Lyric-based song emotion detection with affective lexicon and fuzzy clustering method. In: Proceedings of ISMIR 2009, pp. 123–128 (2009)

11. Lang, P.J., Bradley, M.M., Cuthbert, B.N.: International affective picture system (IAPS): affective ratings of pictures and instruction manual. Technical report A-8, The Center for Research in Psychophysiology, University of Florida, Gainesville, FL (2008)
12. Laurier, C., Sordo, M., Serrà, J., Herrera, P.: Music mood representations from social tags. In: International Society for Music Information Retrieval (ISMIR) Conference, Kobe, Japan, pp. 381–386, 26 October 2009
13. Meng, R., Mao, C., Choudhury, R.R.: Driving analytics: will it be obds or smartphones? Zendrive Whitepaper (2014)
14. Murphey, Y.L., Milton, R., Kiliaris, L.: Driver's style classification using jerk analysis. In: IEEE Workshop on Computational Intelligence in Vehicles and Vehicular Systems, CIVVS 2009, pp. 23–28, March 2009
15. Nesbit, S.M., Conger, J.C., Conger, A.J.: A quantitative review of the relationship between anger and aggressive driving. Aggression Violent Behav. **12**(2), 156–176 (2007)
16. Peter, C., Ebert, E., Beikirch, H.: A wearable multi-sensor system for mobile acquisition of emotion-related physiological data. In: Tao, J., Tan, T., Picard, R.W. (eds.) ACII 2005. LNCS, vol. 3784, pp. 691–698. Springer, Heidelberg (2005). doi:10.1007/11573548_89
17. Russell, J.: A circumplex model of affect. J. Pers. Soc. Psychol. **39**(6), 1161–1178 (1980)
18. Saari, P., Barthet, M., Fazekas, G., Eerola, T., Sandler, M.B.: Semantic models of musical mood: Comparison between crowd-sourced and curated editorial tags. In: 2013 IEEE International Conference on Multimedia and Expo Workshops, San Jose, CA, USA, 15–19 July, pp. 1–6 (2013)
19. Schäfer, T., Sedlmeier, P., Städtler, C., Huron, D.: The psychological functions of music listening. Frontiers Psychol. **4**(511), 1–33 (2013)
20. Schilit, B.N., Theimer, M.M.: Disseminating active map information to mobile hosts. IEEE Netw. **8**(5), 22–32 (1994)
21. Valenza, G., Citi, L., Lanatá, A., Scilingo, E.P., Barbieri, R.: Revealing real-time emotional responses: a personalized assessment based on heartbeat dynamics. Scientific reports 4, (2014)
22. van der Zwaag, M.D., Janssen, J.H., Nass, C., Westerink, J.H., Chowdhury, S., de Waard, D.: Using music to change mood while driving. Ergonomics **56**(10), 1504–1514 (2013). PMID: 23998711
23. Västfjäll, D.: Emotion induction through music: a review of the musical mood induction procedure. Musicae Scientiae **5**(1 suppl.), 173–211 (2002)
24. Viereckl, R., Ahlemann, D., Koster, A., Jursch, S.: Racing ahead with autonomous cars and digital innovation. Auto Tech Rev. **4**(12), 18–23 (2015)
25. Xia, Y., Wang, L., Wong, K.-F.: Sentiment vector space model for lyric-based song sentiment classification. Int. J. Comput. Proc. Oriental Lang. **21**(4), 309–330 (2008)
26. Yang, Y.-H., Lin, Y.-C., Cheng, H.-T., Liao, I.-B., Ho, Y.-C., Chen, H.H.: Toward multi-modal music emotion classification. In: Huang, Y.-M.R., Xu, C., Cheng, K.-S., Yang, J.-F.K., Swamy, M.N.S., Li, S., Ding, J.-W. (eds.) PCM 2008. LNCS, vol. 5353, pp. 70–79. Springer, Heidelberg (2008). doi:10.1007/978-3-540-89796-5_8

Automatic Detection of Hateful Comments
in Online Discussion

Hugo Lewi Hammer[(✉)]

Oslo and Akershus University College of Applied Sciences, Oslo, Norway
hugo.hammer@hioa.no

Abstract. Making violent threats towards minorities like immigrants or homosexuals is increasingly common on the Internet. We present a method to automatically detect threats of violence using machine learning. A material of 24,840 sentences from YouTube was manually annotated as violent threats or not, and was used to train and test the machine learning model. Detecting threats of violence works quit well with an error of classifying a violent sentence as not violent of about 10% when the error of classifying a non-violent sentence as violent is adjusted to 5%. The best classification performance is achieved by including features that combine specially chosen important words and the distance between those in the sentence.

Keywords: Hateful comments · Machine learning · Threat detection

1 Introduction

Over the past years there has been an alarming growth in hate against minorities and women [1,2]. A similar increase in hate speech has been observed on the Internet [3,4], and experts are concerned that individuals influenced by this web content may resort to violence as a result [5,6].

Hateful speech is illegal by international law, signed and ratified by most countries in the world [7] (Article 20). In addition several countries, and most of the countries in the Western World, have similar national laws. There exist examples of individuals who have been arrested for expressing hate or threatening with violence, see e.g. [8–11]. The last three examples are based on violent threats posted on the Internet. It is almost impossible for the police, NGOs, discussion moderators and others concerned with hate speech to keep track of the wast amount of online activities. A tool that automatically detects hate speech and threats of violence could potentially be very helpful.

The main aim of this paper is to evaluate the potential of using different machine learning approaches to detect sentences in hateful online discussions that contain a threat of or sympathy with violence (for short just called threats of violence in the rest of this introduction). More specifically this paper has the following contributions:

© ICST Institute for Computer Sciences, Social Informatics and Telecommunications Engineering 2017
L.A. Maglaras et al. (Eds.): INISCOM 2016, LNICST 188, pp. 164–173, 2017.
DOI: 10.1007/978-3-319-52569-3_15

– A large text material of about 25.000 sentences from online discussion were manually annotated for threats of violence and about 1.500 were found. This large and unique material is openly available for further research.
– Reading through hateful discussions, one observes that much of the same words and phrases are used in different ways to express threats of violence. We present new approaches to construct features that capture these properties in an efficient way. The approaches are based on using the most salient words in violent sentences and constructing sentence features that are combinations of these words.

This paper is a major extension, both with respect to methodology and results, of the one page short paper [12].

2   Related Work

There is little previous work specifically devoted to the detection of threats of violence in text. However, there is previous work which examines other types of closely related phenomena, such as 'cyberbullying' and hate-speech.

Dinakar et al. (2011) [13] propose a method for the detection of cyberbullying by targeting combinations of profane or negative words, and words related to several predetermined sensitive topics. Their data set consists of over 50,000 YouTube comments taken from videos about controversial topics. The experiments reported accuracies from 0.63 to 0.80.

There has been quite a bit of work focused on the detection of threats in a data set of Dutch tweets [14,15], which consists of a collection of 5000 threatening tweets. In addition, a large number of random tweets were collected for development and testing. The system relies on manually constructed recognition patterns in the form of n-grams, but details about the strategy used to construct these patterns are not given. In [15], a manually crafted shallow parser is added to the system. This improves results to a precision of 0.39 and a recall of 0.59.

Warner and Hirschberg (2012) [16] present a method for detecting hate speech in user-generated web text, which relies on machine learning in combination with template-based features. The task is approached as a word-sense disambiguation task, since the same words can be used in both hateful and non-hateful contexts. The features used in the classification were combinations of uni-, bi- and tri-grams, part-of-speech-tags and Brown clusters. The best results were obtained using only unigram features, with a precision of 0.67 and a recall of 0.60. The authors suggest that deeper parsing could reveal significant phrase patterns.

3   Sentence Features to Detect Threats of Violence

Most classification methods within text mining are based on the so called document term matrix, also referred to as bag-of-words or unigram. A document term matrix counts word frequencies. For example the document term matrix for the two sentences:

Sentence 1: "I will kill Muslims and I will kill Jews"
Sentence 2: "We love to kill Muslims"

is shown in Table 1. For example we see that the word 'I' occurs two times in 'sentence 1' and zero times in 'sentence 2'. Further we see that the word 'kill' occurs two times in 'sentence 1' and once in 'sentence 2'. The columns of the document term matrix are referred to as *features* and represent the information from the sentences that will be used in the automatic text classification. Naturally there is information in the sentences that is not included in the document term matrix, e.g. the order of the words. Differences in the word order may change the meaning, e.g. the two sentences "I love Israel not Palestine," and "I love Palestine not Israel" contain the same words, but differ in meaning. However, for the most typical application of text mining, like document summarization or clustering, the unigram matrix as introduced above works quite well. For the problem of detecting sentences with threats of violence, we hypothesize that classification can be improved by adding other specially constructed features as described below.

Table 1. Document term matrix for the two example sentences

	I	will	kill	and	Muslims	Jews	we	love	to
Sentence 1	2	2	2	1	1	1	0	0	0
Sentence 2	0	0	1	0	1	0	1	1	1

3.1   Bigrams of Important Words

We expect that a threat of violence often should contain the subject that wants to perform the violence, like 'I' or 'we', some aggressive words like 'kill', 'bomb', 'nuke', 'gun', etc., as well as the target for the violence, like 'Muslims', 'Jews', 'women', 'bastards', 'sandniggers' and so on. Potentially important features from the sentences therefore are bigrams of such important words. A procedure to find important words is described below. If the important words in the sentences above are 'I', 'we', 'kill', 'Muslims' and 'Jews', we start by excluding the non-important word from the sentences and then compute the bigrams of the remaining words. The result is shown in Table 2. For example we see that 'I-kill' occurs two times in the first sentence and that 'kill-Muslims' occurs in both sentences.

Table 2. Feature matrix for the bigram of important words.

	I-kill	kill-Muslims	Muslims-I	kill-Jews	we-kill
Sentence 1	2	1	1	1	0
Sentence 2	0	1	0	0	1

A natural extension of Table 2 is to use all combinations of the important words, not just the subsequent. The first features of 'sentence 1' will then be 'I-kill', 'I-Muslims', 'I-I', 'I-Jews', 'kill-Muslims', 'kill-I' and so on.

3.2   Bigrams of Important Words with Distance Function

Naturally we expect that a combination of important words like 'I-kill' is more important if 'I' and 'kill' are close to each other in the sentence, because then it is more likely that 'I' is related to 'kill'. Said in another way, if there are several words between 'I' and 'kill', it is more likely that 'kill' is used for another purpose in the sentence, and it is less likely that the sentence contains a threat of violence. To incorporate this in Table 2, we use a weight function. Maybe the most natural weight function is to divide by the number of words between the two important words in the sentence

$$w_1(d) = \frac{1}{d+1} \tag{1}$$

where d is the number of words between the two important words. If the two words are next to each other, $d = 0$. Using $w_1(d)$, Table 2 will be changed to Table 3. E.g. to compute 'I-kill' in 'sentence 1', we see that 'I-kill' occurs two times and both times with one word between, such that the computation becomes $1/(1+1) + 1/(1+1) = 1$. Further, 'we-kill' occurs once in 'sentence 2' with two words between, such that the computation becomes $1/(2+1) = 1/3$.

Table 3. Feature matrix for the bigram of important words using weight function (1).

	I-kill	kill-Muslims	Muslims-I	kill-Jews	we-kill
Sentence 1	1	1	1/2	1	0
Sentence 2	0	1	0	0	1/3

The selections of features above is based on using a set of important words. We chose those words that were significantly correlated with the response (violent/not-violent sentence).

4   Classification Method

We base our classification of violent/non-violent sentences on logistic LASSO regression [17]. Logistic LASSO regression can document excellent classification properties, and is at least as effective as Support vector Machine [18]. A training set is used to estimate the parameters of the model. The fitted model can be used to compute the probability that a sentence (from a test set) contains a threat of violence or not. We classify a sentence using a threshold on the computed probability.

4.1 Evaluation of Classification Method

The first measure is the Mean Squared Error (MSE). Let $y_i \in \{0,1\}$ denote whether sentence $i \in \{1, 2, \ldots, n\}$ contains a violent threat or not, where 1 means violent. Further let p_i denote the computed probability that sentence i is a violent sentence. The MSE is then computed as

$$\text{MSE} = \frac{1}{n} \sum_{i=1}^{n} (y_i - p_i)^2 \tag{2}$$

We introduce one more measure. We denote the portion of non-violent sentences that are classified as violent as Type I error, and the portion of violent sentences that are classified as non-violent as Type II error. We adjust the threshold in the classification such that the Type I error is equal to α, say 0.05. Naturally we want the Type II error to be as small as possible under this restriction on the Type I error.

5 Evaluation

In this section we will compare the different suggested sentence features presented in Sect. 3 with respect to classification performance. Classification based on LASSO logistic regression model was performed using the 'glmnet' package [17] in the statistical software R [19].

5.1 Text Material

The text material consisted of all comments on eight YouTube videos. All the videos were related to religious and political topics that typically create a lot of anger and disagreements in the comments, like the Eurabia theory [20], halal slaughter, Anders Behring Breivik, Geert Wilders, etc.

Each sentence in the material was manually annotated to either contained a threat or sympathy with violence or not. For sentences where it was impossible to decide, e.g. due to terribly poor language, or the sentence was part of a larger argument, the sentence were annotated as 'not violent'. A few comments contained copies of violent passages from the Bible or the Quran. Such sentences were classified as violent if the passage was violent. Sentences in other languages than English were removed from the text material. After the annotation process, the text material consisted of a total of 24,840 sentences where 1,469 sentences were violent. A randomly selected subset of 100 non-violent and 20 violent sentences (based on the annotation from the main annotator) were labeled by an other human annotator for inter-annotar study. The results showed that for 98% of the sentences, both annotators made the same decision, and both annotators found a total of 20 threats of violence.

5.2   Feature Matrices

In this section we present the different feature matrices we want to compare, which are all based on the theory presented in Sect. 3. The first feature matrix is the unigram exemplified in Table 1. We denote this feature matrix UNI in the rest of this paper. In addition to the weight function w_1 in (1), we will also consider the weight function

$$w_2(d) = \exp\left\{-\left(\frac{d}{3}\right)^3\right\} \tag{3}$$

Comparing w_1 and w_2, w_2 gives more weight for small distances between important word and less weight for longer distances.

As previously described, we select important words using correlation with the response (in the training set) resulting in a list of approximately 300 important words depending on which part of the whole material were used as training set. The rest of the feature matrices consist of the features from UNI in addition to

- The feature matrix exemplified in Table 2; and together with UNI we denote this feature matrix C. ("C" (constant) since the score is independent of distance between the important words in the sentence)
- The same as C, but where we use all combinations of important words as described in the end of Sect. 3.1, denoted ACC (all combinations constant weight).
- The feature matrix exemplified in Table 3; and together with UNI we denote the feature matrix W1 (weight function w_1)
- The same as the item above, but with all combinations of important words, denoted ACW1.
- The same as W1, except that we use the weight function w_2. We denote this feature matrix W2.
- The same as the item above, but with all combinations of important words, denoted ACW2.
- We also select a random sample of 300 words (the same amount that we have of important words in the previous feature matrices) among the 3,000 most frequent words in the text material except stop words like *and, it, is, at,* .... We compute the feature matrix based on these words the same way that we computed ACW1 and denote this feature matrix ACW1FW (frequent words). It is interesting to see how ACW1FW performs compared to ACW1 and the other feature matrices above.

Before computing the feature matrices above, all stop words and punctuation marks were removed from the sentences and all words were changed to lower case. In text mining it is also quite common to do word stemming, but for the application of detecting violent threats, different word stems are important, e.g. the word kill is more common in threats of violence than killed. Therefore word stemming was not performed. For computational robustness, we removed all features that were non-zero in three or fewer sentences.

5.3   Classification Performance of the Feature Matrices

To evaluate the performance of the feature matrices we randomly divided the sentences into training and test sets. The training set consisted of 80% of the violent and 80% of non-violent sentences in the corpus, and the rest of the sentences constituted the test set. We fit the logistic LASSO regression model to the training set for each of the feature matrices in the previous section. We use the test set to evaluate the feature matrices by computing the Mean squared error (MSE) and Type II error measures as described in Sect. 4.1. For the Type II error, we set the Type I error to $\alpha = 0.05$. To reduce uncertainties in our results, we repeated this procedure 40 times. Tables 4 and 5 show the average

Table 4. The second column shows the average Mean squared error (MSE) for the different feature matrices over the 40 runs, computed using (2). The others show the results of tests for differences in MSE. The significance codes are adjusted for the number of tests carried out. That is: *** if p-value $\in [0, \frac{0.001}{28}]$, ** if p-value $\in (\frac{0.001}{28}, \frac{0.01}{28}]$, * if p-value $\in (\frac{0.01}{28}, \frac{0.05}{28}]$ and n.s. means not significant.

	MSE	ACW1	ACC	ACW2	W2	W1	C	UNI
ACW1	0.0269							
ACC	0.0277	**						
ACW2	0.0286	***	**					
W2	0.0290	***	**	n.s				
W1	0.0290	***	***	n.s	n.s			
C	0.0294	***	***	***	**	**		
UNI	0.0325	***	***	***	***	***	***	
ACW1MF	0.0344	***	***	***	***	***	***	***

Table 5. The second column shows the average Type II error, in percentage, for the different feature matrices over the 40 runs. The other show the results of tests for the differences in Type II error. The significance codes are adjusted for the number of tests carried out. That is: *** if p-value $\in [0, \frac{0.001}{28}]$, ** if p-value $\in (\frac{0.001}{28}, \frac{0.01}{28}]$, * if p-value $\in (\frac{0.01}{28}, \frac{0.05}{28}]$ and n.s. means not significant.

	Type II	ACW1	ACC	ACW2	W1	W2	C	UNI
ACW1	9.72							
ACC	10.48	**						
ACW2	11.00	***	n.s					
W1	11.04	***	n.s	n.s				
W2	11.11	***	n.s	n.s	n.s			
C	11.16	***	n.s	n.s	n.s	n.s		
UNI	13.89	***	***	***	***	***	***	
ACW1MF	16.11	***	***	***	***	***	***	***

MSE and Type II error over the 40 runs, respectively. For the tests in Table 4, we use paired Student's t-tests where the observations are the differences in MSE in each of the 40 runs. For the tests in Table 5, we assume that the number of Type II errors for a feature matrix in one of the 40 runs is an outcome from a binomial distribution, and tests are performed approximating the binomial distributions with normal distributions. Since we perform several tests, the significance levels are adjusted using the Bonferroni correction [21].

From the tables we see that ACW1 performs significantly better than all the other feature matrices, both in terms of MSE and Type II error, e.g. being the only feature matrix with a Type II error below 10%. Further, the feature matrices using all combinations of the important words perform the best. We also see that the prediction performance significantly depends on the choice of weight function, with w_1 being the best. Finally we see that ACW1MF performs poorly showing that it is not enough just to include more features, but that those features must be cleverly chosen.

Table 6, shows contingency tables for the cases UNI and ACW1 based on the 40 runs.

Table 6. Contingency table of classification results.

UNI		Truth	
		Violent	Not violent
Prediction	violent	10127	8014
Outcome	not violent	1633	151986
ACW1		Violent	Not violent
Prediction	violent	10617	8021
Outcome	not violent	1143	151979

5.4 The Strongest Predictors of Violent Sentences

A great advantage of the LASSO model is that the solution is sparse with respect to features. To achieve the optimal predictions as summarized in Tables 4 and 5, the model consisted of between 400 and 1000 nonzero regression parameters (features). By choosing a higher value of the regularization parameter in the LASSO model, the solution will be even sparser, showing the few features which is the most important to detect threats of violence. The features is shown in Table 7. As expected, several of these strong predictors is a combination of a subject (I or we) and an aggressive word like kill, burn, die and so on. We also have word combinations that point to the target of the violent threat like "you-burn", "kill-you" and "kill-all". We also see that "breivik" is a strong predictor, finding sentences that support the terrible actions of Anders Behring Breivik. Lowering the value of the regularization parameter the set of nonzero features also include word combinations "breivik-hero" and "commander-breivik". It also included features that reduced the probability of a threat of violence like "not" and "never-kill".

Table 7. Features with a nonzero regression parameter for a high value of the regularization parameter.

kill-hell	kill	nuke	burn	and-burn	die
we-kill	you-burn	death-to	deported	deport	i-die
exterminate	kill-and	you-die	i-kill	i-burn	be-deported
breivik	shoot	kill-all	deport-and	kill-to	kill-you
and-die					

6   Closing Remarks

In this article we have shown how text mining and machine learning can be used to detect threats of or sympathies with violence in online discussions. In particular we focus on how specially chosen features of two words can improve prediction compared to the traditional unigram (single words) feature matrix. Our results show that detecting treats of violence generally works quite well using machine learning with Type I and Type II errors of about 5 and 10%, respectively. Using all combinations of the important words and the weight functions w_1 gives the best results.

Parsing the text material may possibly improve our results, however, we expect that automatic parsers will have quite a hard time, since the language quality in such online discussions is terribly poor, full of slang, misprints and erroneous grammar.

One may also suggest to use ordinary bigrams, but then it is only possible to include features of word beside each other in the sentence. Including features of word separated in the sentence is impotant to detecting threats of violence. E.g. in Table 7 a feature like 'i-die' refers to sentences where the two important words are clearly separated in the sentence like 'I would love to see them die'. Also using ordinary bigrams, the number of features will be in the millions compared the only a few tens of thousands in our approach making the problem computationally less challenging and equivalent to ordinary unigram.

References

1. Fekete, L.: Pedlars of hate: the violent impact of the European far Right. Institute of Race Relations (2013). http://www.irr.org.uk/wp-content/uploads/2012/06/PedlarsofHate.pdf. Accessed 12 Mar 2016
2. Wilson, R., Hainsworth, P.: Far-right Parties and discourse in Europe: a challenge for our times. European network against racism (2013). http://cms.horus.be/files/99935/MediaArchive/publications/20060_Publication_Far_right_EN_LR.pdf. Accessed 12 Mar 2016
3. Goodwin, M., Ramalingam, V., Briggs, R.: The new radical right: violent and non-violent movements in Europe. Institute for Strategic Dialogue (2013). http://www.strategicdialogue.org/ISD%20Far%20Right%20Feb2012.pdf. Accessed 12 Mar 2016

4. Bartlett, J., Birdwell, J., Littler, M.: The rise of populism in Europe can be traced through online behaviour... Demos, (2013). http://www.demos.co.uk/files/Demos_OSIPOP_Book-web_03.pdf?1320601634. Accessed 12 Mar 2016

5. Strømmen, Ø.: The Dark Net. On Right-Wing Extremism, Counter-Jihadism and Terror in Europe. Cappelen Damm, Oslo (2012)

6. Sunde, I.M.: Preventing radicalization and violent extremism on the Internet (Norwegian). The Norwegian Police University College 2013:1 (2013)

7. UnitedNations: International Covenant on Civil and Political Rights (2014). http://www.ohchr.org/en/professionalinterest/pages/ccpr.aspx. Accessed 12 Mar 2016

8. TheTimesOfIndia: Akbaruddin Owaisi arrested in hate speech case (2014). http://articles.timesofindia.indiatimes.com/2013-01-08/india/36216031_1_nirmal-rural-police-akbaruddin-owaisi-police-stations. Accessed 12 Mar 2016

9. Skjetne, O.L., Hustadnes, H.: Ubaydullah Hussain is accused of violent threats (norwegian) (2014). http://www.dagbladet.no/2013/11/20/nyheter/ubaydullah_hussain/innenriks/islamisme/trusler/30429704/. Accessed 12 Mar 2016

10. Euronews: Neo-Nazi and black metal star Varg Vikernes arrested in France (2013). http://www.euronews.com/2013/07/16/neo-nazi-and-black-metal-star-varg-vikernes-arrested-in-france-/. Accessed 12 Mar 2016

11. Valaker, O., Holte, M.A.: Bergen blogger arrested (norwegian) (2012). http://www.bt.no/nyheter/lokalt/Bergens-blogger-pagrepet-2732162.html. Accessed 12 Mar 2016

12. Hammer, H.L.: Detecting threats of violence in online discussions using bigrams of important words. In: Intelligence and Security Informatics Conference (JISIC), p. 319 (2014)

13. Dinakar, K., Reichart, R., Lieberman, H.: Modeling the detection of textual cyber-bullying. In: The Social Mobile Web, pp. 11–17 (2011)

14. Oostdijk, N., Halteren, H.: N-gram-based recognition of threatening tweets. In: Gelbukh, A. (ed.) CICLing 2013. LNCS, vol. 7817, pp. 183–196. Springer, Heidelberg (2013). doi:10.1007/978-3-642-37256-8_16

15. Oostdijk, N., van Halteren, H.: Shallow parsing for recognizing threats in Dutch tweets. In: Proceedings of the 2013 IEEE/ACM International Conference on Advances in Social Networks Analysis and Mining, pp. 1034–1041. ACM (2013)

16. Warner, W., Hirschberg, J.: Detecting hate speech on the world wide web. In: Proceedings of the Second Workshop on Language in Social Media, pp. 19–26. Association for Computational Linguistics (2012)

17. Friedman, J., Hastie, T., Tibshirani, R.: Regularization paths for generalized linear models via coordinate descent. J. Stat. Softw. **33**(1), 1–22 (2010)

18. Genkin, A., Lewis, D.D., Madigan, D.: Large-scale bayesian logistic regression for text categorization. Technometrics **49**(14), 291–304 (2007)

19. R Core Team, R: A Language and Environment for Statistical Computing. R Foundation for Statistical Computing, Vienna (2013)

20. Fekete, L.: The Muslim conspiracy theory and the Oslo massacre. Technical Report 53(3), pp. 30–47. Institute of Race Relations (2011)

21. Johnson, R., Wichern, D.: Applied Multivariate Statistical Analysis. Prentece Hall, Upper Saddle River (1998)

Author Index

Printed in the United States
By Bookmasters